David Cohen graduated from Oxford in ~~~~~~~~~~~~~ ...os-
ophy, since when he has worked as a j~~~~~~~~~~~~~ ..aker.
He is the co-editor of *Psychology News*.

DAVID COHEN

Forgotten Millions

PALADIN
GRAFTON BOOKS
A Division of the Collins Publishing Group

LONDON GLASGOW
TORONTO SYDNEY AUCKLAND

Paladin
Grafton Books
A Division of the Collins Publishing Group
8 Grafton Street, London W1X 3LA

A Paladin Paperback Original 1988

Copyright © David Cohen 1988

ISBN 0-586-08667-6

Printed and bound in Great Britain by
Collins, Glasgow

Set in Baskerville

Contents

To Jane

Preface and Acknowledgements

There are some 250 million severely mentally ill people in the world. Some are schizophrenic; some suffer severe depression; some have a mixture of psychological problems linked to alcohol or drug abuse. The World Health Organization's figure of 250 million is, of course, an estimate but it's based on well-documented statistics. It constitutes a huge problem and, on the whole, one which, for a variety of reasons, the world ignores. Madness both fascinates and repels because the idea of the human mind somehow 'going off' is terrifying to most of us. Poor countries tend not to see mental health as much of a priority. Yet, worldwide, the treatment of the mentally ill should be a major concern.

In 1981, I made a film called 'I was in Broadmoor' for ATV (now Central Television) which looked at the way in which this special hospital was run. A Japanese lawyer, Etsuro Totsuka, came to see me. He had been sent by the Japanese Bar Association to study the ways in which the West coped with psychiatric patients. During his tour, he became convinced that Japan treated its mentally ill very badly. Quite ordinary patients were treated as restrictively as those in Broadmoor which was intended only to house very dangerous inmates. My film argued that many Broadmoor patients were not that dangerous. Totsuka took back twenty videotapes of the film and even arranged for my book on Broadmoor to be published in Japanese. They became additional ammunition in a campaign to reform Japanese psychiatry. He felt that only international pressure would change the situation. I stayed in touch with Totsuka and, in 1984, went to Japan to see the situation for myself. I was encouraged to go by Ann Barr, then the deputy editor of *Harpers & Queen*, who eventually published a long account of psychiatric scandals in Japan and, also, by Joan Shenton, another friend of Totsuka's.

In 1986, Central Television said that they would like to have a film about psychiatry in a number of different countries. 'Forgotten Millions', which I directed and co-produced with Joan Shenton, looked at four countries – Japan, the United States, Egypt and India. There were reasons for choosing these particular countries. Japan and America are the two richest countries in the world and both, in different ways, have failed to cope with the problems of their mentally ill. The Japanese lock them up arbitrarily for long periods; the Americans neglect them. The film also looked at two poor countries, India and Egypt where the problems are very different. This is not the book of the film both because I have included two other countries (Israel and Great Britain) and because a fifty-two-minute film, while it can be closely argued, can only convey a very limited amount of information. Nevertheless, this book owes a great deal to the film.

Chapter 1 looks at the problems worldwide, at the extent of 'madness' on the planet and at the failure of psychiatry to cope. Chapter 2 examines psychiatry as an international 'business' in which Western ideas and teaching dominate and lead to less than appropriate care. In the chapters that follow it is clear how Europe and America exported psychiatry to the rest of the world.

Chapter 3 looks at Japan which took its inspiration from Germany in the 1880s and America after the war. Chapter 4 looks at the United States and how its liberal policy of closing hospitals has led to unexpected problems. Chapter 5 looks at Israel which has avoided many of the American problems and has developed special ways of coping in a society where the threat of war imposes constant stress. Israel has a few special dilemmas of its own. Chapter 6 looks at Egypt, a relatively poor country which is trying to provide services for a population that is growing fast and converging on big cities. Much of Egypt's care is private. Chapter 7 looks at India which is both poorer and larger than Egypt. Curiously, it has the scandals on a par with Japan but, also, the best community care of any country. India defies neat analysis. In the research for the film, Joan

Shenton was the first to visit India and this chapter incorporates much material that she originally drafted and for which I am very grateful. Chapter 8 looks at the situation in Britain and examines what we, prime colonial exporters of psychiatry, are doing now. Finally, in Chapter 9, I try to offer some brief suggestions of what could usefully be done.

It has been said that one of the best ways of measuring how civilized a society is, is to judge how it deals with its most inadequate citizens. The fate of the mentally ill shows that, with some unexpected exceptions, we are far less civilized than we would like to think.

Both the making of the film and the writing of this book would have been impossible without the help of many friends. Particularly I should like to thank Etsuro Totsuka who helped with so much of the Japanese research; Richard Creasey, Central's head of features who decided that he wanted a worldwide film; Roger James, the head of documentaries at Central, who interfered most creatively with the editing and helped resolve many problems; Elizabeth Sayce who did such excellent translations of the Japanese interviews; Akiko Domoto of Tokyo Broadcasting who suggested I visit the strange Mr Goda. I am also grateful to Joan Shenton both for her great help with the India chapter and her comments on a first draft of chapter 1. I also benefited much from discussions about the state of British mental-health services with Dr James MacKeith, Dr Stephen MacKeith and Jane Eames.

In New York, I was much helped by Diane Sonday of Project Reach Out; Tyrone Henderson, one of her community workers; Bob Couteau, Barry Klein and Inga Kopulskya of Community Access. Fuller Torrey gave me much of his time as did Davis Pollack of the National Alliance for the Mentally Ill.

In India, Dr Srinivas Murthy and Dr N. Reddy of the National Institute for Mental Health and Neurosciences were generous in their help, as was Dr Helmut Sell, then the World Health Organization man on the spot. Dr S. Sharma let me see his survey on Indian mental hospitals. In Egypt, I was grateful for the help of Dr Gamal Abu Al Azayem; Dr Atif Shonka and Dr N. Kotry of the Egyptian Ministry of Mental Health. In Israel,

Dr David Davidson gave me generous access to the work of his hospital.

Aileen La Tourette read two of the chapters and gave me sharp, useful critical comments. I am also grateful to my agent Sheila Watson for useful criticism. Sandy Lowe helped check a number of references and statistics. Many thanks. I'm also grateful to my two sons, Nicholas and Reuben, who spent their summer holidays of 1986 with me and had to spend some of them visiting Japanese mental institutions. They were good company and Nicholas did most of the word-processing of the manuscript.

1

250 Million

'No, I don't have any bad feelings.' Walter Reed smiled at me as his legs jerked again. 'I'm on the payroll. Every month, I get two pay cheques from social security, one for the left hand and one for the right hand.'

It can't be easy for Walter to be so optimistic. Thirty years of treatment have taken their toll. His limbs are in perpetual agitation as if he's always itching and never comfortable. His speech is slurred. He often falls asleep at six in the evening. His memory is poor and he can't remember all of his medical history. Bob Couteau, director of counselling at Community Access, New York, has tried to piece together Walter's medical records but many documents have been lost. Couteau believes Walter was first admitted to a Mississippi mental hospital in 1956 and that, since then, he has had at least twenty-four spells in hospital. Many institutions have failed to cure him and, in many ways, Walter is a victim of the fashions in psychiatry over the last thirty years. The latest ideas, in their time, kept him in hospital, then threw him into the 'real world' without any preparation and then reckoned him a failure when he could not survive on the streets.

In Mississippi, each week started with what Walter calls 'the electrical hammer', or ECT (electroconvulsive therapy). Sometimes, 'after a fight', Walter was locked in the seclusion room which he nicknamed the 'conclusion room'. Being in solitary left 'a lousy feeling because you picked up all the misery there. Some people had died there.' Drugs should have 'cured' Walter of his hallucinations but he still sees 'the cover' which is 'like a cloud'. Bob Couteau, who is given to Freudian insights, interprets this black cloud as a symbol of repression and depression. When we are miserable, we are 'under a black cloud'. Walter won't accept such a tidy analysis. He loves and hates his cloud and, for him, it doesn't have any simple meaning. Often people are wrapped in it, so they seem to be covered in whipped cream. It's an image which tickles the imagination and leads to debates as to whether it's cute, eerie or sexual. 'There are a lot of sad feelings there too,' said Couteau who wanted to emphasize how much Walter had suffered.

Like most of the mentally ill around the world, Walter has suffered and continues to suffer. But Walter is also right to be optimistic, and street-wise to point to the 'payroll'. In most of the rest of the world, especially the Third World, a fifty-six-year-old schizophrenic like him would probably be dead. Instead, he lives in some comfort in an apartment in New York with an icebox, a respectable bathroom, two leather armchairs, a television and a cleaning lady to keep it all tidy. 'I go out with girls too,' Walter grinned. Bob Couteau sighed that this was a problem; female junkies often lured Walter back to his apartment and proceeded to steal his money without doing him any favours. Walter did not mention any such reverses. He declared: 'I wouldn't say I'm lucky but I do appreciate it because it's hard to find shelter.' He knows he is an exception. Few of the mentally ill find such a relatively happy ending.

When Walter was first sent to hospital in 1956, every large town had its asylum and orthodox practice was to keep patients there, usually for long periods. In 1948, the number of inpatients in American public hospitals was 540,000, in British hospitals, 170,000. Some American hospitals, like Milledgeville which housed 9000 patients, were huge. By 1955, American inpatients had risen to 560,000 with an extra 300,000 patients in veterans' administration hospitals and private asylums. It was assumed that they could not cope outside. In the mid-1950s new drugs and old scandals changed all that.

Albert Deutsch's famous book *The Shame of the States* was published in 1948. It was followed in 1955 by Mike Gorman's exposé of Oklahoma's hospitals, *Every Other Bed*. Both authors concluded that the mentally ill were often kept in conditions that would not be tolerated for animals. They concluded that hospitals could never be reformed: they had to be closed. By 1960, progressive commentators claimed that large hospitals themselves caused illness. In them patients were made to feel low, helpless and persecuted. President Kennedy set up Community Mental Health Centers in 1963 as a remedy. The CMHCs would allow individuals to be treated as outpatients in their neighbourhoods. The federal government even promised to pay for the CMHCs' operations for the first five years. In Britain, the Minister for Health, Enoch Powell, denounced the old asylums in 1959 as Gothic Victorian relics. The modern age would do better.

The final push towards deinstitutionalization came when radical American lawyers started winning test cases against hospitals. These victories forced hospitals to justify keeping patients. They could be detained only if psychiatrists could swear they were dangerous either to themselves or to others. To avoid being sued, hospitals had to discharge people fast. This 'liberation' was hailed as a liberal victory.

The discovery of drugs like thorazine made it seem a sensible victory. Thorazine suppressed the worst symptoms of schizophrenia. Patients stopped hearing voices and became less paranoid. Calmer, they might manage in the real world. In the 1960s, some psychiatrists even claimed that, in a crazy world, the 'mad' had special insights. It was time to listen to them. 'Care in the community' seemed not just humane and optimistic but practical too.

Ironically, a long-term Canadian study, the Stirling Community Study, had already shown that it was not easy to set up a community care programme which was in fact caring or had anything to do with the community. It was the fashion to be anti-hospital so few heeded contrary evidence such as this or paid too much attention to long-term planning. For example, what would happen to the CMHCs after five years when the federal money would need to be replaced by local money? Would neighbourhoods be happy to pay for such facilities? Letting patients go seemed wonderfully progressive and caught the mood of the 1960s. By 1970, hospitals all over America were releasing patients – some out of conviction, others to avoid being sued.

The pattern was the same all over the West, though the pace was different. In Britain, for example, the hospital population fell far more slowly than it did in America, from 165,000 in 1955 to 120,000 in 1965. In Italy, some cities like Trieste closed all their psychiatric hospitals in a few years. Today, there are far fewer patients in hospital in all Western countries than there were twenty years ago. America has only 273,000 psychiatric inpatients; Britain has 70,000; Sweden has 21,420. In Britain, the government plans to cut down psychiatric beds even further.

Released from hospital, Walter Reed drifted to New York where, like many ex-patients, he found he couldn't manage. He lived rough. He started to drink and take drugs. He had to eat out of garbage cans. None of that improved his mental health and none of it was exceptional. In New York, patients were almost evicted from hospital. Creedmoor, the asylum for the borough of Queens, released nearly 3000 patients in a few months. Some went back to their families. But, often, families didn't want to know or had just moved away. Patients were free, which meant free to survive without a home, without friends and without proper after-care. A liberal policy created problems no one had foreseen.

Walter was lucky. In 1983 he was referred to Community Access, a programme that provides accommodation and help for forty-six ex-patients in New York. Most of the city's mentally ill have access to nothing like it. But, for a few like Walter, it does offer a good way of life. Bob Couteau regrets they found Walter when he was so old because, 'He will always need help and be in the mental health system. If we had found him earlier, when he was less damaged, it might have been different.' Walter might have become competent enough to go back to the real world on his own. Nevertheless, both of them know Walter is lucky.

The Extent of Madness

While hospitals in the West are releasing patients, in Third World countries and in Japan the trend is different. In 1960,

India had fewer than 10,000 inpatients; today it has 21,000. Bangladesh had no psychiatric hospital till Pabna Mental Hospital opened in 1957. It has grown from eighty patients to nearly 1000 and is still the only mental hospital in Bangladesh. China has increased its psychiatric beds, especially in cities like Shanghai.

Most dramatically, in Japan, the number of inpatients has trebled from 100,000 in 1955 to 350,000 today. The conditions in Japanese mental hospitals are very like those in the bad old Victorian asylums: they are overcrowded, dirty and often brutal in their discipline. It is one area in which Japan is antiquated rather than hi-tech. Some sociologists claim that Japan's frenetic drive for industrial success requires 'bins' (i.e. loony-bins) in which to dump those who are unwilling to conform to the demands of industry. These 'bins' need to be unattractive to instil the appropriate terror.

Most of the world's schizophrenics and depressives live in poorer countries where there isn't enough food or basic health-care and where mental health has a low priority. Schizophrenia is probably the most common and most serious psychiatric illness. To be schizophrenic is not, as jokes and the movies suggest, to have a split personality so that you act like Dr Jekyll by day and Mr Hyde by night. Rather, schizophrenia involves a variety of symptoms which focus round hearing voices and feeling that one's thoughts are controlled.

In the 1960s, anti-psychiatrists like R. D. Laing, author of *The Divided Self*, and Thomas Szasz, author of *The Manufacture of Madness*, argued that schizophrenia did not exist. Szasz used as evidence the fantastic variety of symptoms of schizophrenia that could be found in the literature. How could you have an illness where the doctors did not agree either on the symptoms or on the right treatment? The macabre truth, Laing and Szasz claimed, was that society labelled as schizophrenics those who troubled it. Rebels were lunatics. These arguments annoyed and threatened conventional psychiatrists who were motivated to set up an ambitious international study of schizophrenia. The results would prove the anti-psychiatrists were quite wrong, misled by their ideological obsessions.

From 1969, the International Pilot Project on Schizophrenia examined the incidence of schizophrenia and whether psychiatrists from different cultures could agree on its diagnosis. Twelve hundred patients in Denmark, India, London, Moscow, Prague, Washington, Taiwan, Nigeria and Colombia were studied. They fell into two groups. Two-thirds suffered from 'first-rank' symptoms: they heard voices, had jumbled thoughts, blunted emotions, hallucinations and felt persecuted. The symptoms were terrifying and totally convincing. In such cases, psychiatrists could agree on the diagnosis.

With 'second-rank' symptoms there was more conflict. Psychiatrists in Washington and Moscow were more likely than others to attribute schizophrenia to patients with vaguer symptoms. But this slight dissent didn't bother the organizers of the project. They had triumphed, showing that most psychiatrists agreed what schizophrenia was. The project also confirmed that about one per cent of the population suffers from schizophrenia. With a world population of 6000 million, there are probably 60 million schizophrenics.

It is fashionable now to mock anti-psychiatry as a radical folly of the 1960s. For all the vigour of their writing, say their detractors, Laing and Szasz were deluded and have been silenced, having failed to establish that schizophrenia is not an illness. Nevertheless, their controversial ideas have affected the mental health community all over the world, more than many psychiatrists like to admit. Laing and Szasz have forced new issues on to the agenda, issues which were not much mentioned twenty years ago, such as the legal rights of patients, consent to treatment, the dangers of giving too many drugs and the right to information. Many Third World psychiatrists, in particular, resist such decadent Western notions but, even in Cairo and Calcutta, Laing and Szasz have had some influence. For me, one of the more bizarre threads running through this book is the way in which some doctors find it hard to concede any rights to their patients other than the right to be treated – without ever questioning the notion that doctor knows best.

Schizophrenia may be the best known, but it is not the only psychiatric illness. The other most common ones are depression, mania, obsessional states, personality disorders, anxiety neuroses and many phobias. There is no clear estimate of how many people suffer from these ills; it may even be more than the World Health Organization's estimate of 250 million. A twenty-year Canadian study in Stirling County has just reported (Leighton, 1986) that 20 per cent of the population needed psychiatric help. Extrapolate and you have a mind-boggling mega-number – 1500 million in need of 'help'. Psychiatry is clearly a good career in which you need have no worry about being out of work.

Despite these large numbers, mental health remains a poor relation of the health services the world over. In health budgets, psychiatry usually has a low priority. In Britain, for example, the amount spent on psychiatry was £1·5 billion (16 per cent of the hospital and community health budget). Yet psychiatric beds take up 60 per cent of the beds in the National Health Service. In Japan, total spending on health is only 6.2% of the health budget and, curiously, as the number of psychiatric beds in Japan has risen, the amount spent on psychiatry has fallen.

Money for research is also relatively scarce. Some American psychiatrists complain about the resources devoted to AIDS. Despite the rhetoric that it is God's punishment of the 'permissive society', governments fund research heavily. Dr Subjud Mukerjhee, an Indian psychiatrist who works at Creedmoor Hospital, New York, regrets that schizophrenics do not die. If only they did, he says, there would be serious money available for serious research. Yet, he adds, schizophrenia is often, a 'living death'. Even the National Institute for Mental Health did not fund basic research generously until pressed to do so by lobby groups, notably the National Alliance for the Mentally Ill, a pressure group of relatives of the mentally ill.

The Shock of Change

In *Future Shock*, Alvin Toffler argued that human beings had never before been asked to adapt so fast to technological and social changes. The strain, Toffler warned, might be too great for many. It would be impractical to attempt here a potted history of recent social changes and their psychiatric impact; but there are some consequences which appear obvious for mental health and the organization of services.

The history of psychiatry is an urban history. In Britain, the first asylums were in London; in France, they were in Paris. In the eighteenth century, it seemed as if cities with their crowded and dirty conditions created madness. The sweet countryside was sane; the foul city crazed. This wasn't just a naïve, romantic view. A famous experiment in psychology looked at rats who were crowded into cages. At a certain density, they became violent, unbalanced, berserk. They didn't have enough space to be normal. To many, the rat experiment was proof of the damage living in cities inflicted. Less sensational studies proved a more modest thesis. City-dwellers with low-income, low-status jobs and low educational qualifications were especially vulnerable to psychiatric illness. Bad housing, poor healthcare, financial anxieties, isolation, all hurt them.

The fastest-growing cities today are mostly in the Third World. Cities like Bombay, Cairo, Mexico City and Manila are expanding fast, attracting 'immigrants' from the even poorer countryside. Cairo's population is 14 million so that now one in every four Egyptians lives there. Most are poor. Understandably, psychiatrists worry about how they are ever going to provide the services they need.

Coming to live in a city can be strange and stressful. Lipsedge and Littlewood (1981) argue that migrations provoke mental illness. Imagine the situation of the Egyptian peasant who has lived for years a hundred miles from Cairo: life on the Nile Delta has not altered much for centuries, the rhythms of village life persist. New technology is limited and hasn't brought many social changes. Pharaoh's peasants might have to learn a few specific skills but would probably feel at home there. Cairo, on the other hand, is a modern city of slums, traffic and bazaars which has changed out of all recognition. It is crowded, fast, impersonal. The physical distance from the village may be just a hundred miles; the psychological distance is immense.

Newcomers have to adapt to the city at a time when family networks are under threat. The Islamic revival advertises the glory of the Islamic family but modernization has different imperatives. Husbands have to live in hostels away from their villages to work in factories; wives are left isolated. The separation is painful; the family is less of a bulwark. People have to adapt to the big city with less support than they are used to.

No one prepares people for these changes just as, in the advanced West, no one prepared people for the impact of unemployment. Jahoda (1981) argued that when someone loses a job, they lose status, their role in the family, networks of support and a way of spending time. It's a kind of bereavement. Rapid social changes also create a sense of unease and of dislocation. What seems to be merely common sense is backed up by considerable research.

One of the most successful attempts to quantify the impact of change is 'life events' research. Basically, this assumes life carries on dully most of the time till we are jolted by 'life events', major happenings. Traumatic life events include divorce, bereavement, moving house, getting a job, losing a job, getting engaged, worrying about health, housing problems and being promoted. Not all these events are bad but they are all extraordinary and force one to adapt. Sophisticated research has shown that, for many people, a combination of too many life events, just too much to cope with at any one time, can trigger major depression and, even, suicide attempts. Toffler would be pleased.

Toffler suggested that the best way to cope was to learn how to learn. Not everyone is so devoted to self-improvement, however. Many cultural commentators see us seeking ways to escape relentless change. It has been argued that the current 'epidemic' of heroin/cocaine/crack is, among other things, an attempt to escape the pressure of changes. If I am stoned, nothing can touch me.

The World Health Organization estimates that perhaps 200 million people suffer from drug and alcohol addiction. Though these are hardly new problems, their scale has forced governments all over the world into unusual action. What was seen as a problem for the decadent West has suddenly become an international issue. Egypt, for instance, is running a publicity campaign warning both that the Qur'ān forbids drugs and that they are lethal. No one is sure how to handle this new 'epidemic'.

In America most new psychiatric admissions are 'young chronics'. For some, drugs brought on psychological problems; for others, poor mental health took them into drugs. Such patients are hard to treat. They often leave hospital bragging that, now they are 'sane', they are free to enjoy drugs. Ironically, because governments have 'declared war' on drugs, they are more willing to spend money on research, treatment and publicity against addiction than on mental health. No government-financed campaign has promoted mental health as vigorously as the British government's £2 million anti-heroin campaign. Some experts argue that psychiatrists should not treat addicts who are not psychiatrically ill. Nevertheless, in most countries, addiction is part of the 'territory' of psychiatry. The talk is of an epidemic and an epidemic requires doctors to treat it.

Attitudes to Mental Illness

It is not surprising that governments have not paid much attention to mental illness as opposed, say, to cancer. Historians of psychiatry have shown how madness has been and still is viewed mainly with fear and, occasionally, with awe as a sign from the gods. Writing of Bangladesh, Dr R. Rahman noted: 'Mental illness is regarded as punishment from God due to misdeeds by the patient or his ancestors and the mentally ill patients are usually cursed and looked down on' (Rahman, 1967). In Japan it is also cause for shame. Even in America, where yuppies flaunt their personal problems and where psycho-therapy comes in a thousand brands (from Aromatherapy to Zen), serious mental illness still carries a stigma. Davis Pollack, chairman of the National Alliance for the Mentally Ill (NAMI) media group, complained that television, radio and the papers poked cheap fun at psychiatric patients in a way that they would never dare with cancer patients or the physically handicapped.

In India, the mentally ill are taken to religious shrines to be beaten. Pamphlets from the National Institute for Mental Health in Bangalore advise local communities that it is not necessary to whip the demons out of those who exhibit psychiatric symptoms.

A leading textbook tells doctors that 'chains, fetters and ropes only worsen psychiatric conditions'.

In Japan, ex-patients are not allowed to have a driving licence, to work as cooks or bakers, to enter public baths or even to act as a tourist guide (who knows what they might say?). A survey in Tokyo showed that 51 per cent of people were frightened of patients 'because you never know what they might do' and only 30 per cent thought that it would not be a 'family disgrace' to have an ill relative. The Japanese reveal common prejudices, only in an extreme way.

Despite much advocacy for patients by groups such as MIND in Britain and others in Western Europe, public attitudes in the West include fear – especially fear that patients are violent. Follow-up studies suggest that such fears are misplaced as patients are less likely to be violent than average, but most societies persist in believing the opposite. The press sometimes whip up sensational fears if, for example, an ex-patient is found guilty of a violent crime. It all creates, and contributes to, fear.

Rejection does not just come anonymously from 'society', it is also very personal. In all the countries I studied, many patients had been abandoned by families. Egypt and India pride themselves on their close family ties, yet I came across many stories of patients who were isolated, abandoned or just locked up in the home. Etsuro Totsuka, a Japanese lawyer who has fought for mental patients, represented one family where the wife had lied to her husband for years. She had told him her sister was a Buddhist nun which was why she had never visited them. In fact, the sister was in a mental hospital but the woman was afraid her husband would never have married her if he had known the truth. A Greek study in 1968 found that, even when someone came from a village and had strong community links, they tended to be abandoned once they entered hospital.

Not all the news is bad, though. Many families *do* remain loyal to relatives. In America, for instance, an estimated 800,000 patients live at home with family. Nevertheless, in all cultures, to be mad is to risk rejection.

It is not just the public and politicians who are intolerant. Doctors themselves do not value psychiatry highly. A study in

1972 by McLaughlin and Parkhouse showed that it was the first choice of only 1.4 per cent of British doctors (Clare, 1976: 380). Often, junior psychiatrists were overseas doctors with little knowledge of English culture. Clare asked, 'Why do British doctors shun psychiatry as a career?' Writing in 1976, he concluded that it was a mixture of poor career prospects (because GPs made more money) and snobbery. The psychologist Liam Hudson (1975) suggested that graduates are attracted to medical specialities that are more technological. It may also be that doctors reflect general social attitudes. Madness, 'the dark side of the moon', is best shunned.

In America, psychiatry apparently enjoys a higher status. Many medical graduates choose it, but that is no bonus for the mentally ill. The best psychiatrists take neurotic cases. I do not intend to belittle such problems but there is a major difference between schizophrenics and neurotics who fret about relationships, anxiety and why they still can't get on with their mothers. Woody Allen, that prince of 'patients', may have complexes but he, like thousands of others in therapy, is not ill. The American fetish for psychotherapy can make it seem an indulgence. Your therapist is part of your mind-and-body maintenance team that will massage you, manicure you and perfume your ego too. Woody Allen may have been uncomfortably close to the truth when he said that the great merit of psychotherapy was that it let him talk for an hour a day about himself without any interruption. Fuller Torrey has argued that for good psychiatrists to devote themselves to such pseudo-patients, the 'worried well', is a dreadful misuse of expertise. It is as if the 'best surgeons spent all their time treating acne' (interview with author).

If the situation is bad in the West where there is at least a tradition of services, it is even worse in the Third World. In November 1985, leading doctors and health professionals from the Eastern Mediterranean met in Damascus to report to the World Health Organization on the state of psychiatry from Morocco to India. Civil servants are not usually that critical but most acknowledged major problems. Afghanistan and Morocco have only two psychiatrists each. Jordan has just 200 psychiatric

beds. Pakistan says it does not have enough money to provide
drugs for all who need them. Libya boasts it now has two
hospitals. A recent study on the Philippines, Taiwan and Thailand notes: 'These countries are unable and unwilling to allocate
economic, educational, administrative, research and manpower
resources to secure the standards of care prescribed by contemporary criteria of service delivery' (*Third World Challenge in
Psychiatry*). That is a stiff, academic way of saying there is a crisis
and that one reason for it is that no society cares enough for the
mentally ill.

The Problem of Abuse

With such negative attitudes, it isn't surprising that nearly every
country has seen abuse of patients. They are neglected, threatened, stolen from and, not infrequently, beaten up. Usually
nurses or attendants commit any violence but, occasionally,
doctors take part. In Japan, ex-patients from Utsonomiya Hospital claimed that the hospital director, Dr Bunnishio Ishikawa
used to hold 'therapy' sessions and smack patients with his golf
club if they dared ask about their treatment. Utsonomiya, in the
words of its current director, Dr Hirahata, 'is the most famous
hospital in the world' after 222 unaccounted for deaths there in
three years. Utsonomiya's story (see Chapter 3) may be shocking
but it is not unique.

In 1984 and 1985, not specially gruesome years in the annals
of psychiatry, patients were killed in Utsonomiya and Otaki
hospitals in Japan. In India, forty-four patients died in one
month in Bihar State Hospital while 500 were left to starve. In
Manhattan State Hospital which looms across the East River
from New York's chic East 80s, patients were harassed. Paul
Lee, a schizophrenic, alleged staff let one man bully other
patients mercilessly to the extent that he openly engaged in
homosexual acts on the ward. Lee claimed the staff did nothing
either because they did not care or because they were warned
about infringing patients' rights. In South Korea, patients
were kept in caves. In Bangladesh, Pakistan and India, the mad
were often manacled, their wrists chained to their ankles. Mrs

Eleyemma Brocklesby Davis, an Indian nurse, had to send patients to the local cycle shop to have their chains smashed apart. In Pabna, Bangladesh, they also arrived in chains. In Trivandrum, southern India, local police raped female patients. In China, ECT was given without anaesthetic or muscle relaxant even though research shows this can lead to broken bones and dislocated joints. In Britain the last ten years have seen serious allegations of brutality at Broadmoor and Rampton top security hospitals and at ordinary hospitals like St Augustine's, Whittingham and Ely.

In every country I visited, patients, talking on their own with no fear of being overheard, complained of a lack of treatment, of neglect, of drugs being over-prescribed even when they complained of side-effects.

In the 1976 edition of *Psychiatry in Dissent*, Anthony Clare noted: 'For too long psychiatrists and those working with them in the psychiatric arena have tended to cover up when they should expose and when genuine scandals have occurred, such as Whittingham, they have more often than not assured the public that such lapses are atypical and rare instead of making plain the more honest view that such lapses are inevitable as long as the psychiatric services are starved of skilled resources, are inadequately staffed and poorly funded.' (Clare, 1976)

Many psychiatrists argue that there are some patients who provoke violence. Journalists with 'tough' stories of abuse, they say, have no idea what it is like to work on wards, day in and day out; staff are poorly trained; patients are paranoid and do not behave like saints. There is some justice in such counter-arguments but, often, it is *helpless* patients who get beaten up. Abuse may be universal but the horror stories only surface in open societies – usually, through the media. So-called 'whistle-blowers' from inside the system are rare. Two nurses at Broadmoor in 1980 publicized abuses but psychiatrists themselves hardly ever make revelations.

An outsider may be forgiven for wondering what would be bad enough to provoke serious criticism of fellow professionals. In 1985, after the Utsonomiya scandal, the International Commission of Jurists visited Japan and produced a damning report about the violation of patients' rights. In 1987 Professor S. Sharma, chairman of the ethics review body of the World Psychiatric Association, said he couldn't comment on 'rumours of violations' because he did not know what Japanese psychiatrists felt about the issue. It would be wrong to offend professional colleagues by premature comment. So, two years after the International Commission produced its report, the world's leading psychiatric body stays silent because Japanese psychiatrists have, conveniently for them, not replied to letters. Professor Sharma did not think this odd or outrageous.

Such failure to respond suggests that monitoring psychiatry really cannot be left to psychiatrists. They find it all too easy to dismiss their critics as crazy – especially if, as is necessarily the case, they are ex-patients.

The World Health Organization has paid no attention to the question of brutality in its many publications. One WHO official told me that in countries where there was hunger, poverty and arranged marriages, issues like patients' rights were an irrelevance. What mattered was delivering services.

In the Alma Ata declaration (which defined the goals for global health up to the year 2000) the WHO committed itself to providing 'health for all' by the year 2000. Everyone ought to have access to psychiatric treatment at least through a primary healthcare centre. The declaration is fine but the WHO doesn't add that, even if such centres are built, psychiatrists may not be able to cure the mentally ill. The slogan 'health for all' conceals many conflicts about how to achieve it.

The Problem of Treatment

Experts disagree as to what is the best treatment. Larry Gostin, an American lawyer who fought hard for reform in Britain when he was legal officer of MIND, has pointed out that this is one of the perennial puzzles of psychiatry (Gostin, 1986). Each generation of doctors and activists proclaims that they have found a new solution. In the 1840s, it was 'moral treatment': provide the 'insane' with clean country air, respect and a decent environment and they would be healed. The history of the famous York

Retreat, a model Quaker asylum, however, shows (Digby, 1986) that moral treatment became what we now criticize as old-fashioned lunatic asylums, where patients were kept in gruelling conditions. Improvement was rare. After the Second World War, the magic solution seemed to be drugs. Now we know that heavy use of drugs tends to create its own problems, such as tremors and dependency; moreover, doctors who rely on drugs tend not to deal with patients' underlying 'life problems'. Emptying the hospitals, the magic solution of the late 1960s, turned out also to have unforeseen problems. The 'freed' patients often would receive no treatment at all; they would be poor, homeless and abandoned. Each new solution has bred new problems. Today's panacea, community care, has turned out to be just the same – a combination of promise and pitfalls. Though we like to think of ourselves as being far more civilized and tolerant than in the past, we have not come so far from the days of Clifford Beers.

Beers was a businessman who went through a psychotic period. In *A Mind That Found Itself* (1907), he described the cruel treatment he received in mental hospitals in 1902. This included being kept for fifteen hours in a straitjacket, that 'instrument of torture': 'When my arms were released from their constricted position, the pain was intense. Every joint had been racked.' Straitjackets are used rarely now – an obvious sign of progress – but Beers was also angry about

the time I was held also in seclusion in a padded cell. A padded cell is a vile hole. The side walls are as high as a man can reach, as is also the inside of the door. One of the worst features of such cells is the lack of ventilation which deficiency of course aggravates their general unsanitary condition. The cell which I was forced to occupy was practically without heat and as winter was coming on I suffered intensely from the cold.

Eighty-five years later, seclusion and padded cells remain an integral part of life in mental hospitals all over the world. I have inspected them from Kent to Bethlehem, Tokyo to Cairo. Some countries (Britain, America, Holland) have rules on how they may be used; most do not. It was explained to me, often, in many different countries, that there were times when the only thing to do with a patient was to isolate him. This would calm him down.

In October 1986, the New York Office of Mental Health published a survey of how seclusion was used in thirty-one of its hospitals. Between 15 February and 14 March 1984, there were 2150 cases of seclusion, with many patients getting the 'treatment' more than once. A total of 804 patients were actually restrained. Most hospitals wrote seclusion orders for two to four hours but some were longer. The report accepts that seclusion is used 'by hospital staff as a means of controlling dangerous, destructive or disruptive behaviour when medication and psychotherapy fail'. Sometimes it is used for less, since the report notes: 'The majority of the episodes were precipitated by violent behaviour rather than by threats or agitation.' In some cases, their threats or agitation were enough. Blacks were put in seclusion more often than either whites or Puerto Ricans. The report only questioned staff, so it was somewhat one-sided. Patients might not have seen the reasons for their seclusion in the same way. They might have been more inclined to Clifford Beers's view – that to be in solitary was a form of punishment and that it was 'a vile hole'. However, those who had been secluded (even though they constituted a substantial number) were never asked to comment. Clifford Beers went on to fight for reform and the rights of patients. I suspect he would recognize many of the current debates.

Most psychiatrists today see themselves as doctors dealing with diseases. They admit social and emotional factors may play a part in causing diseases but it is a small one. Predictably, such doctors rely mainly on drugs and on ECT. Physical diseases need physical cures. It is important not to caricature such psychiatrists. There are sensitive (and insensitive) believers in the medical model. The sensitive ones will also offer some counselling and do their best to explain to patients what is wrong even if they don't have much hope of being understood. Fuller Torrey, who argues passionately that schizophrenia is a brain disease, is not surprised by the lack of insight of patients. They are brain sick and the brain is the organ we use to think about ourselves. To expect anything else is unrealistic. For him, psychotherapy cannot help with serious mental illnesses though he is happy to think of it as a form of education for middle-class neurotics (interview with author).

Torrey's view is contested, however. There are distinguished dissidents all over the world who maintain either that the 'medical model' does not work or that it has been warped out of all recognition. Professor Al Rahawy of Cairo University, for instance, complained: 'I like medicine but the medical model has come to be seen as a chemical model.' It was naïve to think that madness was only a chemical imbalance in the brain and that the schizophrenic, just had his 'chemistry up or his chemistry down'.

Different schools accuse each other of relying too much on drugs or being duped by psychotherapy. Attempting a dispassionate assessment, Clare (1976) concluded that drug treatments coped with acute episodes of schizophrenia but that social and therapeutic help was also needed long-term. Patients remain stubbornly individual. One-third do not respond to any medication. No treatment is universally accepted as effective for a particular cluster of diseases.

ECT can be very useful in deep depressions but often, it, too, doesn't work. Side-effects, such as loss of memory, may be severe. A report from the Royal College of Psychiatrists (Pippard, 1980) on ECT in Britain found that it was often given poorly, making it less effective and more likely to produce side-effects.

The various brands of psychotherapy also have a mixed record. In a famous paper in 1952, Hans Eysenck claimed that psychoanalysis and psychotherapy did no good. In his recent *Decline and Fall of the Freudian Empire* (1986), Eysenck repeats his original attack, even though there is evidence that some therapy is modestly successful, as are drugs and ECT.

Much depends on how you define cure. Few statistical evaluations confront the messy issue of how good the criteria for cure are. How much does a person have to change to be declared cured? And would the family's definition of cure agree with that of the psychiatrist? If not, whose is better? These are all proper, important questions but psychiatrists often shrug them off as methodological frills. Yet, dismissing such issues also protects psychiatrists from examining their own work critically. Dr Subjud Mukerjhee pointed out there was 'too much negativism so that a little improvement is considered enough' (interview with author).

Dr Okasha of Cairo elevated modest expectations into a goal in themselves. Psychiatrists should not encourage unrealistic hopes. Most doctors did not cure: 'The doctor does not get rid of high blood pressure or diabetes' (interview with author). Insulin and other drugs allow the patient to live with the illness, to feel less pain and to manage. Why should psychiatry do better? It sounds plausible yet it also sounds much like Dr Mukerjhee's 'negativism'.

Certainly, many advocates of drugs make only modest claims. Properly administered, they enable many to live with, and within, their symptoms. However, even with drugs and a settled life, schizophrenia is hard to eradicate. It comes back all too easily. Many patients know they are trapped between the dangers of medication (side-effects) and the dangers of non-medication. In the West, at least, some patients get the chance to discuss such issues. Few have this 'luxury' in the Third World.

Travelling from hospital to hospital and clinic to clinic left me with paradoxical impressions. Many psychiatrists and their co-workers try hard and become fond of many of their patients. They moan that, if they let it, the job would consume their lives. Yet many psychiatrists exude a sense of failure. It was rare to come across enthusiasts like the staff at Mokattam Hospital in Cairo or Community Access in New York. Usually, as Dr Mukerjhee said, 'You do your job, collect your money, don't make waves.' Apathy rules. In many professions, success is easy to judge. The surgeon knows whether the appendix is properly removed; the lawyer knows whether he has won the case; the architect can see the building. Psychiatrists deal with far less tangible signs of success, for how do you really know if someone is better? Few psychiatrists acknowledge such inner conflicts publicly but, I suspect, they contribute to the depressing climate in many hospitals. And perhaps the depression of psychiatrists adds to the depression of patients.

The Problem of Patients' Rights

In Britain, when you enter a prison you are read a list of your duties and your rights. Enter a mental hospital in most parts of the world and nothing similar happens. An international comparison of what rights patients lose is depressing.

Patients lose the right to vote in Japan, India and, in some instances, in Britain and the US. In Holland, Egypt and many European countries, they lose the right to administer their own property. In Japan, Egypt and Israel, they lose the right to write and receive uncensored mail. In most countries, outside America, patients do not have the right to refuse treatment. In Britain, the 1983 Mental Health Act requires two psychiatrists to agree that a patient who refuses to consent to a particular treatment needs it. But the first psychiatrist can choose which colleague to ask for a second opinion. He is likely to ask someone with similar attitudes. Cosy collaborations grow up. I am not likely to disagree with you about what your patient needs if, tomorrow, I may need you to approve my treatment. The Mental Health Act Commission report for 1987 found that many detained patients had mail censored, were frightened to complain if badly treated and, in some hospitals like Broadmoor, were overcrowded and sometimes had to stand naked in corridors. The Commission was especially critical of the way in which psychiatrists often dismissed patients' complaints as a sign of illness.

In most countries, if a patient threatened to sue his/her psychiatrist, it would be seen as final proof of madness. In America, fear of litigation makes some states give patients information about their legal rights. Creedmoor Hospital in Queens, New York, for example, hands new patients a detailed pamphlet. It outlines specific rights. Everyone has the right to access to the telephone, to have visitors at all reasonable times, to privacy when visited and to 'send and receive sealed, unopened and uncensored mail'. Interestingly, 'The treatment team may decide that certain limitations are necessary for the well-being of patients and others.' So, even in America, doctors can decide that making a phone call or sending a letter would be counter-therapeutic and the only quick appeal is to the hospital director who supervises the team that made that decision. Again, patients have less right to an independent second opinion than might appear.

American patients have to give informed consent for any treatment like ECT. The hospital has to give them 'a full and comprehensive disclosure of potential benefits and harm' so they can be properly informed. In emergencies, however, the physician can over-ride that consent and, even, put a patient in seclusion for up to a day. Patients' rights are far from secure. They have no say in who their doctors will be. Yet, for all its loopholes, Creedmoor's document is important. All too often patients believe they lose all rights on entering hospital. Few hospitals outside America offer any such information.

The most important civil rights issue is the detention of patients against their will. In many countries, it is seen as an extreme measure and psychiatrists use the fact to bargain with patients. If they agree to treatment, there won't be any need for such drastic action. Good patients, helpful patients, know the doctor knows best and don't want to involve lawyers. In Egypt, a hospital can detain patients for seven days before it has to notify the authorities that they are there against their will. Dr Ahmed Abu Al Azayem explained (interview with author) that during those seven days patients often calmed down and, in that more rational state, agreed to accept treatment. They knew the disadvantages of disagreeing. Their employers would have to be told; their right to control their property would go; the stigma would be great. It was much more convenient to keep the law out of it. In America, a voluntary patient has to give a hospital seventy-two hours' warning that he, or she, intends to leave. During that seventy-two hours, the hospital can apply to a court to keep him/her there. In Israel, a psychiatrist even has the power to detain a patient for a week without having seen him if the family doctor is sure the patient is a danger to himself or others. Such laws make it very easy to bring pressure on patients to stay in hospital.

In Britain every year, there are about 16,000 compulsory admissions. Most last no more than twenty-eight days but some last far longer. Some patients have more than one compulsory admission a year. On an average day, 4,700 are held.

In America, there are 188,000 patients detained. In Israel some 2,000 are held every year against their will. In Sweden, some 3,254 are held so. The World Health Organization, for all its massive studies of psychiatry worldwide, was unable to give me a reasonable estimate of how many involuntary patients there are across the world. It seems quite possible that it is between 1 and 2 million people often held in conditions more like prison than hospital, conditions which Clifford Beer would find depressingly familiar.

Possibly the worst situation is that in Japan. Japan has 350,000 inpatients. According to Etsuro Totsuka, a lawyer who founded the Japanese Civil Liberties Mental Health Association, some 80 per cent are held without their consent. Families can commit embarrassing relatives by taking them to the local hospital. Only one psychiatrist has to accept that they need to be in hospital and that psychiatrist can be the owner of the hospital. Every new patient is a new source of revenue. The Japanese government does not see this as a dangerous conflict of interest. It is telling, though, that Japan not only has more mental patients than any country on earth but that it detains them on average far longer (583 days in Tokyo) than other countries.

Most legal systems (even the Soviet one) specify that someone can be detained against their will only if they are a danger to themselves or others. But, as reports from many countries show, the oddest things can be taken as proof of such danger and the anger that being committed against your will can cause can be extreme. In the USSR it can be trying to get friends to read the Bible; in Britain it may be acting too boisterously if you are black; in Japan, being a beatnik.

Etsuro Totsuka recently helped arrange a meeting in Kyoto at which a number of distinguished psychiatrists called for a basic charter of rights. One of the group, Professor T. W. Harding, reported their deliberations in *The Lancet*. Harding wrote: '. . . in the absence of a clear set of international standards for the protection of the mentally ill, it would be useful to define a set of basic principles.' The following principles were unanimously accepted:

1. Mentally ill persons should receive humane, dignified and professional treatment.
2. Mentally ill persons should not be discriminated against by reason of their mental illness.
3. Voluntary admission should be encouraged whenever hospital treatment is necessary.
4. There should be an impartial and informal hearing before an independent tribunal to decide, within a reasonable time of admission, whether an involuntary patient needs continued hospital care.
5. Hospital patients should enjoy as free an environment as possible and should be able to communicate with other persons.

As the signatories to that document know, many psychiatric patients do not get care that conforms even remotely to these standards. And yet the standards demanded are not that high. Moreover, there is no guarantee that international psychiatry will accept guidelines laid down by a distinguished but rather ad hoc group of experts gathered in Kyoto in the wake of continuing scandals about Japanese hospitals. Many influential organizations were absent: the World Health Organization, the British Royal College of Psychiatrists and the American Psychiatric Association were not formally represented. Nor was the Japanese Association of Psychiatric Hospitals who are unlikely to approve of the Kyoto principles. There was no one from Eastern Europe or from Africa.

The Kyoto document is well-intentioned but it would be naïve to think that it will transform psychiatry. Yet something like it is badly needed. The United Nations Charter of Human Rights, for example, does not guarantee the specific rights that matter to the mentally ill. It is sad, however, that there were no Third World psychiatrists at Kyoto because, though they have imported Western ideas, they have been even slower than their

Western colleagues to take any notice of patients' rights, a point I develop in Chapter 2.

If Kyoto is to mark the start of something, there needs to be far more awareness of what is happening in different countries. There is little of an international literature, though there are, of course, those fat tomes on cross-cultural psychiatry where the intrepid psychiatrist goes trekking for the natives' weird stone-age symptoms. On safari, the mind doctor loves to stalk an 'exotic' variant of depression in Papua New Guinea or a marvellously 'primitive' schizophrenia in the Amazon. Can anything be done to preserve splendid syndromes like running amok or digging up your future father-in-law's vegetables? This symptom is found only in Borneo and is the product of sexual frustration! But few books investigate how psychiatry is practised internationally though there have recently been two useful books one on the Philippines, Thailand and Taiwan (Higginbottom 1986) and one on Botswana (Ben-Tovim). But no book has tried to compare large countries like the United States and Japan with Third World countries.

In this book, I want to focus on the conditions in which people are kept, on the treatments they can hope to receive and on the views both of psychiatrists, of other professionals and of patients who often have a strange mixture of hostility and gratitude.

Walter Reed, for example, appreciates what Community Access does for him and, yet, periodically wants to get away. He dreams of escaping to California where no one will nag him to go to hospital for his injection. Paul Lee also appreciates the help he receives and yet said, 'Yes, I feel bitter, I feel bitter about the lot fate handed me.' American patients are more used than most to expressing their views. I hope, in this book, to listen also to less vocal patients from other cultures.

2
Psychiatric Imperialism

Psychiatry is an international business. One afternoon when I was researching in England for a film on Napsbury Hospital's crisis-intervention service, I accompanied a Chilean psychiatrist and a Scottish social worker who had been called out to an address where a man had gone berserk. We drove to a semi-detached house in north London. An agitated Bangladeshi girl let us in and began to explain. Her husband had taken a knife, threatened her, and then threatened to kill himself. Then he sat on his prayer mat and refused to budge. She was not quite sure why because her Sylheti was very rusty. He had come recently from Sylhet, in the north of Bangladesh, and spoke no English. They could hardly communicate. The Chilean psychiatrist found it hard to understand what she was saying. The Scottish social worker understood her but, being accustomed to the batterings of life, just shook his head knowingly. The 'team' was committed to a model of psychiatry that saw illness as the product of problems in life. How could a South American doctor from a Catholic country make sense of the traumas of someone from a totally different religion and culture, especially if they could not exchange a word? The team had no option but to take the patient to hospital. The man looked frightened and angry as he was led to the car. The psychiatrist, liberal in his views, was dismayed that he had no alternative. The wife seemed grateful.

Travelling back to the hospital, we began to theorize, perhaps because our failure to communicate had made us feel uncomfortable. Coming to Britain and to a new wife had terrified the man. He had withdrawn and become catatonic to avoid the terror of novelty. None of us could begin to explain his behaviour so we took refuge in Toffler. Too much change, too fast, had led to the breakdown. Despite all the nationalities at the scene, no one had the right cultural knowledge to get through to the man on the prayer mat.

That failure highlighted for me the fact that, though psychiatry is increasingly an international business, it is, like most others, a business in which the West is dominant. The only anomaly is that Japan, for once, ranks as a Third World country.

In London, the Institute of Psychiatry has been training foreign doctors since 1925. Robin Murray, its Dean, is a psychiatrist who made his name with research on the psychological problems of doctors. The Institute is a microcosm of the world. There are Arab, African, South American and European students. Murray said they sink their geographical and cultural differences to master advanced psychiatry. Other famous training schools, like the New York Psychiatric Institute, also take students from all over the world and operate on similar principles.

Graduate doctors come to acquire a grounding in what ought to be known as the Western psychiatric tradition. Psychiatry hardly recognizes any other tradition. The Maudsley library emphasizes this dominance discreetly: nearly every periodical on its well-stocked shelves is American, British or German. There are a few eastern European journals but hardly any Eastern ones apart from the *Indian Journal of Psychiatry*, one Arab journal and the *Japanese Journal of Psychiatry* which is entirely biological in its outlook. You would never suspect from the library shelves that some historians claim that the first mental hospital was in Baghdad and that, long before London had its Bedlam, Aleppo in Syria had a mental hospital. Nor would the library allow you to think there is a long, learned Eastern tradition of coping with madness. A recent textbook on Indian psychiatry produced by S. Sharma (1985) illustrates this dominance. Out of twenty-eight chapters, Sharma devotes only one to local forms of illness. In writing of schizophrenia, depressive illness and manic states, he makes no concession to local conditions.

Yet, other cultures may well have much to offer orthodox psychiatry. N. Pereschkian is an Iranian therapist who practices in West Germany. He suggests in a charming but also provoca-

tive book, *Oriental Tales as Tools in Psychotherapy* (1985), a number
of ways in which the West could learn from the East. He is
scathing about gurus like the Bhagwan who made all his disciples
wear orange and carry a picture of him, but he claims that their
ego posturings should not make us ignore everything the East
has to offer. Pereschkian retells about a hundred tales. Their very
foreignness offers therapeutic advantage. It obliges one to take a
fresh look. Take the story of the couple who had been happily
married for thirty years. When they breakfast that happy day,
the wife doesn't eat the doughy part of the bread she usually
does. Instead she eats the crust and gives him the dough. He is
ecstatic. She is surprised. She thought he might be upset but,
after thirty years she felt she had the right to have the crust she
much prefers. Well, it turns out, he prefers the doughy part but
didn't like to say so since he thought she liked that part better
herself. Is such 'silence' a recipe for a happy marriage? Pereschkian claims the tales offer a starting point to help patients
focus afresh on their lives. He treats both Eastern and Western
traditions as equal, something colonial societies could not easily
achieve.

The first country to 'benefit' from the exportation of psychiatry
was India. The first psychiatric hospital was built in 1745 by the
East India Company for those of its servants who went berserk.
Indian patients were accepted in 1817. Asylums were built at
Calcutta in 1787 and then at Delhi, Lucknow and Agra in the
shadow of the Taj Mahal. Many of these elegant buildings
continue to be used as psychiatric hospitals. Hospitals were also
built in Karachi, in Nairobi and Cairo. The British even built a
hospital at Jaffa when they held the Palestine Mandate. The
French set up asylums in Algeria, where the great psychiatrist,
Frantz Fanon, author of *The Wretched of the Earth* (1966), worked.
When the Americans occupied Japan, they followed suit, urging
the Japanese to build hospitals so that patients would no longer
be kept at home (where they were sometimes housed in cages).
Building such hospitals encouraged native doctors to look to the
West for their ideas. Many became very 'professionalized' and
began to look with scorn and hostility on traditional ways of
managing insanity. As a new professional class, doctors were in

competition with traditional native healers and had to quash such unqualified 'amateurs'.

The directors of these colonial hospitals were nearly always European psychiatrists like Colonel Berkeley Hill and Major Brocklesby Davis who ran the asylum for the European mad at Ranchi. Few colonial psychiatrists spoke native languages. And few acknowledged this might put them at a disadvantage in diagnosing the 'natives'. For example, till the 1960s, it was confidently stated that Africans did not suffer from depression. The black man was too unintellectual and too happy-go-lucky to suffer the Hamlet melancholies. If he felt a bit low, all he needed to do was dance to the bongo-bongo drums and, by Sambo, he'd be as happy as a golliwog again. Psychiatrists clung to this stereotype just as their psychologist colleagues trumpeted that Jews should not be allowed into America because they would lower the intellectual tone and IQ level – all nice evidence of how easy it is not to see the evidence.

Today, few psychiatrists believe that Africans cannot summon up a depression but modern training still reflects Western culture and concerns. Few Asian and African countries have specialist training. Even in Japan, a doctor may be the director of a psychiatric hospital without any qualification in psychiatry. A doctor who wants to get a good post-graduate qualification that will make him marketable internationally usually has to go to the West. If such a student comes to the Maudsley, he or she will receive the latest background in neurology, brain chemistry, the use of drugs, controversies about ECT, psychotherapy and the use of social workers. But there will be little cross-cultural material, little attention paid to questions such as what may provoke madness in his, or her, culture, and alternative ways of coping in a poor country.

The training doctors receive, moreover, is likely to alienate them from significant aspects of their own culture. They may come to see their mission as introducing the benefits of Western medicine to their backward compatriots. Good Indian hospitals use exactly the same techniques as good Western hospitals. The same appears to be true in most of South East Asia, according to 'Psychiatry in South East Asia' (Neki, 1973) which lists a familiar compendium of drugs, ECT and occupational therapy though in both cases even this care tends to be given to the middle classes.

It is worth asking why psychiatry has remained so 'imperialistic'. Partly, it's the result of success. Since the eighteenth century, Western psychiatry has appeared to be quite successful. Historians like Scull in his *Museums of Madness* and Foucault have argued that this success is not due to curing patients but to controlling them. Fast-growing industrial societies, like Victorian Britain, had to keep their outcasts on a tight leash. For a long time, doctors had to compete with non-medical lunatic asylum superintendents for the role of providing social control. The doctors won because they had more status and to involve them suggested a veneer of care. Despite these unflattering origins, by 1900, many psychiatrists clearly thought they were in the business of treating patients. And, in many ways, care has become more humane. There are few straitjackets in the West. Patients are not kept in chains or subjected to bizarre tortures like being dunked in cold baths. Solitary confinement is used less. Some patients do get better. The Western model is certainly not a total failure.

But psychiatry has remained imperialistic for less idealistic reasons too. It is in the interest of psychiatrists. The post-industrial world has seen the development of international professional élites who can ply their trade anywhere on earth. The architect can build anywhere; the engineer engineer anywhere; the pilot pilot anywhere. Why shouldn't psychiatrists do the same. Unlike architects, engineers and pilots, alas, the psychiatrist does not work on inanimate objects that can be separate from the local culture. Psychiatrists work on human, social beings who are tied into their societies. For most doctors this is not an important issue. A heart, gut or intestine is the same in Accra and Accrington. Psychiatrists have the misfortune of being the only group of doctors who ought not to be able to practise internationally. They have responded to this dilemma by pretending that local cultural conditions don't matter very much.

While researching this book, I was struck by the number of expatriate psychiatrists. I met Indian psychiatrists in London and New York, I met Egyptians in London, Israelis in America, Germans in India. It would be nice to think that this mix led to a more creative psychiatry. The opposite is the case. International psychiatry can function only by excluding local differences, so the practice of the trade is curiously standardized all over the world. The last skill an ambitious Third World doctor who wants to practise in America needs is expertise in how his, or her, native culture affects the expression of madness. The fact that many black doctors face prejudice only exacerbates this trend. Unsurprisingly, they often see themselves less as native Indians or Bangladeshis and more as members of the international medical technocracy. Their roots come to matter less than their roles.

There are many idealistic doctors, but doctors are only human and the difference in salaries is huge. The average Egyptian doctor picks up 400 Egyptian pounds a month; the average Indian doctor 1000 rupees. Two hours with a New York psychiatrist costs more! According to Robin Murray, the temptation for doctors to leave Third World countries is enormous.

Even more surprising, radical psychiatry has not confronted such international issues. The intellectual heirs of R. D. Laing and Thomas Szasz have become insular. This isn't the place to examine this in detail but two books, *Critical Psychiatry* (Ingleby et al., 1981) which was subtitled 'The Politics of Mental Health', and a different *The Politics of Mental Health* (Banton et al., 1985) reflect that insularity. Both are chic, Marxist and oddly blind to the Third World.

Ingleby and his co-authors in *Critical Psychiatry* accuse psychiatry of being obsessed with trying to prove it is a biological science. He claims it is naïve to think brain states 'cause' mental illness because mental illness is a social 'construction': societies define what is sane and insane.

Ingleby then provides evidence from America, Britain, Italy and even Norway to suggest that the only proper cure will be a variation of psychoanalytic Marxist therapy. Liberation will involve seeing through the class structure. He makes no reference to any country that isn't rich. One stunningly self-indulgent chapter requests sympathy for the dialectical agonies of Norwegian social workers who fret about whether entering the Common Market would make them more neurotic! The chapter on America, written by Joel Kovel, never deals with the fact that the homeless mentally ill, like Walter Reed in Chapter 1, are a major political scandal. Kovel even examines the Community Mental Health Centres (CMHC) without acknowledging that they fail to cope with the poor, the blacks and Hispanics. Instead, since CMHCs challenge the professional 'hegemony' of psychiatrists, he praises them for making the first inroads in 'the medicalization of politics'. Fuller Torrey, outwardly a much more conservative psychiatrist, has condemned the CMHCs for concentrating on narcissistic neurotics who want their egos adjusted while the seriously mentally ill get ignored. Ingleby's book also never deals with the economic facts of life as psychiatrists in poor countries see them. A psychiatrist may see 150 'state' patients a week. His pay will be low. The doctor wants to confirm himself as a professional with a good standard of living; he 'needs' private practice to live as he has been taught a professional should.

Positive action can change that need but it has to be recognized as a problem first. Dr N. Reddy explained to me that the staff at NIMHANS (National Institute for Mental Health and Neurological Sciences) in Bangalore are not allowed to have any private practice. They are paid better salaries than in state hospitals which permit private work. The policy was good, Reddy argued, as they had found that doctors tended to favour their private patients, to abuse public facilities and 'making money becomes the main aim'. Dr Murthy, one of Reddy's deputies, said he was only too glad not to be distracted by private practice. The prestige and, in Indian terms, decent salary were compensation enough.

Ingleby also suggests that 'psychiatrists have been bamboozled into being agents of the state' whose purpose it is to cure people so that they can be returned to productive labour. Ingleby does not seem to have taken into account the rise of unemployment. The state may actually welcome those who are too disabled to feature in the job market. America may be capitalist but it is happy to shunt its mentally ill into shelters and on the streets where they drop out of employment. Japan, which might fit a Marxist analysis better is ignored totally by Ingleby, even though there is huge social pressure to conform and work productively.

Fail to please Nippon Inc. and you might be sent to hospital. Even there it is far from clear that hospitals try to get people back into jobs. The lack of a real international perspective among authors who are very critical of the assumptions of psychiatry is bizarre.

The Politics of Mental Health, written by five Marxist feminists, again makes no mention of any poor country and the conditions in which psychiatry has to function. Without much of an international radical perspective, it is easy for most doctors to accept as conclusive the evidence that mental illnesses are similar in different cultures. That was the drift of the International Project of 1973, which compared how psychiatrists in different countries diagnosed schizophrenia. The Stirling County study found few differences between French and English Canadians. Leighton (1986) and his team also studied Eskimos and Indians. They found a similar range of problems though there were subtle differences in expressions of symptoms. Arab psychiatrists certainly believe in general similarities and subtle differences. 'The culture shades the symptoms,' according to Gamal Abu Al Azayem who found that in Egypt patients had delusions of being persecuted by angels and devils rather than by missiles and lasers which are popular hallucinations in the West. Mohammed Kamal, who runs the Bethlehem Hospital, finds his patients complain more of psychosomatic problems. They moan they have a 'heavy heart' rather than they are depressed. In China, doctors report a number of exotic conditions.

The training that doctors receive worldwide is apt to minimize the importance of cultural differences. The human body is the same from Anchorage to Australia, after all. Graduates in psychiatry will learn that, while there are exotic local variants, the basic psychiatric diseases are the same. This may be true but it does not mean that the correct, and/or possible, treatments ought to be the same, especially when no form of treatment seems to work for all of the patients all of the time. It is easy – and, perhaps, slack – to assume that variations in symptoms and in public attitudes are so small as not to matter.

In the rest of this chapter I want to look at five areas where this bias of training affects treatment and narrows the perspective of psychiatry. Three of these show how Western assumptions rule. The other two are less simple. All psychiatric training is medical and tends to ignore social attitudes yet it is clear that public tolerance affects how a particular society handles mental patients. Then, the West has also developed the notion of consumer rights in health. Imperfect as these are, the rest of the world does not have them: sadly, there is little sign that Third World psychiatrists want their patients to acquire them.

Poverty

The Alma Ata declaration stated that poverty damages mental health. Western psychiatrists do not often have to deal with famine and malnutrition. Malnutrition retards emotional and intellectual development; it may well cause depression. Recent results suggest that a vitamin deficit may be one causal factor in schizophrenia. To realize the extent to which Western psychiatry ignores the facts of hunger, look at the list of stressful 'life events' that are said to be possible triggers of major depression. There is no mention of lack of food or poor diet. The reason is simple, I suspect; Western psychiatrists rarely encounter famine. Yet, charities like Oxfam and Save the Children find that such problems do more to damage mental health than such classics as 'executive stress'. Dr Kotry, director-general of mental health in Egypt, pointed out that difficult economic circumstances lead to psychiatric suffering even in an Islamic country where the Qur'ān requires charity. In theory, no one is allowed to starve in Egypt, but anxieties about food persist. Indian psychiatrists also argue that economic problems cause anxiety. Hunger is not an area to ignore.

Poor countries often have relatively large health budgets but they are even less able than rich countries to spend much on psychiatric care. In America, a well-run community mental-health centre may offer psychiatrists, psychologists, psychotherapists, an educational psychologist for children, a grief counsellor to cope with bereavement, a social worker to negotiate decent housing and now a case manager to make sure you keep all your appointments with all the above. After all, what will your therapist feel if you miss too many appointments? Are you rejecting him/her? In Africa, no community can afford such a galaxy of skills and neuroses. Dr Helmut Sell, the regional adviser for psychiatry to the World Health Organization, explained to me that when he had been the one psychiatrist in Botswana, he had a catchment area of over one and a half million people. He would drive into the desert and might, if lucky, see a patient once every six months. Many of those in need did not know he existed. There were no nurses. 'I taught families how to give patients injections and how to recognize when they might be needed.' What else could he do? There is little point in recommending sophisticated community services when most underdeveloped countries can't hope to afford them. The question should be, what are the best possible psychiatric services for different countries given what they can afford? Doctors may not like some of the answers. The World Health Organization argues, for example, that paramedics may often be of more use in developing a spread of psychiatric services. They need far less training and are far less expensive than psychiatrists. But there is a drawback. The treatments paramedics are best at giving are usually pills and injections.

Poverty also affects what counts as good treatment. In the West, doctors have become rightly anxious about the prescribing of drugs. In the 1970s, Britain saw an epidemic of attempted suicide which was linked to the habit GPs had of prescribing tranquillisers too freely. Patients took valium in large quantities. There were 200,000 attempted suicides by 1980 when sustained publicity began to influence more conservative prescribing. In 1981, the American Psychiatric Association, not an organization noted for its radicalism, warned that many major tranquillisers had side-effects such as tardive disykensia, the tremor that Walter Reed suffers from. But while the West has become chary of drugs, almost all Third World countries judge the success of psychiatry in terms of how effective they are in the delivery of drugs. As there is no hope of delivering psychotherapy or counselling services the criterion for success tends to be the amount of drugs used. The Western 'medical' model triumphs. Even in India where impressive attempts are being made in some areas to deliver community psychiatry, the emphasis is on drugs. In a study of satellite clinics near Bangalore, Reddy and his colleagues found that 63 per cent of patients could be treated on the spot without hospitalization (Reddy, 1986). Drugs made that possible and so their consistent use was not much questioned. The Bangalore programme relies heavily on paramedics who tend to reinforce drug use.

I am not arguing that medication is bad, merely stressing that, in the West, many see that drugs are not the only answer. It would be ironic if community psychiatry's success in the Third World should be judged largely in terms of the consumption of tranquillisers. Psychiatrists should try harder even if, in the face of poverty, they plead nothing more subtle can be tried. Psychiatrists obviously cannot solve such dilemmas but, at least, they ought to be aware of them.

Religion

There are also philosophical differences. Is it right to exclude religion from psychiatry? And what is the proper balance between the rights of the individual and the rights of the family?

In his *The Manufacture of Madness* (1972), Szasz pointed out how religions have often persecuted the mad. Medieval lunatics received little Christian charity. In *King Lear*, Edgar, the good son of Gloucester, who fakes madness is driven to live in a hovel on the blasted heath. If there is a warm, welcoming 'community' he never finds it! When Lear and the other 'fools' turn up, they all become outcasts. In the seventeenth century, Christian communities persecuted so-called 'witches' whose delusions were possibly schizophrenic. There is little tradition of using Christianity (or Judaism) creatively as part of the healing process. The great Jewish psychiatrists from Freud onwards have tended to identify themselves as 'Jewish atheists'. Freud in *The Future of an Illusion* (1932) claimed that as human beings grew up they would stop needing the father-figure in the sky. Faith was a form of dependency. The morality churches imposed led to neurosis. Even the minority of spiritual psychiatrists like Jaspers and Jung did not think formal religion could help patients. An awareness of spirituality, perhaps; going to church, no! Michael Argyle, the social psychologist and author of *Religious Behaviour* (1952), told me once that as a practising Christian he was most eccentric among psychologists.

In Islam and some other Eastern countries, there is more respect for religion among psychiatrists. Certain Islamic countries have experimented with using mosques as bases for community care. In Egypt, Dr Gamal Abu Al Azayem makes his patients pray five times a day in the mosque he has had built in his hospital. He likes to claim that he relies on faith rather than tranquillisers. That may be a trifle exaggerated but he also encouraged me to visit Fayoum, a town 100 kilometres across the desert from Cairo where the main mosque provides an astonishing range of medical services: counselling, surgery, even renal dialysis is available. Those with drug and alcohol problems are exposed not just to medical remedies but to social and spiritual pressure. The imams hector 'sinners' to stick to the Qur'ān which forbids all stimulants. Gamal claims this combination of medicine and morality works rather well. Similar ideas are being tried in Pakistan. I have argued that many Third World psychiatrists dismiss traditional native healers. In Fayoum, what is happening is different. It's an alliance between orthodox medicine and orthodox religion. To the West, it is alien and smacks of unpleasant moral pressure. Nevertheless, it is a model that deserves to be studied, especially because it is linked with conflicting views of individual rights.

The Individual

From the Renaissance on, Western 'man' has gloried in being an individual. The cult of the individual flourishes now as never before. It is considered psychologically healthy to 'assert oneself', to do 'one's own thing' and not to be held back by antique guilts. To be handicapped by hang-ups is to torpedo one's life. This creates a particular frame of reference for the concept of cure in Western psychiatry. Take a neurotic conflict. A man aged forty decides that he is no longer happy with his marriage. It makes him depressed. He and his wife married young. They are not very compatible now. He has had homosexual fantasies. He has had two affairs with other women. At home, he is bad-tempered, depressed and lethargic. Nevertheless, his wife wants him to stay. This is a rough patch they will get over. A psychotherapist treating him as an individual might well advise him to 'explore' himself, his options and his conflicts. Going back to the marriage would be defeatist and might turn him into 'less of an individual' than he could be. (The phrase is interesting, as is much psycho babble. We are asked to be 'more' ourselves as if we are an expandable material). An Islamic psychiatrist would see his task differently. It would be to fit the man back into the context of his family. Making the marriage work would be a priority. Such conflicts involve the therapist making choices about what is, and is not, healthy behaviour. Considerable evidence suggests that psychiatrists and therapists are often highly directive. In theory, therapy teases out what the patient wants. The expert listens, interprets, plays back what the patient tells. In practice, from Freud on, psychiatrists have tended to give practical, immediate advice. As experts on living, it is expected of them. Yet psychiatry doesn't recognize that what is a happy ending in one culture may be a disastrous patch-up in another. Again, it is an area that requires attention – especially as views of the family differ radically.

Western psychiatry developed in the nineteenth century when the family was a strong institution. Since the Second World War the nuclear family has become fragmented. There is far more divorce, many more single-parent families, far more open homo-sexuality and many more elderly people are sent from their homes to institutions. Experts disagree, and the pyramids of evidence make it easy to disagree, as to whether these trends are psychologically healthy or not. The strong family could be tyrannical. Father ruled; children obeyed. Those who rebelled risked total rejection. It was oppressive. Others counter that the family offered acceptance and love as the last resort, a haven against the assorted traumas of a harsh world. You knew you always could go back home to mother.

In the West, the family is changing. In the UK, 11 per cent of children are born to one-parent families. Mothers go to work. The extended family and the authority of elders that went with it, is a thing of the past. In the East, especially under Islam, the trend is the opposite. Traditional values are back in favour. Experiments with a more Western, liberal approach now look like betrayal. In theory, the old-fashioned family thrives where the father is the patriarch, wives quake and sons obey. Islamic women are not likely to go to consciousness-raising groups and complain that marriage is not fulfilling them. Teenagers will not know they are teenagers with all that implies by way of staying out late, questioning parental rules and dabbling with sex. While filming in India, I asked the well-educated sons of Indian doctors what kind of 'social' life they had; they looked baffled. One eighteen-year-old said it was important to be in bed by nine o'clock. Going out with girls was something unknown. One psychiatrist said he was sure most men were still virgins when they married. The individual is bound closely to the group and to behave as the group expects. To us, it may seem reactionary; to people like Gamal (who is in the position of being the patriarch) it seems wise, humane and practical.

For psychiatrists, there are many parodoxes here. First, even the most Islamic of psychiatrists who accuse the West of imperialism, prejudice and weakness nevertheless seem to use the Western medical model. Second, the vision any culture has of what is a 'normal' family and what are the 'normal' roles for individuals to play in it, must affect the kind of therapy that is offered. In an Islamic society, it hardly makes sense to ask a child if he thinks a parent is behaving tyrannically, for example. Curiously, Arab and Indian families may be similar to those Freud and other analysts treated round 1900 when patriarchy reigned. Psychiatric training needs to recognize and explore such differences, especially if they are becoming more polarized.

One should not idealize the non-Western family. Some Eastern stories I was told echo Europe a few decades ago when the rich were always willing to ship off their mad relatives to sanatoriums to be a safe distance away. The extended family may not be quite that supportive. First, a Middle Eastern monarch began to behave more bizarrely as he got older. Keeping the old king at court meant witnessing his less than regal behaviour so it was decided to let one of his sons assume the throne while he was sent to an Egyptian hospital. There, he lived in a luxury villa with a swimming pool and servants, all mod cons for a mad king. As long as he was out of the way, let him have comfort. The less grand are less generous. I was introduced in Egypt to a young man in his thirties. He sat, in a kaftan, on his bed, totally withdrawn. His doctor, Dr Okasha, said it was not surprising he was almost mute. His family had kept him in a room for about twenty years because they believed he was retarded. They were too ashamed to seek help. The boy was not violent and did not fight being imprisoned in the room. They fed him well, of course. But, for twenty years he did not leave his room. Only when a half-brother began to worry that this might be unkind did the family decide to seek help. In Banawadi, a village fifty miles from Bangalore, Mrs Shivamma had also been kept locked in a room for days at a time over a period of twenty-five years because her family could not control her. Her daughter said: 'She scratched children and always scolded so we had to lock her in a room but we always gave her food.' The extended family can offer more care but it also has more power; power which can be used cruelly. Psychiatry badly needs to examine the many variations of family life and obligations. They influence both when a patient will break down, when the family will seek help, what form that help will take and how easy it will be to return the patient to the community. As different cultures evolve very different ideas of what is a 'normal' or 'good' family, such comparisons become even more crucial.

Treatment and Tolerance

The evidence on how tolerant different cultures are towards mental illness tends to be anecdotal. This is understandable – the issue is very complex – but unfortunate, since the level of tolerance influences the fate of the patient more profoundly than most doctors admit. It is no good trying to put ex-patients in the community, for instance, if the local community is too hostile.

Helmut Sell trained in Germany and was a psychiatrist both in Botswana and in Algeria. 'Mentally retarded children very rarely survive in traditional cultures. Children who have Downism, for example, which can be detected early simply do not survive' (interview with author). He did not think that parents 'did it with an axe but they gave the child a little less food, a little less water and in the desert that's enough.' He argues that follow-up studies show that the severely mentally ill are also left to die unless they get treatment that makes them economically 'viable'. Romantic notions of savage tribes caring for their mentally ill were liberal trash, Rousseau-esque delusions. It is important not to idealize out of liberal guilt. In some societies, Sell added, he had witnessed elaborate rituals of rejection; in northern Iran the mentally ill go through a ceremony of crucifixion. Sell has travelled widely as the regional officer for the World Health Organization in Delhi. His anecdotes come out of many years of practising psychiatry in the rough and he relishes the fact that they clash with the pious view that many Third World psychiatrists like to present of their culture.

In Egypt, all emphasized the splendid tolerance of their country. The Qur'ān commanded them to be kind to the mentally ill and they were more than kind. 'We accept them', said Dr Al Rahawy, 'much better than other so-called civilized cultures. We think they are blessed and, then, we allow here for more eccentricities.' There were no rigid norms of behaviour in Egypt. People did not have to conform to a code. Eccentricity thrived. Dr Okasha repeated the same idyll of the tolerant society. Dr Gamal rhapsodized, too, though he added that with modernization the tradition of rural tolerance was fading. 'In the cities the families now want them to go to mental hospital with the quick change in the social life.'

In India, too, psychiatrists like to stress the tolerance of villages. Dr S. Murthy argued that tolerance came easily because Indians do not blame people for falling mentally ill. They are beset by demons. Yet, much as they harped on tolerance, they also conceded that many ill people were restrained. 'It is not unusual when we go into the village to find people locked in a room or in chains. There is no other way to restrain them.' Murthy and other psychiatrists tended not to see this as a form of brutality but as an inevitable reaction to crazy behaviour. Murthy claimed that once the crazy behaviour passed, people were accepted back into society as if nothing much had happened.

Local variations in attitudes are perhaps most obvious in Israel. Dr Moshe Avner started practising in Liverpool and is now the director of the Shermenache Hospital near Hadera in central Israel. His hospital takes patients from northern Israel. These include European Jews, Jews from North Africa who were brought up in an Arab-influenced culture, Christian Arabs from Galilee and Muslim Arabs. Avner suggests, anecdotally, that there are cultural differences in tolerance. European Jews tend to be more ashamed of serious mental problems. More than Arabs, they will want serious cases hospitalized.

Psychiatric courses need to study whether such differences in social attitudes are real. Third World psychiatrists like Okasha offer reasons for tolerance. Pressures in the Third World are less intense. To succeed in New York's go-getting society, you need to keep a job which will mean getting to work on time, coping with colleagues (many of whom are bound to bitch), coping with the boss (who may well be incompetent, insecure or insufferable) and coping with your own insecurities.

Certainly, economic pressure and negative attitudes towards mental health co-exist in Japan which is, of course, very different from saying one causes the other. A Tokyo University survey found that 67 per cent of Japanese believed economic pressure contributed to breakdowns. Despite that and despite the fact that 78 per cent felt sorry for patients, 49 per cent would refuse to discuss any such problems, should they occur in their family, with their doctor. It was best kept secret.

The few surveys of public attitudes that have been conducted in Britain and America suggest that people are becoming theoretically more tolerant of the mentally ill, but such surveys do not reveal how people behave in real life. The true test is how people respond if a sheltered home for ex-patients is planned in their street.

For all our education, the reaction is often automatic. House values will come down; the children will walk in fear. Everyone is sympathetic to community care, but why does it have to be here? If Third World attitudes really are different, we need to

know – both because it allows for services to be planned
differently and because it would mean the West has something
to learn. But the issue has not been studied very methodically. It
needs to be.

Consumer Rights and Patients as Persons

During colonial times Western psychiatry also exported legal
attitudes, and even specific laws relating to mental health. The
British Lunacy Act of 1890 was a model for Acts in different
parts of the empire. It inspired the Indian Lunacy Act of 1912.
Even countries which were not part of the empire modelled
legislation on British laws. Egypt's law specified the conditions
under which patients could be detained against their will. In
many circumstances, patients could be held for long periods (a
year or more) without any review of their case.

In Britain, America and much of Europe, these old laws have
changed. In countries that were colonies, there has been little
such progress. India is still largely bound by the 1912 Act, Egypt
by its 1944 Mental Health Act. The position in those countries
ossified perhaps because there was no pressure from outside
psychiatry. Coalitions of academics, lawyers and ex-patients won
legal reforms in the West. Psychiatrists tend to splutter at the
presumption of these 'lay' people. The pressure group, MIND, is
typical of such organizations. It has parallels in the Scandinavian
countries, Holland and in America both in the Public Citizen
Health Group and in the National Alliance for the Mentally Ill.

It is not surprising that psychiatrists should be suspicious of
pressure groups. They challenge their authority and take seriously the testimony of patients whom doctors see as deluded.
New laws in Britain and America have had the impertinence to
let non-psychiatrists monitor what psychiatrists do. Bodies like
the Mental Health Review Commission in the UK and the Joint
Committee on the Accreditation of Hospitals in the USA judge
how effective and fair care is. They also inquire if patients are
getting their rights. These rights range from the mundane – such
as having a phone in the ward – to access to lawyers and a voice
in their own treatment. The rise of self-help groups, like the

Schizophrenia Society or the National Alliance for the Mentally Ill, also has challenged psychiatrists. Medical decisions have been contested at law, with MIND winning cases at the European Court of Human Rights. In America, a veritable litigation industry is at work. Lawyers now advertise for patients to tell them, free, of how doctors have mishandled them because there may be money in that misdiagnosis.

Questioning the authority and wisdom of doctors is not new. The French playwright Molière satirized the pretensions of doctors in the 1660s. But the rise of 'scientific' medicine enthroned doctors as experts, wise men. Popular dramas like 'Dr Kildare' and 'Dr Finlay's Casebook' hallowed the doctor. Western docors have now had to resign themselves to being scrutinized by critical pressure groups and better-informed patients who raise issues like whether psychiatrists over-use tranquillisers and under-use techniques like listening and counselling.

Western psychiatrists remain ambivalent about such developments. Many would prefer to return to the good old days when the docile patient accepted that the doctor knew best. More liberal doctors realize, however, that there is much to be gained from informed consent which can make the patient a knowing ally in treatment. Unfortunately, psychiatry as taught in most Western medical schools still gives little sense of the patient as something of an equal – a subject rather than an object to be ladled out treatment. In Egypt, one doctor quipped that there his patients saw him as God whereas in England he wasn't worshipped. Uppity neurotics asked him to justify his treatment decision. Dr Okasha was less flamboyant but still said that he thought it was much better for patients to trust their doctor totally. A view echoed by Dr Ahmed Al Azayem who said that, as doctors, their only concern was to heal their patients. That meant taking tough decisions and recognizing that the patient, being mad, could not hope to make any sensible comment on his treatment. I noticed, however, that this did not stop Dr Ahmed quoting the reactions of patients to ECT when these were favourable. Patients found it worked so well, he beamed, they asked for more. Criticism of treatment, however, was a sign of delusions. Dr Ahmed is not alone in such ambivalence to patients' opinions.

Third World psychiatrists tend to claim that what is crucial is that the patient should have access to treatment. Consulting patients is a mark of the weakness of the West. By definition, a schizophrenic cannot know what is good or bad treatment. Such attitudes affect the practice of psychiatry deeply and, ironically, reflect a colonial attitude to patients. Poor savages, they have to have their lives ruled by the doctor-sahib. The training psychiatrists receive hardly ever gets them to confront the extent of their power, or the paradox that they are not just curing, but controlling. In the Third World those powers are most absolute.

Another important aspect of the rise of the consumer approach to mental health is that it is struggling, albeit confusedly, to develop a positive view of mental health. It is not easy to do this because it is complicated and because it is easy to mock new psychotherapies which offer a manicured Me. In *The Development of Play* (1987) I argued that a unique form of modern play is playing with ourselves. Ads for new therapies such as mind–body suspension, holistic massage, aromatherapy and so on in *Time Out* and *The Village Voice* promise a better you if only you'll follow Brand-A Therapy. In *Critical Psychiatry* (edited by Ingleby, 1981) Kovel acidly snapped that the rivalry between therapies such as primal scream and EST is like the rivalry between Ford and Chrysler. The promise is that you will be more assertive, more assured, happier and have a better sex life. All this psychobabble has made it seem that positive mental health is a fad. Kovel added a jeremiad: all these therapy-fetishes showed the spiritual desolation of later capitalism when people have 'stomachs full and hearts empty'. To which I cannot resist adding Bertolt Brecht's aphorism: 'First grub, then philosophy.'

The fun we can all have at the expense of 'psychobabble' (which we can indulge in only if we have grub) should not blind us to an important difference. In the Third World, mental-health professionals deal almost exclusively with the seriously mentally ill. The Third World has few psychologists, few psychotherapists and relatively few social workers. There is too much acute need for anyone to concentrate on positive mental health for the non-sick. The idea of positive mental health developed in wealthy America, where the mental hygiene movement of the 1920s to 1950s aimed to produce the perfectly balanced person, open to life and love. Psychoanalysis and its satellite therapies has had a great impact on our view of ourselves. To be mentally well, I must have no hang-ups, no neuroses, no complexes, no obsessions and be conversant with all my conflicts. If I have a trace of any of these, I am not all I could be. Oh Lord, give us this day our daily insight! The Third World has not yet aspired to this vision of psychological perfection. Somehow, people manage without the self-consciousness and self-talk of the West.

Societies like India, Pakistan and Egypt have little time for such 'playing with oneself' and that 'lack' affects the nature of their psychiatry. Few patients look to psychiatrists for more than prescriptions, injections, a word of comfort. In Egypt, I watched one doctor interview a patient who had just attempted suicide. He had known her for eleven years. For the first time, he learned that she had been neglected as a child and that her brother, in what was meant to be a loving family, had taunted her for years. The doctor did not seem embarrassed never to have uncovered such key facts. Egyptian psychiatry could not afford the 'luxury of psychotherapy'.

Different expectations affect how psychiatrists see their career prospects. In America, the best psychiatry graduates hope to set up in private practice which offers more money and more job satisfaction. What can you do in a large hospital but prescribe tranquillisers as you scurry from one ward to another. The psychiatrist cannot exercise his sensitive talents properly. Some non-Western graduates are led to emigrate by a similar mix of motivations. They want to get richer but rich countries also provide better facilities in which you can be a better psychiatrist.

From the early 1970s on, experts both in Britain and America complained that foreign graduates were being recruited to work in hospitals. Fuller Torrey noted that foreign psychiatrists were cheap labour. Elmhurst State Hospital in New York City had thirty-five psychiatric residents, all of them foreign. Torrey and Taylor (1973) also found that while 50 per cent of American psychiatrists were in private practice, only 5 per cent of foreign graduates were. The rest were in state hospitals. In 1976, Clare discerned the same problem in Britain. Some x per cent of junior psychiatrists were foreign, though few consultants were.

These analysts worried about the impact of such trends on the quality of care in Britain and America. From a global perspective, the anxiety is very different. Robin Murray, Dean of the Institute of Psychiatry, said that if a doctor spent more than three years out of his native country after getting his Royal College certificate, he was unlikely ever to return there. The international nature of psychiatry is depriving poor countries. It has been estimated that there are eighty Bangladeshi psychiatrists in Britain but perhaps only eight in Bangladesh itself where there is only one psychiatric hospital. Egypt has 200 psychiatrists working in the country but far more working in Saudi Arabia, the Gulf and other countries. There are at least five Egyptian psychiatrists in London's Harley Street who cater largely to rich Arabs who have become dependent on valium!

All this means that psychiatric imperialism continues to thrive. It affects the quality of care, ignoring local culture and encouraging psychiatrists to see their patients less as persons than as things who should be grateful such mighty beings as doctors care for them. In the subsequent chapters, we shall see that far too few psychiatrists see the dangers of such an approach and even fewer realize the extent to which their role gives them power over other people.

3

Japan: 'I'm sorry, I didn't count the bodies . . .'

'One day I complained that I hadn't seen the sun for over a year. OK, said the nurse, we'll see what we can do about that. They took me out an hour later and handcuffed me to the cage which was outside.' Ignatius Yasui, who was then in his mid-forties, stood there for ten hours. 'It was hot and my skin got burned. I couldn't protect it. When they finally let me go, one arm was', he mimed a large circle, 'horribly swollen.' Ignatius Yasui added that really he ought to have known better than to complain in Utsonomiya Hospital, sixty miles from Tokyo, but he had always been stubborn. He seemed less stubborn the first time I met him when he forced a melancholy smile and said, 'I am a broken man.'

In Utsonomiya it was routine for nurses to beat patients in public. A second patient told me later that, in his thirteen years there, he knew more than ten patients who had died after being attacked by staff.

Japanese newspapers exposed two cases in 1984 where patients had died after being clubbed by nurses wielding iron pipes. The exposures forced Dr Bunnishio Ichigawa, the owner and director of the hospital, to resign. Many Japanese doctors and lawyers argue that Utsonomiya is not that exceptional. Japanese attitudes to mental patients and the peculiar organization of services have led to a situation in which cruelty is common. The 1970s saw a series of psychiatric scandals. In three hospitals owned by the Juzenkai Corporation, 859 patients (out of a total of 2100) died in one nine-month period. At Utsonomiya, there were some 222 deaths in the three years before March 1984.

Even more bizarre than Utsonomiya is a *bushoan* in Fuji city. It is not a hospital but purports to be a Buddhist community.

Parents send delinquent children or, according to Mr Goda, the owner, a construction engineer who went bankrupt, 'those who have violence in the home'. The families of inmates pay 10,000 dollars to keep them there for six months. Goda employs no doctors and no nurses, even though he concedes that most of his inmates are either mentally ill or addicts. None of them has been certified insane, yet they are, effectively, in jail. 'If they escape, we catch them ourselves or do so with the help of the police.' In most countries – and, indeed, possibly under Japanese law – Goda would be guilty of unlawfully imprisoning people. Yet he courts publicity. When I arrived to film there (he was quite willing to let me do that) I found the local television station on hand to film my filming. Goda's openness about incarcerating over two hundred people reflects Japanese attitudes not just to the mentally ill but to all who fail to conform.

The West has long accused the Soviet Union of abusing psychiatry. Many Japanese claim that, although abuses in Japan have nothing to do with political opinions, the suffering of patients is as great. In 1984 the Japanese Civil Liberties Union complained to the International Commission of Jurists (ICJ) and the International League for Human Rights. In a report released in 1986, the ICJ said Japanese psychiatry was seriously inadequate and demanded action from the Japanese government.

Usually, even when hospitals are very poor, brutality is left to the lower professionals. Nurses and assistants actually beat patients; psychiatrists turn a blind eye. These niceties do not seem to apply in Japan. Many patients have died in suspicious circumstances; psychiatrists have falsified death certificates to prevent police investigations; two directors of hospitals have been charged with killing patients.

The University of Tokyo established courses in psychology and psychiatry as soon as it opened in 1879. One of the leading Western texts of the time, Bain's *Mind and Body*, was translated in 1882. Its translator, T. Inoue, warned that it was not enough to import Western technology. Japan had to absorb the new sciences of the mind, for it was the Western mind that had fashioned all those technical marvels.

In 1890, Professor Kure left Tokyo University to study the latest advances in European psychiatry. He visited Britain, France and Germany. He studied under the great German psychiatrist, Emil Kraeplin, and brought his system back to Japan imposing it on Japanese medicine. 'When I was a student in the late 1950s,' Dr Moryama, a chubby fifty-three-year-old lecturer at the university, explained, 'we were still learning Kraeplin's system. We learned that schizophrenia was incurable, for instance.' Kraeplin believed that psychiatric illnesses were essentially organic and that patients had to be viewed as a species of deformed humanity. R. D. Laing analyzed one of the quotations Kraeplin used to demonstrate how a patient was quite out of his mind. Every phrase Kraeplin had used as proof of total insanity could be reinterpreted. Laing argued convincingly that the patient was protesting at his diagnosis and at the way Kraeplin was showing him off, a mangled specimen of mangled mind, for students to peer at. Not surprisingly, Kraeplin believed schizophrenics were often dangerous and frequently had to be kept secure in cells, straitjackets and locked wards.

In 1900, when the Japanese decided to modernize their mental-health law they drew heavily on Kraeplin. They built prison-like mental hospitals but they also decided to allow families to continue to care for their insane although, having learned that mentally ill people might be dangerous, families could keep their disturbed relatives only if they held them in special cells or cages in the home. Local officials had to call each week to make sure families had not succumbed to temptation and allowed them out. In 1919 a new law encouraged yet again the building of mental hospitals, but as late as 1950 there were only 200 such hospitals in the whole of Japan.

Though the Americans tried to introduce such ideas as counselling and psychotherapy into Japan during their occupation, it was hardly one of their priorities. By 1950, however, the Japanese themselves had decided that it was barbaric to keep the family lunatic imprisoned behind the living-room. So the law was repealed. Henceforth, a sign of liberal times, the sick would be treated in hospitals. Not surprisingly, though, Japanese public opinion continued to fear and despise lunatics.

* * *

Ninety-seven per cent of all mental-hospital beds in Japan are private. Hospitals admit that, to keep funds flowing in, they have to ensure that no bed is ever vacant. Many doctors personally own their hospitals. Japanese law makes it easy to commit patients against their will. There is no appeal against the judgement of one doctor. Critics claim that profit-conscious hospitals employ too few staff. The more able patients are sometimes roped in to cook, clean and, at times, dispense medicines. Occupational therapy is also lucrative: patients are often sent to work in local industries. As this is called 'therapy', the hospital collects their wages but passes on only a few hundred yen and a packet of cigarettes. Despite a catalogue of well-authenticated abuses since 1968, the Japanese government refused to consider reforms until recently. Late in 1987 the Diet, the Japanese Parliament, considered a new mental-health law but the Japanese Ministry of Health does not think sweeping reforms are necessary. There has not even been a major national investigation into malpractices. Spokesmen for the Ministry of Health told me they thought it unlikely that many other hospitals were like Utsonomiya; they *hoped* it was unlikely; but, in all honesty, they could not say. The data were missing.

Such complacency is not all the government's fault. No political party has been much bothered by the evidence of abuses. Until recently, the Japanese public was happy to assume that all lunatics were dangerous. The country was producing its economic miracle; few questioned the need to work hard, profit and prosper. Those who could not pull their weight in yen did not get much sympathy. These attitudes, however, are beginning to change, partly because of the continuing revelations – 1984 saw one scandal unearthed after another and 1985 was no better – and partly because some Japanese are starting to question the values which have ruled them since 1945. Polls conducted by the Ministry of Trade showed that between 1953 and 1984 the number of Japanese who saw leading a 'straight and narrow life' as a priority declined from 49 per cent to 9 per cent; the number who saw leading a 'relaxed life with time to enjoy hobbies' as a priority increased from 9 per cent to 38 per cent. All this suggests a shift in values which may come, in time, to affect attitudes to mental health, though there are few signs of it at present.

And, for all the abuses, Japanese psychiatry wants to shine in the eyes of the world. Dr Ichigawa, the director of Utsonomiya who would smack patients with a golf club if they asked what was wrong with them, made an odd request of one inmate in about 1979: he offered him the riches of ten packets of cigarettes to write a glowing account of his treatment. Dr Ichigawa wanted to read it at a World Congress of Psychiatry conference to that body which took so long to condemn Soviet psychiatry.

The background to the latest revelations was gruesome. On 24 April 1983, fifty patients on the Shinkannikkai ward of Utsonomiya Hospital were eating dinner. It was four in the afternoon. Among them was a thirty-two-year-old man who had been admitted in 1969 as a schizophrenic. Japanese newspapers do not identify psychiatric patients even after they are dead so, throughout, this patient has been known only as Mr A. Mr A. complained about the quality of the food to one of the nurses. A quarrel started. After a few harsh words, a twenty-four-year-old male nurse took the patient into an adjoining room. He told him to wait. The nurse then went to collect a three-foot-long iron pipe from the nurses' station. Armed with it, he proceeded to hit the patient on the back and the hips. Diagrams in Japanese newspapers explained in meticulous detail how the nurse stood behind the patient to club him. Mr A. screamed for the nurse to stop. Then he ran back into the big hall where patients had, not surprisingly, stopped eating. Mr A. begged for help but, for the next twenty minutes, the nurse continued to club him in full view of some fifty patients and staff. No one lifted a finger to help him.

After twenty minutes, the nurses allowed the patients to carry Mr A. back to his bed. Very soon his face turned blue and he began to vomit. At eight o'clock in the evening, he died. Japanese law requires a doctor always to be on duty in a psychiatric hospital, but many hospitals ignore this ruling. When Mr A. died, there was no doctor at the hospital. By the time the nurses had called the medical superintendent, Mr A. was dead.

At about eight-thirty that evening, Dr Bunnishio Ichigawa finally arrived. He pronounced Mr A. dead. He told his staff that he was rather tired and left it to his deputy, Mr Matzumoto, to tell the relatives that Mr A. had died of a weak heart as a result of frequent epileptic attacks. Once he had given his instructions, Dr Ichigawa returned home. If the incident made him anxious, he did not show it. The next day, Dr Ichigawa wrote out a death certificate stating death had been due to a heart attack.

When Mr A.'s family saw his body, they noticed many bruises and injuries, especially about the head. Mr Matzumoto was not a doctor (he had been an officer in the local police till his retirement). He told the family that Mr A. had hit his head against the toilet door. The family had no reason to doubt his word. Mr A.'s body was burned, as is common in Japan.

Six months later, Utsonomiya Hospital saw another violent quarrel. Mr B. was a thirty-five-year-old man who had been admitted four months earlier as an alcoholic. He was known to suffer from cirrhosis of the liver. On 30 December 1983, a friend visited him. Mr B. asked this friend to do his best to arrange a discharge because the hospital was so atrocious. When his visitor left, Mr B. was visibly upset. He returned to his ward and, after lunch, began to argue with another patient who had been in Utsonomiya for many years. Three staff joined the established patient in taunting Mr B. After a few minutes, they went into the nurses' station and collected wooden clubs. Three members of staff and one patient then proceeded to club Mr B. They stopped after a few minutes but, in the evening, just before bedtime, some staff members decided to assault Mr B. again.

The next day Mr B. lost consciousness. Dr Ichigawa ordered he be moved to a medical ward where he vomited a large amount of blackened blood. At six-thirty-five that evening, the patient died. Dr Ichigawa told his family that Mr B. had succumbed to cirrhosis of the liver. Given his alcoholic history that seemed all too likely. When the hospital handed over the body, the family was told it had already been prepared for cremation – there was no need for them to examine it further. Again, Dr Ichigawa signed a death certificate which stated that death was due to natural causes. There was no reason to suppose that there would be any investigation. Cremation is the norm in Japan and it would have been reasonable for Dr Ichigawa to assume that Mr B.'s body would be burned.

News of these two deaths did leak out to the Japanese press. On 14 March 1984 most of the major newspapers carried articles alleging there had been two brutal deaths in Utsonomiya. On 16 March, Dr Ichigawa told a press conference that he had seen the bodies and that the death certificates were true and accurate. Unlike most Japanese families, however, Mr B.'s did not cremate its dead. The police decided to exhume his body. Japanese television hired helicopters to film these grim scenes as police undid the grave. Between December and March the weather in Japan had been extremely cold, so Mr B.'s body was well preserved. It showed all the signs of having taken a vicious beating. The police began to mount an investigation. Again, television pictures showed the odd sight of perhaps 200 Japanese detectives queuing to enter the gates. Within six weeks, a nurse was charged with murder.

Dr Ichigawa was also arrested. He had failed to report these two cases as unnatural deaths, which Japanese law obliged him to do. Under interrogation, he also admitted that he let unqualified staff dispense drugs to patients and, sometimes, allowed them to give injections. Qualified staff were hard to get, he pleaded. Dr Ichigawa was charged and obliged to resign as director of the hospital. However, the Ministry of Health did not force him to sell it, so, bizarrely, he remains the owner of Utsonomiya Hospital.

The Japanese press made the allegations front-page news. The international press carried a few small stories. With so much publicity, the Japanese government reacted by saying that Utsonomiya was an isolated instance. Japan has over 1,500 psychiatric hospitals; a few had to be bad.

One man who was especially sceptical of the government's assurances was Etsuro Totsuka. Totsuka is a small, intense lawyer who has just turned forty-four. He laughed as he explained, 'I know that one of my defects is that I talk too much about things I think are wrong.' He spent his first ten years as a lawyer fighting one case: he co-ordinated a group of lawyers who sued the pharmaceutical firm, Ciba Geigy, over SMON, a drug they had marketed since the 1930s. SMON had appalling side-effects including paralysis, tremors, blindness and sometimes death. Totsuka and his colleagues represented over 6000 victims in what they think may have been the largest law suit in history, and won damages of 492.5 million dollars from Ciba Geigy. The company admitted it had not paid enough attention to animal experiments which warned, if anyone had been interested, of the dangers of SMON.

After his victory, Totsuka decided to follow the tradition by which Japanese travel in order to learn. He joined a party of twenty politicians, lawyers and doctors who went to Europe to see what provisions existed for dealing with the criminally insane. One of the British psychiatrists he met was John Gunn, who holds the chair of forensic medicine at London's Maudsley Hospital. Gunn explained that only 5 per cent of psychiatric patients in Britain were held against their will. The rest were voluntary patients. Gunn wondered what the situation was in Japan. To his embarrassment, Totsuka found he could not answer. He promised Gunn that he would find out and write from Tokyo.

On his return to Japan, Totsuka found that the mental health law allowed three kinds of admissions. The smallest number of patients were voluntary admissions. Even today, most psychiatric hospitals in Japan have only one or two open wards at best. Most patients go straight into locked wards and over 50 per cent of them stay for more than three years. In such circumstances, it is perhaps not surprising that few volunteer for treatment. Totsuka found that only 20 per cent of patients were voluntary patients.

In British law there is a clear distinction between voluntary and involuntary admissions. In Japan, Totsuka discovered, the situation was far more muddled. Japan has some forty-seven prefectures or areas of local government, much like an American state or English county; each prefecture has an administrative head, its governor. If a person seemed to be a danger to himself, a danger to others or just in need of treatment, the governor of the local prefecture could commit him to hospital. Everyone accepted that this was an involuntary admission and it accounted, Totsuka found, for another 18 per cent of patients.

But a person could also be committed under Article 29 of the 1950 Mental Health Law. Article 29 states that if a responsible member of the family thinks that a person should be sent for treatment and if they can get a doctor to agree, then that person can be sent to hospital even if they object. According to Totsuka, any admission under Article 29 is *ipso facto* against the patient's will. Adding it to the previous figures, he calculated that a further 62 per cent of patients were being treated against their will.

Often, the Japanese government admitted, families did commit patients. But Western countries with their tradition of individualism couldn't understand the special dynamics of the Japanese family. People are closer to each other; they belong; they feel responsible for each other. This 'line' sounds oddly similar to the one put forward by the Egyptians who claimed it was this sense of family that led to greater tolerance. Coming from a Middle Eastern Jewish family myself – and being aware of the nice myths that surround the sweet, loving, chicken-soup Jewish family – I took these rosy Egyptian declarations with a pinch of salt.

Being Japanese himself and coming from a large family, Totsuka was less impressed by these tributes to family love. He suspected that many families were only too glad to dump troublesome relatives in institutions. Between 1955 and 1975, the number of private hospitals rose from 206 to 1450. The number of patients increased from 44,000 to over 300,000. The latest figures for 1986 show patients have risen to 350,000. As Totsuka examined the figures more critically, he became worried and angry. 'It seemed more than likely that 80 per cent of the 340,000 mental patients were effectively being held against their will on involuntary orders.' The government liked to say that admission by family consent was not involuntary, but Totsuka thought that untrue. Most patients admitted with the consent of their families were being put away because they were a nuisance. No wonder most had to be kept on locked wards.

In the course of researching the situation in Japan I talked with thirty patients. The following, highly précis-ed, accounts come from them and so are not 'objective' evidence. Nevertheless . . .

Mr Jon (aged thirty-eight) was admitted to Aoba Hospital for eight years after his brother had him committed.

Mr Yamada (aged twenty-four) described his relationship with his parents as 'bad because I am a very passionate person.' They minded that he did not like school and refused to work hard. They objected to his passion for rock music. Finally he broke some windows in their house and they summoned the police. The police put him in the cells for twenty-four hours but he was not charged with any offence. His parents then took him to Otaki Mental Hospital. The hospital admitted him. According to Yamada, his parents told him he had to stay there for life. Hospital policy, he alleges, was to take in all the drop-outs of Japanese society. 'The hospital director said I was normal but that I was the scum of the earth.' All patients were seen as scum. Eventually, Mr Yamada escaped with the help of a lawyer, having witnessed much violence against such 'scum.'

Mr Z. (aged twenty-four), interviewed in an isolation cell at Yowa Hospital where he was playing the guitar, said that he had made difficulties for his parents because he did not like to work. The staff said he was violent.

Mr K. (aged fifty), an ex-businessman, had admitted himself to hospital because he was very depressed after going bankrupt; his wife divorced him.

Mr Suzuki (aged seventy-nine) had been a soldier in the Japanese army. He protested when his son-in-law drank too much and beat his wife. He went, at their insistence, into hospital because otherwise they would summon the hospital doctor, he would arrive in the hospital car and the neighbours would know. To avoid such shame, Suzuki agreed to go into hospital where his doctor saw him for two minutes before calling him 'an imbecile'. Suzuki is, in fact, a rather dignified old man.

Mr P. (aged twenty-eight) had been in hospital since the age of nineteen and was sad that his family visited him only once a year.

At Kitakumegaya Hospital, I met two old men who had both lost most of their teeth. One had been in the hospital for twenty-eight years, the other for twenty-seven years. The second smiled ruefully: 'I dream of the outside world.' He felt he had missed so much in life. The other snapped: 'Bah, you wouldn't last six months in the outside world.' Dr Yokota, the young medical superintendent, agreed that his hospital was full of patients who had been forgotten and who, given reasonable treatment, could have gone back into society years ago. Now, for many, it was too late.

In Mr Goda's 'reformatory', there were other 'undesirables'. Mr R. (aged twenty-four), who was in a private 'reformatory', said he had experimented with drugs and shamed his parents. Mr H. (aged twenty) was in the padlocked, windowless cell of that institution. He had also experimented with drugs and, after being committed there by his parents, had run away home. His parents called the police to send him back to the institution.

Japanese families also resented doctors asking them about relationships within the family. Family life was not a medical matter; going mad was a private tragedy which had nothing to do with family dynamics. It is possible to believe that many Japanese families might well, in a crunch, avail themselves of the law which allows them to initiate admission.

After visiting England, Totsuka began to drum up interest among radical, and not so radical, lawyers. The abuse of the rights of patients was a major civil-rights issue. When the Utsonomiya scandal broke in March 1984, Totsuka and his friends were ready. On 23 March, Totsuka and two other lawyers went to the hospital and asked to see the superintendent, Dr Ichigawa. He refused to see them and they were bundled out by nurses. Five days later, Totsuka returned with ten lawyers. By now, they had applied to the Tokyo High Court for 539 writs of habeas corpus for all the patients in the hospital. They found that the hospital had barred its entrance and put heavy chains around its iron gate. Burly nurses patrolled the perimeter. 'It was impossible for us to serve the writs on the hospital. We also brought 539 letters with us, one for each patient. But we didn't know the names of most of the patients. The Japanese constitution guarantees everyone the freedom to receive mail, but the hospital refused to accept these letters. Since they did not have names on them,' Totsuka did allow himself a wry smile, 'the hospital said these were not letters.'

The revelations led to intense public pressure. This gave Totsuka the leverage to persuade the local prefecture to deliver 102 of these letters to patients whose names had been discovered. Since the local prefecture could withdraw the hospital's licence, Dr Ichigawa had no alternative but to let them act as postmen. The letters invited patients to write to any of the eleven lawyers if they wanted to be legally represented. Clinically, Dr Ichigawa told the Ministry of Health, getting such letters would only upset patients and aggravate their illnesses – a point that the then Japanese Minister of Health, Mr K. Watanabe, solemnly read out in Parliament. Despite these dubious clinical doubts, the letters were delivered.

International pressure, Totsuka thought, would also help. He had learned the value of international co-operation during the SMON case. He was instrumental in persuading the Japanese Civil Liberties Union to raise the matter of patients' rights both with the International Commission of Jurists and the International League for Human Rights. The former were sufficiently impressed by the evidence to cable the Japanese Prime Minister, Mr Y. Nakasone. Their text noted their concern and anxiety. One section read:

... it is likely that many more such incidents of grave abuse exist than have been made public. Furthermore, there is evidence that officials routinely fail to investigate deaths or other suspicious incidents occurring in mental hospitals. If such an investigation is conducted it is sometimes suppressed.

The Japanese government did not take these interventions very seriously. Prime Minister Nakasone replied tartly that everything in Japan was quite proper. If he had not been so dismissive, the ICJ might not have decided to investigate further, an investigation which has severely embarrassed the Japanese government.

It is a sign of the increasingly international aspect of mental health that the Japanese government could not refuse an investigation, even though it must have known it would be highly critical given the long history of revelations of abuse.

Kazuo Okuma is a journalist for *Asahi Shimbun*, the paper

preferred by Japanese intellectuals. He is an angular-looking man with what I came to recognize were very typical Japanese inhibitions about speaking English. As a young reporter in 1969, Okuma was sent to cover student unrest at Tokyo University. He became friendly with a student nurse who made serious allegations about the Tokyo hospital where he worked. Okuma got himself admitted as an alcoholic – just by turning up drunk at the hospital entrance – and after a month inside published seven articles on the conditions inside. It was cold, dirty and brutal; there was no therapy. Okuma did not name the hospital in his articles but he did note that he saw patients left freezing in cells, that they had to drink out of toilet bowls and that they were often beaten. When the articles appeared, the association of owners of psychiatric hospitals met and took legal advice on whether they could sue *Asahi Shimbun*. They were advised that only the specific hospital Okuma had been in could sue. That would mean naming it in court. Silence seemed wiser.

Kurioka Hospital is in Osaka, Japan's second largest city. It was named after its owner, Dr Yohiyuki Kurioka. Early in 1969, a patient at the hospital was killed. Patients were not allowed to write letters to relatives, but one inmate was so outraged that he stole some paper and described what had happened. He wrapped his letter inside a sock and also put a bar of soap inside. He explained in a note to anyone who found the sock that the soap was a present. The sock was found; the letter was read; the police were alerted. On 11 October 1969, a few months after Okuma had published his articles, the superintendent of the hospital, Dr Kurioka, and two nurses were charged with manslaughter of a patient. In 1980, eleven years later, the Osaka District Court found him guilty. Totsuka told me: 'One can only be amazed it took so long to try him. One can only be amazed that, during the whole time, the Ministry of Health did not suspend his licence to practise as a psychiatrist.' Dr Kurioka is still appealing against the verdict.

In the same year, at Yomatogawa Hospital in Osaka, two deaths aroused some suspicion. The hospital promptly changed its named to Yasuda Hospital. In August 1979, Okuma unearthed evidence of another scandal there. Three nurses assaulted a patient who had defied hospital rules by sleeping during the day. At Yasuda, patients had to wake up at six-thirty and then either work or be involved in therapy. Only during the ninety-minute lunch-break were they allowed back on their mattresses, the traditional Japanese futon which is rolled up when not in use. The delinquent patient had not merely napped but had unfurled his futon. Two days after the beating he was dead. The death certificate noted that he had died of a heart attack. No suspicious circumstances were reported.

Okuma discovered that the nurses' station at Yasuda was a virtual armoury. As in Utsonomiya, there were wooden clubs and iron pipes to hand. But there was also a refinement. At Yasuda, the nurses had bows and arrows. Sometimes they threatened patients with being used for archery practice. The nurses never actually hurt anyone with an arrow but they did kill a dog, which patients were then forced to eat. The local police, Okuma said, admitted that this certainly infringed the laws against cruelty to animals.

Like Utsonomiya, both these scandals could be dismissed as isolated tragedies. The third scandal Okuma reported in the 1970s was on a grander scale, involving money as well as violence. On 2 September 1974, *Asahi Shimbun* reported on the Juzenkai private medical corporation which ran three hospitals near Kyoto. They housed 2124 patients – mainly psychiatric cases. In the whole of Kyoto, there were some 5000 patients. Of the 2124 in Juzenkai's care, 859 died between January and September 1973. True, many were over sixty-five but Kyoto's other psychiatric hospitals, with many geriatrics, saw only seventy-eight deaths in the same period. Totsuka believes that the care of old people is likely to be the next 'boom' area. As Japan loses some of its traditional values, families will not want to keep older relatives, a process hinted at in *An Artist of the Floating World* (1986), Kazuo Ishiguro's novel about a famous artist who grows old and isolated.

Rumours also suggested that the Juzenkai Corporation was making vast profits and had become involved in take-overs on the Tokyo Stock Exchange. These allegations highlight the capitalist twist to the saga: in Japan there is much money to be made out of madness. Between 1959 and 1970 there was a boom in mental hospitals. At the start of the decade there were 400 hospitals; by its end, 1400.

It is hard to know whether mental hospitals increased to meet the needs of patients or whether patients increased to meet the needs of mental hospitals. In Japan, the fees for mental patients are largely paid by insurance companies. The latest figures suggest that it costs 10,000 dollars a year to provide keep for a hospitalized patient. With 350,000 inpatients, this means that mental health is a 3400-million-dollar business. Furthermore, this figure is only likely to 'improve'. The Ministry of Health expects mental-hospital beds to expand at the rate of 5000 a year and, while in the rest of the developed world psychiatric inpatients are spending less time in institutions, the proportion of Japanese patients who are likely to be in for more than three years has risen from under 45 per cent in 1960 to over 55 per cent today. The share of funds allocated to mental health has actually fallen, Totsuka calculates, as the number of patients has increased.

While radicals like Totsuka accuse mental hospitals of making huge profits, the hospitals plead poverty. Dr Satoshi Shikiba is executive director of the Japanese Association of Psychiatric Hospitals. The association represents more than a thousand of the private hospitals. Dr Shikiba pointed out in 1984 that it cost only 200 dollars a week to keep a patient in his hospital: in America, it would cost 4000 dollars. Moreover, hospitals faced a financial crisis. In the 1960s, during the boom years for building new hospitals, many had spent huge sums of money to get themselves started. They needed a full complement of patients to keep on financing themselves. Totsuka told me that even 'conscientious' doctors, as he calls them, worry a great deal about the number of occupied beds in their hospitals. If vacancies rise, even by a fraction, they become very anxious. Shikiba did not raise the question of how well maintained most hospitals are.

I visited three 'good' hospitals – Yowa, Kitukemegaya and Kamihotano. The doctors complained that it was hard to keep the hospitals clean. Yowa and Kamihotano had peeling walls, discoloured patches of damp, and the furniture was often broken.

Kitukemagaya Hospital had gone bankrupt three years previously as its owner had speculated in cemeteries. It was now under new management and there were signs of investment. For example, one ward was freshly carpeted. But that was an exception. Dr Shima, the director of Yowa Hospital, let me see only one ward. Bedrooms were often overcrowded. One man, Mr K., grinned as he gestured out a space of about eight feet. 'This is my palace,' he smiled. There was damp and muck in every corner I peered into, though it was often hidden as patients had to keep all their possessions in their eight-foot preserve. Each room looked as if a jumble sale was about to take place. Owners are conscious of profit and do not easily spend money to keep up 'the plant'. Even these 'good' hospitals have 'cells' into which patients are put. The chief nurse, Mitchiko, explained that she would need to put patients in isolation less often if there were more staff on the wards.

Dr Shikiba said that his association had been very shocked by the revelations at Utsonomiya Hospital and that it had expelled the hospital. It would have to reform itself before they allowed it back in. He denied that it showed a general crisis though, very openly, he did admit that one problem of Utsonomiya's was, perhaps, a bit more widespread. This was the practice of sending patients to work, calling it occupational therapy, and collecting most of their wages. Dr Shikiba added that, while nearly all wards in Japan were locked wards, patients were only too happy to go outside to work. The money did not matter; getting out was a relief. Now that many hospitals were introducing open wards, patients were less and less willing to work. 'Recreational therapy is now very popular,' he said. In Japan, recreational therapy seems to mean playing baseball or volleyball in the hospital garden – rather like 'entertainment therapy' often means watching television.

Dr T. Doi, who was Professor of Psychiatry at Tokyo University and is now director of the Japanese Institute for Psychiatric Research was, like Dr Shikiba, not inclined to blame the hospitals. 'I hope,' he said to me, 'that you are not political, because that is what we are always afraid of.' Given his anxiety, Doi would be probably upset that he reminded me of a slimmed-down version of Mao. He said that it was wrong to suggest that the existence of hospitals 'created' patients. As Japan had become more and more of an urban society, it had become impossible for families to care for their sick in the time-honoured ways. They had to find institutions to send their relatives to because they were living in a modern world.

More radical psychiatrists referred not to 'urbanization' – a nicely bland piece of jargon – but to industrialization and the pursuit of profit. Between 1955 and 1970 in particular, the Japanese economy boomed: annual growth rates averaged 10 per cent. This period saw the huge leap in the number of mental hospitals. A society so geared to production just could not care for its less productive members.

A different slant on that period came from the Japanese Productivity Centre, an association funded by leading companies. Dr Hiroya Kobuta, one of its directors, explained to me that as early as 1967 they had tried to make companies aware of the risks of stress and breakdown among workers. In the heady 1960s, none of their members was much impressed. Only in 1977, after a spate of psychosomatic diseases, did the centre manage to get its members to back a study of the psychological state of workers.

Dr Kobuta told me, 'It took us a lot of money to perfect 598 questions which cover all the ground we needed. We have now studied about 130,000 workers and we find that we have to warn about 10 per cent that their psychological state is not that good.'

He emphasized that they were not mentally ill in any formal sense, but needed counselling and treatment to prevent worse problems from flaring up.

At the Nissan motor company, which employs 59,000 people, the head of medical services, Dr K. Nishihara, confirmed Kobuta's view. Until the late 1970s, industry had been concerned about the physical well-being of its employees but not about other ills. In the late 1970s, he instituted seminars on stress and how to cope with neurotic, unproductive employees. All managers had courses in stress because an unhappy worker was likely to be an inefficient one. Nissan showed me statistics which revealed that only 699 of its 59,000 workers sought any kind of counselling or advice in 1983. Of these, 103 were admitted to hospital with schizophrenia. Dr Nishihara said it was a low figure. I suspect, on the basis of other Japanese figures, that it is artificially low and reflects employees' fears. Admitting to a mental problem may not boost one's career prospects.

Social attitudes are unhelpful.

The Japanese patients I met felt very isolated. I met Ignatius Yasui, the man who had been caged in the sun at Utsonomiya, through Dr Moryama (a psychiatrist at Tokyo University who had led a revolt against the conservative establishment). Yasui made a dramatic entrance, wearing a red sweater and jeans. He had a mop of greying hair and informed me, quite accurately, that he spoke English, French, German and Italian and would like to know in which language I wanted to conduct the interview. Turning to Dr Moryama, he said he had been his '*salvatore*'. The saviour doctor smiled. Ignatius explained he was a Catholic and shook my hand very vigorously. Anyone who was going to expose psychiatric hospitals in Japan was doing valuable work.

Ignatius explained that he was an artist. His family had always objected to his calling because 'being an artist is not a proper job'. He said that he had successfully sold many works to collectors both in Japan and abroad. His family felt, however, he was squandering money. Ignatius said it was his money but his family said it was their money. The crunch came when he was in his mid-thirties. His elder brother, 'who never visited me once when I was in hospital', contacted a Dr Takemura at Tokyo University. While I could not confirm all Ignatius's artistic claims, he certainly exhibited at the Japan Society in New York in 1966. Both Dr Moryama and Etsuro Totsuka (who had been representing Ignatius for a period) confirmed the rest of his story. Having listened to his brother's account of Ignatius's symptoms, Dr Takemura agreed that he ought to be committed. Dr Takemura did not actually see the 'patient' before signing the committal order under Article 29 which provides for admission 'with the consent of the family'. The family was not merely consenting but asking for hospital treatment.

'I was taken in handcuffs to the provincial hospital and, four or five days later, transferred to Utsonomiya. The beatings started as soon as I arrived there and, often, they took place in public. If you cried, or protested, you were beaten more. The purpose of the beatings was quite simply to keep patients obedient.'

Two other patients were also admitted to Utsonomiya in irregular ways. Mr I. had spent many years living as a bachelor and working, quite successfully, in a variety of engineering businesses. He then lost his job and began to drift. He had a friend living near Utsonomiya and hoped this man would put him up. The friend refused and Mr I. took to sleeping rough in the local railway station. He did not cause any trouble, though, and took care to sweep the part of the station where he slept. This devotion to hygiene endeared him to the local police who arranged for him to be admitted to a nearby home for the elderly. Mr I. was the youngest of the residents. He taught other residents how to play volley-ball and, he smiled as he told me this, once a week he would get hold of some saki or whisky and have a pleasant tipple. There was much wrong with the home. Its elderly inmates had to consume their meals in fifteen minutes; the food was not good; they had to eat in silence. Mr I. was asked to be their spokesman and complain to the institution's owner. Within a few days of making these complaints, Mr I. was told his drinking had caused him severe liver problems and he needed to go for a check-up at Utsonomiya Hospital. 'I had no idea it was a mental hospital,' he said. Once in the hospital, he was told he needed psychiatric treatment. He got out after two years, 'but I have been very saddened.'

Mr N. is a tall man with a high, domed forehead. He wore white overalls and severe steel glasses. When we talked through an interpreter, he often looked away as if he hoped to summon precise details from the periphery of his vision. He apologized and told me that during his time in the hospital he had unfortunately not counted the unnatural deaths. Unlike Ignatius or Mr I., Mr N. admitted he had had a drinking problem. His wife had suggested he go in and, now, he had lost her. He had been in Utsonomiya for thirteen years. 'Every day from eight in the morning until two in the afternoon, until the last few months,

I gave massage to other patients.' Mr N. was paid the princely
sum of 20,000 yen (£60) a month which probably made him the
richest of the patients. But even this position did not make him
feel secure. He also volunteered to sweep the lobby of the hospital
every morning, between six-thirty and breakfast, 'in order to
show I was a diligent person. It was the only way to survive in
the hospital.'

With his diligence, Mr N. became a trusted patient and was
fairly free to move around the hospital. He often went down to
the cells that adjoined each ward. Most wards have a row of
about six isolation cells which are used to detain difficult patients.
Psychiatric hospitals all over the world have these, but they are
supposed to be used only for short periods, under strict rules. At
Utsonomiya, patients often spent three months in isolation,
according to Totsuka. During his walks through the hospital, Mr
N. recalled that he had once heard screams coming from a cell.
He peeped in through a window slit and saw nurses hitting a
patient. Yasui, too, was once beaten up in a cell after planning
an escape. He lost consciousness and came to forty-eight hours
later when, he recalls, a nurse kicked him and said, 'Oh, he's still
alive.'

Everyone accepts that Utsonomiya did not, and still does not,
have enough qualified staff. As a result, the hospital used trusted
patients as *haisins* or dish-servers. They not only helped serve the
food, but also often dispensed drugs. In many hospitals under-
staffing is a general problem; Dr Moryama and Totsuka believe
that such practices are common in many other hospitals. Mr I.
explained to me that often dish-servers were told by nurses to hit
other patients. They had to hit them because 'otherwise the
nurses would have hit them'. Moreover, they often saved
patients' lives because they 'did not hit them as hard as nurses
would have done'.

Two practices at Utsonomiya were, perhaps, especially odd.
The hospital had nearly twenty part-time doctors on its books,
but many of these doctors went there less than once a week.
Totsuka claimed that many patients saw a doctor only once,
soon after they were admitted. Utsonomiya had close connections
with the Department of Psychiatry at Tokyo University. Sixteen

university psychiatrists were among its part-timers. These psychiatrists tended to visit the hospital only when Dr Ichigawa had an interesting case to demonstrate. In the best tradition of Kraeplin, the case would be wheeled in and questioned. A Ministry of Health official confided that he had known that Utsonomiya was a bad hospital because he had attended a conference where Dr Ichigawa explained a number of tests that had been performed on an alcoholic. My anonymous contact at the Ministry of Health said, 'I accused him of using the patient as an experimental animal. But what could I do about it? Nothing.'

Apart from these demonstrations for Tokyo professors, the only approach to conventional therapy were *kaishins*. These 'group meetings' saw sixty patients assemble to meet the superintendent who sat at a desk in the middle of the room. Dr Ichigawa usually had a tape-recorder on his desk and held a golf club in his hand. 'You were not allowed to discuss your illness,' Mr N. told me. 'The superintendent would call you and ask what kind of work you were doing.' Those who had no work were promptly assigned some. 'If you raised the question of what was wrong with you, he often hit you with his golf club.' One patient had presumed to ask to be discharged. 'The superintendent turned to the nurses and told them to "take care of him",' Mr N. said. He assumed, and claims everyone else assumed, that the patient was to be beaten for his impertinence. Certainly, the patient was bundled away to a cell. He was forty years old and had, Mr N. believed, no medical condition. A day later, he was dead.

When I asked if I could visit Utsonomiya, the Ministry said it would not arrange it but would not forbid it either. No other journalist had persuaded the hospital to let them in. I was not too optimistic when I set off with Totsuka and three other lawyers.

Utsonomiya is near a big car-manufacturing plant in the suburbs of the city. From far off, the buildings look like a drab council estate till you notice the windows are barred yet, bizarrely, draped with laundry.

When you step into the lobby of any Japanese hospital, you take off your street shoes. A hospital is a home, so slippers are worn, and each hospital has a huge stock of plastic ones which are generally too small. The lobby was clean, bright and even rather attractive. Ranged against the back windows were five wooden sculptures including a nude boy, a fan of peacock feathers and a large stump of gnarled wood. (Gnarled wood is an art-form the Japanese regard highly.) Three large paintings hung on one wall. White-coated nurses criss-crossed the lobby. The whole effect was that of a quiet air terminal.

When I visited both in 1984 and 1986, the chief doctor at Utsonomiya was Dr Tomijiro Hirahata. Dr Hirahata is well into his seventies. He has a brown, lined face and a sage smile. When Dr Ichigawa bought control of the hospital, Dr Hirahata was its superintendent. He had been demoted to deputy superintendent, a demotion he accepted with apparent good grace. He had worked on throughout the Ichigawa years, but patients claim they saw him only when they were admitted. I wanted to ask Dr Hirahata about that, but he brushed away my request for an interview saying he spoke very bad English so any interview 'would be very silent'. These last words were spoken in English. Dr Hirahata is a well-known haiku poet. He was arrested before the war for his pacifist poems.

Japanese manners are a miracle of form. There was no animosity, no bristling between him and Totsuka as we took our seats in his office. No one would guess that a few months before Totsuka and his group had been thrown out and the gates had been guarded against them. To my surprise, Dr Hirahata had no objection to his chief nurse showing us round.

While the lawyers were seeing their clients, I waited in the gardens. Nurses in white coats came and went. One nurse in impeccably ironed white trousers marched a patient briskly across the garden. The shaggy-baggy patient shuffled to keep up. The nurse said nothing and did not even turn round to ensure his charge was still there.

We were eventually taken to see three wards – two of them locked. All the corridors were dirty and stank slightly. When we arrived in each ward, we found the nurses sitting together in the nurses' station. In the first two, they busily got up the moment they saw us and scrambled to look therapeutic, joining patients in the main room of the ward. In the third ward, the nurses continued to watch the closed-circuit television which kept an electronic eye on the patients. This monitored ward was the open ward.

The nurse then took us to see one of the men's locked wards. Here too the nurses sprang into activity. The nurse in charge explained that, after the scandal, they had introduced more occupational therapy. Patients in the ward were busily folding pieces of cardboard into white boxes. Every minute or so, they added to the stacks of boxes on tables in the middle of the room. The work seemed utterly repetitive but the nurse assured us that patients loved doing it. So it seemed did the nurses. Once we were in the ward, two set about making white boxes too. They sat at the tables just as if they were patients, and folded most diligently; but they made no attempt to talk to patients, to show them what they were doing or in any way to interact with them. The nurse in charge of the ward explained that patients now spent four hours a day making boxes. They got paid 1500 yen (some £6) a month.

None of the patients tried to talk to any of the lawyers. While we were marvelling at the box-making we asked the chief nurse to take us to see the cells. He hesitated a little but, eventually, did so. I was allowed to see one row which had been recently refurbished – after the scandal broke – but they were still dank and dangerous. A tiny window slit allowed nurses to peer inside. A chief nurse proudly displayed the new lino on the floor and the thin, grey felt with which the walls had just been lined. Before the scandal, the floor and walls were both of pure concrete. He asked us to admire these improvements.

When I walked into the row of cells, a man was howling. No nurse was close by. I was told he wanted some water. The chief nurse told an assistant to get a glass. Very gingerly, they opened the door a fraction and handed the patient the water. The chief nurse turned to me with a smile as if to say that this showed how well they cared for their patients. Admittedly suspicious, I could not help noticing that the nurse held the door open in such a way that he could instantly slam it shut on the patient. After a minute, the patient handed back the glass; the door was banged to.

After we had finished the tour, there was another display of impeccable Japanese politeness. Totsuka insisted that he must return to thank the chief nurse for the tour. This nurse was, in reality, an enemy, since Totsuka had done much to publicize the hospital's faults. Yet, in the garden, flanked by the laundry draped from the barred windows, they gravely bowed to each other. And the nurse made sure we got comfortably into our taxi.

No visitor to an institution can reasonably expect to get more than a superficial impression. Utsonomiya was an overcrowded hospital with grim cells, run by nurses who generally seemed to ignore their patients. This, one must remember, is an impression I got on a guided tour. The chief nurse controlled what we saw – probably after consulting with Dr Hirahata. He never suggested that the overcrowding was a problem. I can only assume that our tour showed what Japanese psychiatrists thought was acceptable. When I returned in 1986, Dr Hirahata was eager to explain the many improvements. The number of patients had decreased to less than six hundred so that 'the most famous hospital' was now operating legally. He took me on a tour of the hospital. Though there are fewer patients, this has been achieved by closing some wards. Those wards in use still seemed overcrowded. At one point, Hirahata stopped by an isolation cell. The woman patient was clearly pleading with him. He shook his head in anger. She persisted in saying she wasn't ill. She had to stay in the cell till she saw sense and accepted she was mad. Another patient walked naked without staff doing anything. At the end of the tour, Hirahata agreed to let me return with a film crew. We fixed 14 November for the filming but he then wrote to say filming would have to be delayed. Then, when I rang him, he said that it was nothing to do with him but the hospital policy was to have no filming. It wasn't his fault.

The Ministry of Health conceded in 1984 it did not really know how many hospitals were like Utsonomiya. It was left to a provincial journalist, Masakasu Honda, to start systematic research – a survey of all the psychiatric hospitals in one area. Honda began by accident. His job at the Gumma branch of the

Asahi Shimbun was to monitor police activity. One day he was listening in to the police radio when news came that four patients had escaped from the local Tanaka Hospital. Honda got their names and discovered which of them had relatives living nearby. He managed to contact them before the police did.

Over the telephone, Honda asked why they had escaped. They made a series of allegations of brutality and corruption. Having taped the conversations, Honda drove to meet them: a face-to-face interview would flesh out the story. But it was 50 kilometres to their hiding place, and he was too late – the police had recaptured them and taken them back to hospital. One relative had been frightened neighbours would find out there was madness in the family and had informed the authorities. The police, in return, promised a tactful operation.

The allegations were sufficiently convincing for *Asahi Shimbun* to run Honda's story. As with the Juzenkai Corporation hospital, the Tanaka had a high death-rate. It had some 478 beds (roughly 10 per cent more than its authorized maximum) and, in the three years from 1980 to 1983, 218 patients had died there. Eighty per cent of the patients who died were aged over sixty-five, but that still left a hefty death-rate. Eventually, the superintendent of Tanaka Hospital admitted to Honda that in 208 cases he was not absolutely certain that the detention of the patients was completely legal.

Honda decided that it was not enough to publish about Tanaka alone. Systematically he began to investigate the other nineteen mental hospitals in Gumma prefecture. As Okuma had found ten years earlier, his paper would not allow him to concentrate exclusively on this assignment – there were still weddings, funerals, dances and trials to write up. In the six months that he has been investigating, Honda claims to have found evidence of brutality and financial corruption in five other hospitals.

Asahi Shimbun so far has published his revelations of a high suicide rate in one hospital and patients being robbed of goods and money in another hospital. Again, he has found evidence of hospitals sending patients out to work, calling it occupational therapy and pocketing most of their wages. Honda's patient digging suggests that in one typical prefecture nearly a third of the hospitals are beating and/or cheating their patients. He wanted to ensure, however, that I realized there were some decent hospitals too.

Even odder has been the reaction to Mr Goda's *bushoan* in Fuji city. Japanese television in a broadcast in March 1986 revealed that conditions were cruel. Goda likes to boast that his regime is strict and that his inmates are deliberately kept bored. They have to attend eight religious services a day to break their spirit. One person was killed. Later, in 1987, three inmates died in a fire. Yet, despite the negative publicity and the fact that there is no authority for keeping individuals behind his bars and barbed wire, neither the police nor the government takes any action.

Initially, the Japanese government was not eager to change its mental-health law or to investigate the general state of psychiatric care. Only the Socialist Party did anything to highlight the issue. 'The Communist Party', Totsuka smiled, 'is very retrograde when it comes to human rights, especially for psychiatric patients.' He added that it had close links with Moscow, and the Kremlin was hardly likely to encourage a purge of psychiatry. After much pressure from lawyers and some doctors, the Socialist Party put forward a sixteen-point plan late in 1984. It called for a reform of the law on admissions, the right for patients to see lawyers, investment in rehabilitation facilities and proper policing of the staffing in hospitals. The Socialist Party claimed that it discriminates against mental patients to have a law which says psychiatric hospitals need only a third of the doctors and a half of the nurses other hospitals need. The government 'took note' of the plan in a debate in Parliament, but said then it would be far too premature to consider any action. Throughout 1985 and 1986, Totsuka continued his campaign. In 1985, he was one of the key speakers at Mental Health 2000, a conference organized by MIND. He told the conference that: 'No improvement for the mental patient's rights is expected. To our regret, the government is very reluctant to amend the law appropriately.' He pointed out that the ICJ report 'referred to scandals in at least twelve mental hospitals before and after the one in Utsonomiya Hospital.'

Totsuka also offered evidence of the scandals at Otaki Hospital. Mr Yamada, who had been committed by his parents (see page (66)), was in the bathroom in May 1984 when he saw a nurse argue with a patient who didn't want to bathe. Mr Yamada then saw the nurse beat the patient repeatedly. Two days later, the patient was dead. Totsuka added: 'This incident was reported by *Asahi Shimbun* on 15 July and is emerging as another big scandal.'

Again, perfectly sane patients were being detained. Totsuka suggested that the lack of

any legal framework, coupled with the unrestricted autonomy of psychiatrists has led to continuing or even worsening abuses.

This is one area in which any developing country would be wise to decline aid from Japan. Legislation to uphold the human rights of mental patients is urgently needed. A model legislative code will be helpful for mental patients not only in Japan but also in other countries.

Soon after the end of Mental Health 2000, the International Commission of Jurists published its report on Human Rights and the Treatment of Mental Patients in Japan. It said that the Japanese mental system 'must be regarded as seriously inadequate'. It highlighted 'a lack of legal protection for patients' and, also, the 'preponderance of long-term institutional treatment'. Its survey of the current situation echoed much of what had been described to me.

The International Commission went on to ask for a number of urgent reforms. They wanted to see the setting up of a review board to consider all involuntary admissions within a month of the patient being admitted into hospital. An independent tribunal system ought to be set up with both lawyers, doctors and lay people on its panel to carry out these reviews. Secondly, all mental hospitals should be regularly inspected to check on conditions, staffing levels and receive patients' complaints. Third, all patients had to be advised of their rights and given free access to the tribunals and to someone who could represent them. Fourth, every 'incident leading to personal injury' ought to be logged and investigated where appropriate. Every death should be routinely investigated with an autopsy.

The International Commission argued that the Japanese Ministry of Health needed to stimulate community-care programmes and fund them properly. It pointed to the economic paradox which made it far more profitable to hospitalize patients than to look after them in the community. For those who follow the controversies about community care in Britain, the paradox is ironic indeed. Progressives who argued for community care in the 1970s know now that community care, if it comes cheap, is no care at all. The International Commission wants Japan to avoid that particular pitfall. The report urged a sensitive programme of releasing long-term patients into the community. Crucially, too, it pointed to the need for better education for psychiatrists, psychologists, social workers and the general public. It was not satisfactory to have no special qualification in psychiatry. Psychologists and social workers needed training which was 'more orientated towards rehabilitation and outpatient care. At present their skills are mainly directed towards institutional care'. The public needed education, too, to change its attitudes and for 'diminishing the stigma of psychiatric illness'. Highlighting the economics of it again, the International Commission wanted those with mental disabilities to have the same financial welfare rights as the physically disabled.

The Japanese government did not initially welcome the report. But the continuing bad publicity for Japan, the pressure from the United Nations and what Totsuka believes is a growing sense of shame, have meant that it is now studying how to set up the tribunal system demanded. There were plans for the Diet to discuss mental health law reforms early in 1987, but then Japanese political life was overwhelmed by a debate on whether or not to impose a sales tax to placate foreign countries complaining of Japan's trade surplus, which led to the downfall of Mr Nakasone, and the issue was postponed until the end of the year. The new law finally introduced in late 1987 does provide some safeguards such as the right to have a telephone in wards. Totsuka wanted an independent commission to take complaints and review cases. The law does not go so far. It is some success, Totsuka believes though there is no evidence yet of the Japanese government funding mental health care properly. The publicity has led, he told me in a recent visit to London, to a great deal of interest from other Asian countries. He has had letters from psychiatrists in India, the Philippines and Thailand to say that the abuses in Japan are only the 'tip of the iceberg'. He now plans to study psychiatry in the rest of South East Asia.

Totsuka told me he felt very isolated at the start of his campaign. Now, he feels less so. He hopes to persuade Japanese politicians to grant proper legal rights to patients. Ironically, in the USA, it was just when lawyers started to win such battles in the 1960s that they laid the foundations of the very different crisis in psychiatry that the US is now facing.

4

America: Pamper the neurotics and neglect the sick

In the late 1970s, a small man would shuffle into shops and offices in New York and offer his services as a 'business consultant'. Rikki sounded educated and peppered his conversation with technological terms. 'I read the *New York Times* every day,' he pointed out. Despite that, 'I was always refused.' Rikki smiled. He is a small, wiry man in his forties and not without some common sense, so he wasn't that surprised. He knew he looked very rough. He had been living on the streets for thirteen months: 'I was sick on the streets.' He slept in Central Park and in the hangar-like city shelters.

Rikki had had no medical or social-work help after he had discharged himself from a veterans' administration hospital. He had walked out because, 'I had been attacked and was frightened of being attacked again.' Once out, he simply disappeared into Manhattan and, in his isolation, got worse. His father died and Rikki started to hallucinate again. 'When I go crazy the birds talk to me, the television talks to me, the trees talk to me,' he smiled as he sat on the edge of his hospital bed. Perhaps in reaction to living rough, his hallucinations became more frightening. He became obsessed with ESP. 'I used to think that I was controlled by ESP and, also, that I could use my ESP powers to control others.' He once imagined using his mighty mind to control fifty people. Central to this fantasy was a system which involved ESP 'chits' which individuals signed. Once a person signed an ESP chit they could be telepathically controlled by evil forces. For all his fantasies of power, Rikki was also terrified and had no one to turn to. One day, he found himself in the subway. He was sure the man in front of him had signed the ESP chit and was, therefore, at the beck and call of sinister powers. He might attack. The other innocent-looking subway passengers might be in league with him. As they waited for the subway, the traveller made a fatal mistake. 'He stepped on my toe.' Rikki added, without a trace of regret, 'I pushed him in front of the subway train. I ruined my life.' Rikki said, with pride, that he had never been in trouble before and had no history of violence. Isolation on the streets had made him dangerous.

In May 1986 an even more dramatic incident occurred. Juan Gonzales, who was hallucinating and said he felt persecuted, was refused admission to Columbia Presbyterian Hospital which sent him instead to a city shelter. The next day he went berserk with a gun on the Staten Island ferry, killing two people and injuring nine. The victims and the bereaved blamed the lack of hospital beds. His failure to obtain treatment ought to have provoked a major review of New York's psychiatric policies but it has not. New York State and New York City are continuing as before – and defending that position.

Rikki was found insane and sent to hospital. The murder got him admitted, in fact, to Creedmoor Psychiatric Hospital in Queens. For ten years he has been held rather than treated. Drugs have left him with serious side-effects, much like Walter Reed's. Rikki moves restlessly all the time: his legs swing back and forth, out of his control. His speech is slow and slurred. He shakes his head from time to time for no apparent reason. Bob Couteau regretted that Community Access had not found Walter when he was younger; Rikki might have not become violent if he had had care. There is no evidence that New York is absorbing the lesson of such cases.

Though Rikki is on an ordinary ward, over 50 per cent of his fellow-patients have committed an act of violence. William assaulted a woman in Grand Central station, for example. Some patients had attempted suicide. It made it seem as if extreme, violent action was required to get a hospital bed.

In Chapter 1, I argued that many of America's current problems are the result of well-meaning reforms. But the reforms have not all been counter-productive. They have left patients in a much better legal position, should they actually squeeze any care out of the system. A patient can challenge a decision to detain him quickly; many hospitals have lawyers on call; treatment usually requires the patient's consent. Unfortunately, the one right patients don't have is the right to treatment.

'I have argued that the organization of psychiatry in this country is more psychotic, even more crazy, than the people who have these diseases themselves,' said Fuller Torrey (interview with author). But, of course, it is the mentally ill rather than psychiatrists who suffer. Many psychiatrists, in fact, have a curious, divided attitude. They accept that much is wrong and that patients get a raw deal, but they also complain of their own raw deal. Who cares about their agony, their burn out, their stress? You have to be an American shrink to know how hard it is to be an American shrink.

American psychiatrists have become fascinated by their own psychological problems which shows, perhaps, just how American they are. Since the 1920s, popular psychology has done well. Books on how to live the perfect, balanced life from John B. Watson's *The Psychological Care of the Child* (1928) to Wayne Dyer's *Your Erogenous Zones* (1984) have been bestsellers. Watson pioneered the fashion of using academic psychology expertise to tell people how to achieve the best work life, social life and sex life. Watson recommended greater openness about all problems. His advice has been heeded. The Donovan Show, one of the networks' big hits, depends on individuals hanging out their hang-ups. It is OK to be a drunk, a compulsive gambler, a wife-beater or to have a fetish for young priests as long as you talk about it. Woody Allen has made a career out of revealing his neuroses.

This compulsive openness hasn't improved the lot of the seriously mentally ill. Stigma and discrimination persist. This is a strange anomaly to which sociologists should pay attention. Why do Americans accept serious neurotic problems (Oh God, not the end of another relationship; not another blow to my ability to trust; not another phobia; pass the valium), why do they accept it is no shame to have a psychiatrist and, yet, treat the severely mentally ill as badly as anyone else? Sociologists, *please* attend.

Deinstitutionalization

In 1948, in his angry book *The Shame of the States*, Albert Deutsch painted a dire picture of the psychiatric hospitals of the north-east United States. He wrote:

In some of the wards there were scenes that rivalled the horrors of the Nazi concentration camps – hundreds of naked mental patients herded into huge, barn-like, filth-infested wards, in all degrees of deterioration, untended and untreated, stripped of every vestige of human decency, many in stages of semi-starvation. The writer heard state hospital doctors frankly admit that the animals of nearby piggeries were better fed, housed and treated than many of the patients in their wards.

In 1949, the film *The Snake Pit* dramatized the plight of patients. In 1955, Mike Gorman published a series of articles about treatment in Oklahoma and then gathered these into an angry book, *Every Other Bed*. Academics had caught up by the 1950s and published research papers showing that institutional life was damaging. In bad institutions, patients were abused; in good ones, they became dependent and found it hard to leave. They lost many skills they would need in the outside world. Hospitals created their own sickness, a critique rammed home in two bestsellers of the 1960s. The sociologist, Erving Goffman, published *Asylums* in 1961. The book was based on St Elizabeth's Hospital in Washington DC which Goffman had been invited to observe. Ken Kesey's novel *One Flew Over the Cuckoo's Nest* (1962) saw patients rejoice as they got out of hospital and finally tasted freedom. The message was clear: hospitals hampered healing. Free patients and you would cure them.

All this seemed so clear that few campaigners (and, in England, I was certainly one of a number of film-makers whose programmes took this line) examined in detail what would happen once the hospitals were shut. It was assumed that facilities such as day-care centres and sheltered housing would, almost magically, arise. Closing expensive hospitals would release money for care in the community. In the liberal enthusiasm, few did realistic accounts. Governments do not like spending money on mental illness. It earns few votes.

No one imagined that the money saved on hospitals would *not* be spent on facilities in the community. Yet that is precisely what has happened in America, Britain and even Italy. The savings have not been transferred.

In New York in 1955, there were 93,000 people in psychiatric hospitals. Today, there are 20,000. Few hospitals, however, have actually closed. Most have contracted in size. Despite the fall in the number of patients, 80 per cent of the state's mental-health budget is still devoted to hospital care. Unions have been effective in protecting hospital jobs. The State of New York Office of Mental Health's five-year plan envisages that by 1990 there will be even fewer hospital beds. Short-stay beds are planned to decrease by 9 per cent to 2584; long-stay beds to decrease by 27 per cent to 12,667. The only planned increase is in acute short-stay beds provided in local general hospitals. There will be 10 per cent more of them. In ten years, the state hopes to have only 7000 psychiatric beds, a plan condemned by the *New York Post* (8 December 1986) as 'an unhealthy mental-health plan'.

Fewer beds makes it harder to get those in need admitted. Dr Steve Mollins took a would-be suicide who was talked down from the rafters at the Franklin Armoury shelter (see page 100) to the emergency room of a Bronx hospital. 'They asked him how he was feeling. He said he was feeling better so they sent him back.' A week later, the man tried suicide again. Bob Couteau, in charge of counselling for Community Access, claims clients have to prove to a succession of psychiatrists they are sick enough to deserve a hospital bed: 'People can find the hours it takes terrifying and stressful and you have no guarantee you'll get in.' If they do admit, hospitals keep patients only for a maximum of twenty-eight days because the insurance cover then runs out.

Dr Steven Katz, the Commissioner of Mental Health for New York State, suggested that the failure to hospitalize Juan Gonzales which resulted in the dramatic deaths on the Staten Island ferry was a tragic mistake. Every system will have such mistakes. He admitted that 'We are now seeing a backlash.' But it is an odd backlash. Hospitals have become more cautious about who they release rather than more liberal about who they take in. In the six months after the Gonzales incident, for all the urgent talk about not refusing treatment, social and community workers said they did not find it any easier to get patients into hospital. The inability of New York to react reflects the general confusion and malaise.

Probably the most comprehensive recent assessment of American psychiatry is Fuller Torrey and Sidney Wolfe's report, *The Care of the Seriously Mentally Ill* (1986). They compiled this for the Public Citizen Health Research Group, a branch of Ralph Nader's Public Citizen consumer organization. I talked to them in Sidney Wolfe's office which, he grinned, is piled so high with papers it's impossible to find anything. Yet, during the course of our talk, he somehow managed to dig out whatever reference he needed. Wolfe trained as a doctor but works full time for the Public Citizen Health Research Group. He explained that his main contribution had been putting the statistics into some kind of order. Fuller Torrey had done most of the fieldwork and added the style that makes the report not just devastating but good to read.

With almost wicked glee, Torrey and Wolfe point out that the number of psychiatrists in the USA has risen from 4000 in 1948 to 35,000 today. Qualified clinical psychologists have increased from 4000 to 60,000. The federal government's mental-health budget is 2.3 billion dollars, while states pay 750 million dollars. The 'mental-health industry' is, indeed, worth megabucks. Yet the quality of care offered in and out of hospital is still very poor. Megabucks have not bought megacare. *The Care of the Seriously Mentally Ill* is more angry than witty. Its opening paragraph is worth quoting in full as it reveals the outrage and despair both authors feel:

In 1843, Dorothea Dix appeared before the Massachusetts Legislature to decry 'the state of insane persons confined within this Commonwealth in cages, closets, cellars, stalls, pens, chained, naked, beaten with rods and lashed into obedience.' In 1985, witnesses testified before the Senate Subcommittee on the Handicapped regarding sexual abuse of persons confined in mental hospitals including 'kicking or otherwise striking patients, sexual advances and rape, verbal threats of injury and other forms of intimidation.

Not much had changed in 140 years.

Torrey and Wolfe make the accusation that: 'It is increasingly difficult to avoid the reality that we have done an abysmal job in caring for the seriously mentally ill.'

Using the Freedom of Information Act, they gathered data from twelve different sources. These included the reports of state departments of mental health, those of the Joint Commission on Accreditation of Hospitals (which judges if a hospital is good enough to qualify for Medicare or Medicaid), surveys by the Health Care Financing Administration, reports to the National Institute of Mental Health on services in particular states and on how grants to community health centres had been spent. Torrey and Wolfe also obtained Department of Justice papers where there had been malpractice allegations. They also talked to groups of ex-patients, to local chapters of the National Alliance for the Mentally Ill and to twenty senior practitioners in every state. Fuller Torrey visited twenty states himself to carry out on-the-spot investigations. Despite a major fact-finding enterprise, Torrey and Wolfe's final report runs only to 105 pages which includes twenty pages of historical introduction and five pages of notes and bibliography. This is partly a miracle of compression but, partly, the result of the strange format in which they decided to publish their results. Instead of a comprehensive guide to facilities, Torrey and Wolfe assumed they had to package their information cleverly to make an impact. So they devised a rating scale for the states, a sort of Michelin Guide to Psychiatric Care. They rated how good inpatient and outpatient care was in each state. Wisconsin came top, Hawaii bottom. They also scored each state for 'Direction'. Was it making progress, stuck in the status quo or slipping into even worse chaos? The state of Alabama, for example, ranks twenty-ninth. It scores 2 out of 5 for inpatient care and 2 out of 5 for outpatient care. Its 'Direction' is, alas, directionless for it is bogged down in the status quo. Visitors to Alabama are 'surprised by the improvement' in the large state hospitals like Bryce and Searcy, but the state finds it hard to attract professionals, and local politicians aren't interested in the issue. Five states were 'moving ahead strongly' while another fourteen were 'making steady progress'. The others were either mired in the status quo or declining into something even more rotten.

Torrey and Wolfe reserve some specially acerbic comments for the State of New York. Albert Deutsch, they point out, argued that New York was one of the states that spent most on mental health but 'in the easiest and stupidest way by pouring money into bricks and mortar'. Forty years later, not much had changed. New York spends one billion dollars on its thirty-three state hospitals but only 25 per cent of that sum on community-care programmes. Torrey and Wolfe attack local health-service unions for preferring hospital jobs and conclude that 'the ongoing New York City–upstate tag team wrestling contest will have to be resolved'. Moreover, 'the heavily bureaucratized State Office of Mental Health will have to assign its many chiefs back out to the clinics to learn how the patients and Indians really live'.

Torrey and Wolfe try to explain what led to this national 'mess' and spread the blame widely. The failure to accept schizophrenia as a 'true brain disease' was especially damaging. It offered false hopes of easy cures: released patients would be well. Torrey is sardonic about the sloppy idealism of *Asylums* and *One Flew Over the Cuckoo's Nest* and what he sees as facile attacks on hospitals. The report states:

You can psychoanalyze patients, change the social conditions and release them all into the community but these actions alone will produce little or no improvement in their condition. Indian Chief [the hero of *Cuckoo's Nest*] will not be spearing salmon in the Columbia River but rather will be a mentally ill homeless person in Portland sitting with frostbitten toes and hallucinating beneath a bridge.

Attacking the hospitals made the states pay less attention to them so the actual plant deteriorated. Doctors had too much faith in new drugs and in the willingness of ex-patients to take them. Once the law changed, making it hard to commit people against their will, there was no way to force someone who was not dangerous to take medication. Fuller Torrey is not surprised that schizophrenics should refuse drugs since they are sick in the brain and 'the brain is that part of the body we use to think about ourselves with'. In theory, they were meant to get outpatient care in the community mental-health-care centres. In practice, they did not.

Torrey and Wolfe throw some sharp barbs at the community mental-health-care centres. Local neighbourhoods did build them but then proceeded to exclude the really sick. Their clientele was the 'worried well' who fret about their relationships, their potency, why their teenagers won't talk to them and other defects in the American dream. The neurotics get pampered; the really sick neglected.

The Shelters

In the shelters, you see the results of that neglect. I have never seen anything as noisy, as frightening, as utterly wretched as these shelters. What is perhaps most amazing is the propaganda New York bureaucrats peddle which claims they exist to help the vulnerable. Dickens would have found the hypocrisy familiar.

In the winter of 1985, Ed Koch, the Mayor of New York City, ordered that if the temperature fell below freezing, the police should pick up anyone sleeping outside and take them to city shelters. Humanity demanded that should be done; the cold could kill. The American Civil Liberties Union argued that the city had no right to take such action. Many people slept rough because the city shelters for the homeless were so *unsafe*. There were rapes, muggings, even murders. Better to freeze than to face a night in one. The opposition never succeeded in making a major issue out of the coercion and Koch carried out his plan. Some nights, over 600 people were taken to city shelters. Diane Sonday, the director of Project Reach Out that tries to 'reach out' to the homeless mentally ill, told me she dreaded the coming winter. Mentally ill and other homeless people would die from the cold, from starvation and from sheer neglect in a city which boasts an army of psychologists and psychiatrists and prides itself on its liberal conscience.

By December 1986, these paradoxes were becoming painful. The ever-more-humane Mayor Koch had ordered New York police to evict vagrants from Grand Central and Penn stations, their traditional refuges. In the elegant malls and less elegant tunnels, tramps often doze propped up against walls, or sit in nests of plastic bags. Some scavenge the garbage, others pace up and down restlessly. I watched an old woman wrapped in a white coat walk to and fro, to and fro, for most of an hour, covering and re-covering the ten yards between the entrance to tracks 20 and 22. She stopped occasionally to hug herself. She muttered to herself. The New York police did not like Mayor Koch's orders. Throwing helpless people on to the streets did little for their image but they did it, nevertheless, and some individuals did it with gusto. I saw one officer pull a man to his feet in Grand Central station, give him a lecture on how dirty he was and bundle him to a station exit. The television news regularly showed pictures of police forcing tramps out on to the streets. Koch's policy – to the shelters whether you like it or not – has predictably led to a boom in these bizarre institutions.

In 1970, New York made do with one shelter in the Bowery for middle-aged white drunks. Skid Row is bigger now. Today, there are twenty-two large public shelters and many smaller private ones. In the large shelters which can house up to a thousand people, conditions are appalling. Tokyo may hospitalize its outcasts; New York and most other American cities 'shelterize' them. The name *shelter* is ironic. The shelters provide little real shelter.

The shelters are, according to Fuller Torrey, the sad result of the 'well-meaning policy of deinstitutionalization'. Initially, many of the homeless were ex-patients who could not manage in the outside world, but now there is a new population of people who have never been in hospital but who need treatment. Both streets and shelters are full of individuals who show symptoms of acute mental illness; some are withdrawn, some are very exhibitionistic. The diagnosis doesn't matter too much as the care doesn't exist.

The presence of so many mentally ill is beginning to make New Yorkers uncomfortable. In November 1986, the *New York Times* carried a large article mapping the 'mad people' its reporter saw on a walk down Broadway. The reporter, a psychology PhD, was staggered by the varieties of lunacy on display. It is odd he was surprised because there are disturbed people on every street. I saw them sleeping in the gutters outside smart hotels like the Waldorf, pissing down stairwells close to elegant shops on

Lexington Avenue (including a dress shop called Therapy!) and outside fancy restaurants. In most cities, the poor are in their ghettoes. In New York, they share the streets with the relatively rich who, so far, have not felt their consciences prick too much. Fuller Torrey offers a bizarrely precise formula for when 'the average man on his way to lunch' finds all this too upsetting: 'When you get more than one hallucinating person per half acre then the ordinary person begins to ask what has gone wrong and he gets distressed.' That distress is not entirely selfish. True, the man on the street would rather walk to lunch without encountering too many people per acre whose hallucinations might put him off his high-fibre delicatessen, but there is a nobler side to his distress. Wouldn't the worrying lunatics be better off back in hospital and, ipso facto, off the street?

Torrey argues as if there was a deliberate policy of emptying hospitals, but others think there has been a disaster precisely because there was no policy. Sociologist Phil Brown (1985) has argued there was no coherent policy. There was pressure from the media, mental-health lobby groups and some liberal politicians to empty the hospitals but many other interest groups fought the proposals. It was incoherence, the failure to follow any policy through properly, that has created the present 'disaster' in which America has achieved a notable double – poor hospitals and poor community care.

In New York I went to see Crosby Inman, the man in charge of the psychiatric services offered by the East 3rd Street shelter. Outside the building black garbage bags swarmed over the pavement. Men and women lolled against the bags; a few foraged casually inside them. One man was dressed as a court jester in green-and-white patchwork trousers. His face was clamped in a grin. Many others looked vacant or drugged or simply trembled. They would have made good faces for a frieze of zombies. Such scenes easily make you nervous, especially if most of the surrounding houses are boarded up. Five policemen leaned against their cars, lazy but ready for action. Tyrone Henderson, a black community worker, pointed out acidly that the shelters were 'like concentration camps. They exist to contain the people because imagine what would happen to New York if they got out of control.'

Tyrone's view sounded less melodramatic as soon as I walked inside. The moment I went up to the large semi-circular counter which dominates the entrance hall I was asked what I wanted – very roughly.

I said I had an appointment with Mr Inman.

'ID,' demanded the man behind the counter.

I explained that an interview had been arranged by the Human Resources Agency, the part of the New York City administration responsible for the shelters.

'I need ID,' insisted the man.

I showed him my passport.

'That's not ID,' he barked.

'It's a British passport,' I said. He looked at the document doubtfully and snapped that it was his job to check everything. Critics accuse shelter staff of paranoia. In November 1986, two security guards stabbed residents in different shelters. Officially, the guards are supposed to be unarmed. In practice, many carry arms unofficially. Tension is high. When I turned up to film, by appointment, at the Franklin Armoury shelter, four security guards barred the door, yelling we couldn't come in.

I waited for Mr Inman. Some fifty men, mostly black or Hispanic, wandered around the counter. Others were leaving a 'recreation area' which had to be cleaned. Security guards watched, many with hands on their truncheons. Their swagger contrasted with the slow, shambly walk of most of the 'clients', many of whom looked drugged or stared vacantly just like the men outside.

Notices on the walls advertised Detox groups and one warned that 'sometimes it's not so nice to share' because of AIDS. I hovered anxiously; the city is very sensitive about its shelters which do not have the right image for gorgeous Gotham. Had they changed their mind about letting me visit?

Reception man suddenly became less hostile. He gestured that I should come inside the counter. He had to be very careful. It was nothing personal. But now, one of the deputy supervisors knew I was expected. I would be escorted up to Mr Inman's office. The deputy ordered the lift man to deliver me personally to Mr Inman. This was no place for a stranger to wander in on his own.

Not many people sleep in the East 3rd Street shelter but, during the day, it is full. Stairways, halls and corridors are crammed with people waiting, though it is not clear what they are waiting for. Often they are asleep. They look eerie, lying on tables, lying in corners, propped up against walls. A few glanced up as I was escorted past but most stayed slumped. The clutter of weary bodies was like a scene out of downmarket Kafka. They had nothing to get up for till the next meal which would mean a long time queuing. In theory, they were waiting to be seen by various experts in various rooms who can offer anything from employment counselling to AIDS advice because East 3rd Street takes in the homeless, the jobless, the helpless and the mad. Though they arrive with apparently very different problems, most come to look sadly similar.

There were random bursts of energy. An elfin-looking man with a tiny beard bumped into us as we came out of one room.

'What's in there?' he demanded.

'Job counselling,' said Inman's assistant.

'I'd like that,' he said, but didn't go in.

Crosby Inman is a social worker who has spent twenty-three years in New York. He is a bureaucrat of care. His office is on the top floor where inmates are not permitted. He came to the shelter because he 'thought it was a challenge'. He regretted that, of course, facilities were not perfect. 'There was a lag,' he conceded, because the number of people in shelters was growing so fast. Services could not keep up. But 'I like to feel the system works reasonably well,' he soothed. People did get fed every day; they were given clothes; they were given basic medical care. 'On all these basic necessities,' he smiled, 'we do excellently.' Moreover, for some residents they managed to provide Detox groups or advice on how to get jobs. 'We are continuously expanding the programmatic piece,' he declared, which appeared to mean there were more and more programmes available. Derelicts had never had so much expertise lavished on them.

Inman is in charge of only one of the facilities of one shelter.

To criticize him too much would be unfair. At the Franklin Armoury shelter in the Bronx, its director, Joseph Eady, a black social worker, radiated a similar complacency. When I came out from using his personal toilet, however, I heard him yell 'Shit!' frantically down the telephone. Once he saw me, he cut the conversation short and reverted to his assured smile. According to critics who staff the psychiatric facilities, Mr Eady is frightened – and rightly so.

The Franklin Armoury is a massive shelter. It looks like a castle gone to seed. The streets around are burned out. A patch of grass opposite is carpeted with broken bottles and the trees hung with what I took to be huge white flowers. These turned out to be dirty disposable nappies slung out by residents of the one inhabited block nearby. The blackened buildings have never been repaired and are grimly fascinating. When we filmed, I wandered through the decay looking for evocative angles and came across a graveyard of cars hidden by tall grasses. The desolation inside the shelter matches the desolation outside.

The armoury itself looks like a huge warehouse. On the main floor there are twenty rows of beds, each bed about a foot from the next; 585 men sleep here. From the gallery the view is extraordinary, an endless panorama of beds. In the middle of the beds, a space has been set aside for recreation and eating. There is no privacy. Each man is given a locker but many residents complain that guards rifle the lockers. The guards clearly bully the residents, yelling at them and, not infrequently, shoving them. No one can get in without passing through the metal detector and being frisked. Everyone acknowledges frisking is necessary because many people would try to bring in guns and knives, but it is done roughly. The giant, noisy dormitory is frightening. The guards themselves say they are frightened. There are only twelve of them on duty on each shift. They receive no specialized training and are paid 3.50 dollars an hour, just above the minimum wage. After the stabbings in November 1986, the city promised to reconsider its policy of awarding security contracts to the lowest bidder among the city's rival security corporations. Nothing has come of that yet. 'If things get out of hand, all we can do is call the police and hope they get here pretty fast,' one guard shrugged.

Mr 'Eady assured me that he rarely needed to summon the police.

Dr Steve Mollins, who runs the psychiatric support services in the shelter, has a very different view. He and his mobile psychiatric team had terrible difficulties getting established there. They have a large office at the top of the armoury. The guards and shelter staff are suspicious. Residents have to ask permission to go up there. In practice, they are discouraged from going. One ex-resident was dragged away from the office while taking part in a therapy group. The shelter staff said he was a subversive influence and had the muscle to ban him.

A few weeks before I visited the Franklin Armoury, a resident had climbed on to the rafters high above the floor. He threatened to jump. The police came. He started to tie a sheet to one of the rafters and threatened to swing to and fro. He would soon die if he did that. After hours of panic and, according to Mollins, 'everyone on the floor was trying to talk him down, residents, police, staff, guards', he finally came down. Mollins was sad that the staff and the security guards who had been helpful during the crisis decided to leave the sheet hanging from the rafters as a warning, a gruesome reminder of how far the shelter could push residents.

The guards and the critics like Mollins are, at least, more realistic than the politicians and bureaucrats who pretend the shelter system is meeting the needs of the homeless and the mentally ill. The system relies on coercion, on tough security guards and the police who are an emergency button away. Despite all the criticism, 200 extra beds are being put in the armoury. Mollins argues that the city and the state deliberately keep the shelters 'terrible places because they think millions of people are waiting to live here'.

The shelters exercise a strange fascination on the city's social scientists. They are too remarkable not to study and they have been studied and re-studied by academics and also by reformed residents. Tyrone Henderson is a large, tough-looking man in his thirties who was born in Harlem. I met him in the offices of the

New York Institute for Psychiatric Research. Tyrone had worked as one of their interviewers on one of the studies. His old boss, 'Moose', more formally known as Dr Stuyvingen, greeted him with affection. Tyrone smiled that he had been a good client for social workers till he decided to deal with his drug problem and get an education. 'The pain of that wasn't goin' to be worse than the pain of what I was dealing with on the street.' God had helped him change but, also, he had become increasingly fed up with being helpless. He acted strong but his life was in a mess. He had lived rough after he had lost his home in Harlem and then stayed a short while in the shelters. The residents needed to be heard. To academics like Moose, Tyrone's past made him an attractive employee. 'He'd know how to talk to people on the streets,' Moose said.

As a researcher, Tyrone started at the Fort Washington shelter, another armoury where over a thousand men sleep. 'My first experience was a mass confusion,' and it was a menacing confusion with National Guard units on call outside. Perhaps 80 per cent of those he saw inside were black or Hispanic. The New York Institute for Psychiatric Research survey (NYPI, 1986) found formally that 78 per cent of shelter residents belong to minority groups.

They have to live under petty rules as well as oppressive conditions. 'The shelters insist that if you're not in by seven, you lose your bed. Residents have few rights and they make it seem that being helpless is a crime,' Tyrone pointed out. Many inmates had failed in the world precisely because they could not conform to rules. Here, there were more rules than average, many of them trivial. Staff could use a complex disciplinary system against 'bad' inmates who could be banned for a night, a week, a month or, in theory, for life.

The size of the shelters makes them, according to Tyrone, a culture of pecking orders. The strong prey on the weak. 'There are drug cults, alcoholic cults. Everyone pairs off into groups and the fragile mentally ill are preyed on, especially by the drug cults. It becomes a place where you can take out your anger however you see fit.' Shelters for women are as violent. In some shelters, residents have to work. They sweep corridors or clean kitchens for a pittance – 12.95 dollars a week. 'They claim it's job experience and to keep you active but it's really a matter of slave labour,' Tyrone argued.

Even a critic like Tyrone accepts that clever individuals can use the shelter system to get help for themselves. But few have the motivation, for 'most are broken and are getting nothing more than a bed.' As the shelters become a permanent feature of New York, many workers worry about 'shelterization'. Dr Mollins argued that when people first go to shelters they think, 'This is a shitty place. I must get out of here.' But if they fail to do so quickly, they become depressed and resigned. The skills it takes to survive in the Franklin Armoury are not much help in the real world. Inmates have been saved from being institutionalized only to be shelterized.

Ironically, poor as the system is, it has had to be forced both on the city and the state through a series of law suits. 'Every year since 1979,' Ellen Baxter told me, 'there have had to be legal battles to establish the rights of residents.' Baxter runs an impressive hostel on West 178th Street for ex-patients and other homeless. She explained that lawyers had to take the city to court to define the amount of space there has to be between beds (eighteen inches), the number of toilets and showers for every twenty residents, the number of towels, pillows and, even, how many bars of soap. The Coalition for the Homeless has the right to send monitors into the shelters to check that these minimum standards are kept. 'We find nearly always that they are not being kept,' Baxter smiled wearily. Toilets often have no doors. One state law insists, for example, that no shelter should sleep more than 200 men. That is flagrantly being broken. If you raise such points now, the official reply is that the situation is an emergency. In an emergency, anything goes.

All those I interviewed agreed that many disturbed people avoid the shelters because they frighten them. John, from Ellen Baxter's house, said you felt at more risk inside than outside. Tyrone Henderson rattled off a list of places where one could find people sleeping rough in New York. Favourite locations included Central Park, the subway system, especially the No. 2 and D train, a small patch of the Riverside in the upper 80s.

Only newcomers chose to sleep in Grand Central station or the Port Authority, though Tyrone did not know why. The street dwellers may be disturbed, but they understand and don't interrupt the flow of the city. 'You see them at six in the morning getting ready on the subway and moving out of the way of the commuters,' Tyrone said. Central Park has the surreal spectacle of joggers doing their fitness rituals round tracks, benches and trees where derelicts sleep covered in carrier bags.

Social scientists have tried to unravel the origins of the shelter population. Are they ex-patients, people who ought to be in hospital, or an assortment of the poor, sick and inadequate? Lovers of academic wrangles can revel in disputes as to whether 50 per cent, or just 33 per cent, of shelter residents are psychotic and whether 25 per cent, or just 15 per cent, are suffering from psychiatric symptoms as a result of living rough. Through the arguments about details, most observers agree that a large proportion of shelter residents are mentally ill and get inadequate or no care. There are other, mostly grim, points of consensus.

1. The shelter population in the big cities like New York, San Francisco, Boston and Washington DC is growing. On any one night in New York, some 20,000 are housed in city, church and synagogue shelters.

2. It is too simple to claim that the residents of shelters are those who were thrown out when the hospitals were closed. Many residents are young (aged under thirty). They include many patients who have never come into the hospital system (like the man who swung from the rafters) and are unlikely to do so unless they become violent.

3. A large proportion of residents suffer from psychotic symptoms and are seriously mentally ill. A smaller but still substantial group have moderate mental symptoms like depression.

4. Living in the shelter system often brings on depression, a perfectly normal reaction to an abnormal environment.

5. A majority of shelter residents are black or Hispanic. Middle-class neurotics rarely find their way into these particular lower depths.

6. The length of time people spend in the shelter system is increasing. Once in, it is harder to get out. This is due both to

the lack of effective help available and also to the continuing housing crisis in big cities.

7. Lastly, and perhaps the supreme irony, those who actually enter the shelters are not the most helpless or the most scared.

State Care

When I met Steven Katz, the Commissioner of Mental Health for New York State, he exuded confidence. First he attacked the Torrey–Wolfe report. It was far too pessimistic. 'Torrey got a lot of stick for it,' he added. Katz's view is likely to be coloured by the fact that New York, which likes to regard itself as a pioneer of mental-health services, was only rated twenty-sixth best state. Katz laughed at that and said that, of course, Torrey hadn't visited facilities himself. Katz shrugged and said that the states which came bottom, the Alaskans and Hawaiians, 'would be really sore'. He was above such pettiness, he implied. Later, Fuller Torrey countered that he had visited facilities and was a little surprised that I had taken away the impression he and Katz were friends. 'I've never met the man,' he said, adding that he did not expect the report to please bureaucrats.

Katz had been the psychiatrist in charge of Bellevue Hospital and 'initially I turned this job down. It's not something I wanted to do.' But friends and colleagues, he smiled, pressed him. He is a small, suave man who commutes between Albany, the state capital, and the city. 'This is the hardest job I've ever done.' The politics are complicated. The city of New York has the most pressing, and visible, mental-health problems in the state and, traditionally, the state and city administrations quarrel. Katz did not dwell on these problems but many of his critics said he was a nice man who lacked the political muscle to deal with the byzantine rivalries facing him. I found it curious that he did not even have his own New York office so that we had to meet in a city planner's room. Experts on office politics would see that as a definite failure to make an impact on the bureaucracy. If you can't commandeer an office of your own, what hope do your policies have? Katz insisted it would be wrong to be only critical, wrong to focus only on bad shelters and bad hospitals. Creative programmes also existed. He had a vision or, at least, a five-year-plan.

'The state has taken over acute care and what we've tried to do is to provide comprehensive care.' New York State now had 5000 people in various kinds of community accommodation, including a programme called Residential Accommodation (RACCA) some of which is run by a private organization called Catholic Charities. It was 'for adults who don't need a highly structured hospital environment'. Critics allege that RACCAs are simply a way of dumping patients. Katz also enthused about foster care in the more rural parts of New York. A mother whose children have left home lodges, and looks after, up to four pati·nts. 'Real progress is being made in psychosocial rehabilitation. People are now excited about the ability to get people back to work.' The state was encouraging a new 'profession' of case manager: 'They're assigned to a patient and it's their job to be that person's manager, to be a friend and companion.' A good case manager will know the way round the system.·

Even the much-maligned shelters had their niche in Katz's vision: 'We're setting up mobile psychiatric teams in shelters, special clinics for the mentally ill.' He did not accept that all the homeless were mentally ill which would let 'everyone else off the hook. It's counterproductive to make it just a mental-health problem.' Katz painted a rosy picture of a state that 'has developed and is initiating a restructuring process to develop a continuum of care.' There would be a niche for you on the continuum however ill you were.

The hospitals are the one facility over which Steven Katz has complete control. They are run by the state alone without interference from the city govenment. Eighty per cent of its budget is spent on them. Nevertheless, the treatment they provide is poor. The Torrey– Wolfe report said that they were often decaying and apathetic. Hospitals may have radically fewer patients but they have not become radically better.

In New York, Creedmoor is the main hospital for the borough of Queens, and Manhattan State for the borough of Manhattan. They are both typical city hospitals. Manhattan State Psychiatric

Centre is on Ward's Island in the East River. The next island holds a maximum security prison. The taxi driver had never heard of the hospital. To reach it, you drive off the Triborough bridge into an urban wilderness. Parts of the hospital are surrounded by wire netting and barbed wire. Paul Lee who spent some months there, after being evicted from his apartment and attempting suicide, said it was the worst hospital he had known, far worse than the hospitals in North Carolina. Violent and non-violent patients were crowded on the same ward. Mike D'Amato, another ex-patient, is one of a group who are suing the hospital. He received little useful care there, he feels, though he was grateful for the medication. He agitated for patients' rights and found some staff harrassed him. Some of his possessions were stolen and, eventually, he was beaten up in the hospital grounds by someone he couldn't identify because it was too dark. When he got to his feet and rang the ward for help, he was told no one could assist him. He had, though he was injured, to make it back on his own.

No one complained of violence in Creedmoor but many people complained of apathy. The main block looks exactly like that of Manhattan State, a huge, yellow-grey building with barred windows. It could be a prison. Creedmoor's grounds cover over 300 acres and, when the hospital housed 7000 patients, it must have had the atmosphere of a small town. Its streets are named from 1st Street and Avenue A. As we drove through the grounds, Rita Amatulli, the hospital director of public relations, explained that the hospital used to do its own laundry and catering, and there was even a section that repaired vehicles. Little of that small-town feeling remains with 1300 patients. Empty, half-gutted buildings that were once wards dominate the grounds. Some are now used by other social work agencies but the campus looks eerie and deserted. Rita was not sure if we could drive from one building to another without leaving the hospital grounds because she did not know which agency now 'owned' a large iron gate. The gate divides the campus in two. To her irritation, it turned out to be closed.

Advocates of 'deinstitutionalization' hoped it would improve the quality of care for those who had to remain in hospital.

Creedmoor is no advertisement for that optimism. The wards are still overcrowded and doctors themselves complain of apathy. Building 38, the male ward, is meant to sleep thirty-five patients; it has been sleeping up to forty-five. Conditions in the main dormitory are not as cramped as in Japan but patients have no privacy. A few decorate the wall above their bed with posters or stick drawings on their lockers. Most did not bother to strive for a personal touch. In theory, each patient should have an individual bedroom but many bedrooms have been converted into offices for nurses, social workers, recreation officers and other 'caring' professionals. Patients can survive without bedrooms but professionals can't manage without offices.

By ten o'clock, patients are meant to be active, though 'active' can mean playing bingo or watching morning television. A thin, black patient with a gold bracelet was either so bored or so exhibitionistic that he asked me to watch him dance in the middle of the room. Groups discuss the news in the papers in a desultory way but the main focus is on ADL – 'activities of daily living'. New York state now emphasizes the need to teach patients how to cook, clean and dress themselves so they can cope when they leave for an apartment of their own. There happen to be very few low-cost apartments available, but patients must be prepared for the improbable good fortune of being found one. Life, the ward staff explained, had improved dramatically. ADL offered patients a chance for independence.

The care at Creedmoor dismays Subjud Mukerjhee, an Indian psychiatrist who was educated at Cambridge. He runs the special treatment unit which has an impressive list of backers including the New York Psychiatric Institute and Columbia University. Placing a high-level research unit in a state hospital is rare. After four years, Mukerjhee has been saddened by much of what he has seen. Creedmoor is not a particularly poor hospital but patients tend to get the same treatment month in, month out. For most patients, there is no thought-out therapeutic strategy, no attempt to change treatment if it is not producing results. 'You get a great deal of apathy and ennui so that there is a crisis-management attitude and everything is all right as long as the patient doesn't throw chairs.' Patients suffer as a result of such 'negativism'. The aim is less to cure than to create tranquillity. Mukerjhee's views are very traditional and he blames the situation on the fact that many wards are not really controlled by physicians. Doctors visit from time to time but the day-to-day running of the ward is in the hands of nurses who can't be expected to have the vision of doctors. But the inexperienced, unmotivated doctors who work in state hospitals abdicate all too often. Yet a little variety, a little energy, can achieve much. Dr Mukerjhee has been studying patients who resist treatment. Often, they have resisted exactly the same treatment for years 'because not much new has been tried'. As part of his lateral thinking, Mukerjhee has been trying ECT on manic patients. Something close to 60 per cent respond well, an exciting result. He intends to study the differences between those who respond and those who continue to resist. State hospitals are appropriate for such fundamental research, Mukerjhee believes, since the most difficult patients eventually end there. But there has been little such research which has contributed to the overall lack of research into schizophrenia. Mukerjhee thinks his research unit ought to set a good example and inspire morale. He drives himself, and his staff, hard. One pinned-up memo told them they had to be rigorous in not taking extra days off.

If there is apathy in the hospital, there is confusion in the grounds outside. Creedmoor has tried to make good use of its newly empty spaces. Two wards were turned into a city shelter. Many of its inmates were ex-patients who must have been somewhat confused to be still in the hospital grounds but with no doctors and no nurses. However, the neighbourhood protested against the shelter and, as a compromise, the wards have now been converted into yet another novel facility, a RACCA which houses up to 168 people. Some are just homeless but many are mentally ill; some have been discharged from hospital. Most bedrooms are shared by two people and, though they are small, they are decent. Though conditions are better than in the city shelters, there are few of the facilities residents need. Fuller Torrey is startled by the irony. Creedmoor has discharged patients into the magic community. But the 'community' is actually just another part of the hospital grounds. And the real community is hostile.

After its protests helped kill the original shelter, local residents insisted on the RACCA having security staff in uniform. To appease neighbours, the RACCA has promised that residents would be tightly controlled. Everyone has to sign in and out of the building; as in the city shelters, a tannoy booms out if a resident is wanted. Though it is in the hospital grounds, there is one nurse for 168 people, no full-time doctor and no therapeutic care. A third of residents attend day-care centres. To Fuller Torrey, the RACCA is not liberal progress but neglect.

Sam Joseph, another Indian, who is director of the RACCA, took the job without realizing how few facilities could be offered to the mentally ill. He claimed – and the residents I talked to agreed – that the RACCA is not too bad for those who can arrange activities for themselves outside during the day. But at least a third of residents just stay in the building doing nothing much. 'I'm worried by that,' Joseph said.

Communication between the agencies on the Creedmoor campus is not good. Joseph thinks there might be activities his residents could join in. Unfortunately, he has been unable to find out anything precise even though he has been in his job for a year. The hospital is run by the state: the charity is private. That adds to the communication problem, he told me.

Joseph had never met Rita Amatulli, the hospital's director of PR. She had never been in the RACCA and seemed to think it was improper for her to set foot inside. She escorted me to the door and said she would pick me up, as if from a foreign country, an hour later. Joseph, for his part, knew nothing about the lavish facilities being created on the other side of the RACCA, literally next door to him. There, Creedmoor Hospital has just opened a modern ward for thirty patients who will get concentrated preparation for outside life, a veritable feast of activities of daily living. The ward (which is as large as the RACCA) has immaculate kitchens, dining-areas, workshops and sitting-rooms where patients can master all the skills of Cordon Bleu independent living. Only, with no housing to go to, most patients may well graduate to the RACCA next door. Or worse. Neither there, nor

in the shelters, nor on the streets, will they have much use for creative decoration, city gardening, vegetarian cookery or the other fancy skills they have been taught. But Creedmoor advertises this programme for a select few as proof of its commitment to community care.

This failure to provide a proper long-term programme for most patients probably does more damage than anything else. And the sagas of Creedmoor highlight an unexpected problem. 'Patients', 'clients', 'outcasts', 'inadequates' seem to turn up in a number of different institutions and to move between them. The institutions have little contact with each other. It is not just a bureaucratic muddle; there is also a genuine intellectual puzzle. In Britain, for example, critics of community care say that, if you close hospitals, more people will end up in jails for minor offences. Desperate, they will do whatever they have to to get themselves institutionalized. It is not easy to know if this is true, since it means tracking individuals a little like one tracks migrating birds. What little research has been done suggests, however, that the movements of people in and out of different institutions are more complex than easy theories suggest.

Diane Cournos of the New York Psychiatric Institute has studied the jail, hospital, shelter and nursing-home populations. She told me that she has found that roughly one per cent of the population of New York is in some form of institution. She was very excited when she found that, over ten years, the prison population had risen by 64 per cent while the hospital population had fallen by 65 per cent. She held the neat theory: ex-patients had not managed outside and gone into jail. Infuriatingly, the data showed this equation was wrong. The extra bodies in prison were not ex-psychiatric patients; they did not seem to be people who ought to be in hospital but failed to get in. There always seemed to be one per cent of people who could not cope except in an institution but the individuals who made up that one per cent seemed to change. Cournos confessed that she was mystified to know just what her findings meant but the strange dance of the numbers – some institutions attract more clients, others go into decline – highlights how hard it is to understand shifts in their populations. Cournos's findings are a reminder of our lack of knowledge. That, in turn, makes it hard to plan better facilities.

Families

One obvious effect of emptying hospitals is that it puts pressure on many families. Often, for ex-patients, the only place to go to is back home. Though some families refused to have their relatives back, many others welcomed them. They then found there were hardly any services in the community to help them. It has taken about fifteen years for American relatives of the mentally ill to 'mobilize' but, now, they are beginning to do so in a flamboyant, aggressive way that would be unimaginable in Britain, Japan or Third World countries.

Davis Pollack retired as a doctor a few years ago but he is still full of energy. His wife is a psychiatric social worker. I went to see them at Brighton Beach where New York's subway system ends. Brighton Beach is a retirement suburb. The street I walked down could have been in nineteenth-century Europe. Old women sat on chairs on the pavement while kids milled around. They chattered in Russian, Polish and Yiddish – anything but English. At the end of the street there is an apartment block for elderly Jewish people. Davis and his wife had come to visit her mother. A few minutes after I was announced he strode out of the lift. He could not invite me up, he apologized. The mother was very suspicious. A strange man might be the monster who would drag her away to the old people's home. Would I mind waiting while they made arrangements?

Two minutes later, Mrs Pollack, a lady with an impressive hair-do, appeared in the lobby. There was no problem, no need to make arrangements. They had found a room where we could have our meeting. She took me up to the games-room with tables set for cards, chess and draughts. Flanked by their files, the Pollacks began to explain the work of NAMI, the National Alliance of the Mentally Ill, an alliance they joined because of the illness their children suffered from.

Five years ago, Davis began, a number of families with

mentally ill relatives met in Madison, Wisconsin. 'We met to share experiences and to share pain.' There was no special purpose behind the meeting but it was a heady occasion. Many of those present were relieved finally to meet others who knew what it was like trying to live with, and love, someone who was schizophrenic. The strain was made worse by the stigma. 'There is still a lot of stigma,' Davis said ruefully. America was less enlightened than it liked to think. Mrs Pollack added that her mother 'never mentions that two of her grandchildren are ill. One she says is diabetic and the other she doesn't mention at all.' Her mother was typical. The Pollacks mentioned celebrities with mentally ill 'loved ones' who did not want to 'come out' yet. Privately, they supported NAMI. Publicly, they kept quiet in case it damaged their careers. In Madison, in 1979, no one felt embarrassed or guilty. They had all felt isolated and all felt guilty because various shades of Freudian psychiatrists blamed families.

Very crudely, Freud claimed that childhood experiences determined adult life. If your childhood experiences were bad, you became disturbed. From the 1950s on, theories offered variations on this theme of parental guilt. There was that unflattering figure, the schizogenic mother whose maternal (or infernal) behaviour drove her children mad. The schizogenic mother was followed by the schizogenic family. Two books, *The Families of Schizophrenics*, and *Death of the Family* became key texts for anti-psychiatry. David Cooper and his better-known colleague R. D. Laing claimed that confused family dynamics led to schizophrenia. Parents gave their children mixed messages such as, 'I love you', but also, 'You are a disgusting slut.' Schizophrenia wasn't a real illness but an attempt to cope with such confusing, contradictory signals. Laing's books on schizophrenia became bestsellers. He was always careful to say that parents were not wicked but the products of their own problematic childhoods. But few families of schizophrenics noted the qualifications in the scientific small print. Laing was a dramatic writer who told a dramatic story. The mad were not really mad at all. They were victims of sick and evil families.

Davis added that families often felt angry and paralyzed by such theories. The title of a recent book sums up their fury well.

Maryellen Walsh, a member of NAMI, has a schizophrenic brother and son. She called her book, *Parents are Psychovermin: Why are You being Blamed?* It might be unwise for Laing and others who blamed family dynamics to attend a NAMI meeting; they might not get out unscathed.

'There's also the question of how the media portray schizophrenics,' Davis added. He was for a while chairman of NAMI's public-awareness task-force. He campaigned not just for more coverage but for a change in the image of the mentally ill. He complained aggressively about articles, radio and television programmes which poke fun at madness. The lunatic has long been a figure of fun and, despite America's psychological awareness, the media teem with jokes about being mad. If blacks, women, Jews and gays can fight stereotypes, why not 'lunatics'? The oldest out-group of all deserves sensitive handling too.

Davis is not frightened of seeming humourless. Ignorant and easy jokes contribute to stigma. No one guffaws about physically disabled people now. NAMI often writes of the mentally ill as being another category of the 'disabled'. Such smoothed-down use of language makes me slightly uneasy. 'Disabled' sounds more wholesome than disturbed. But the Pollacks said that NAMI's success had enabled families to speak out, to vent their pain and to argue to both experts and legislators how vital the family was. 'Often they are the basic care-givers because it is, after all, their loved one,' Mrs Pollack said. Some 800,000 American mentally ill live with their families. Thirty-five per cent of the member families of NAMI have made specific arrangements for someone to look after their 'disabled' family member when they are no longer able to do so. Proof of love, Davis pointed out, that R. D. Laing should note.

Science has also contributed to the self-confidence of families. New studies claim to show conclusively that schizophrenia is an organic disease. Some schizophrenics suffer from an excess of dopamine, a neurotransmitter in the brain which oils the passing of messages from one brain cell to the next. If neurotransmitters don't work properly, cells transmit information too fast, too slowly or in a scramble. Fuller Torrey, adamant in his view that schizophrenia is a brain disease, emphasizes the evidence of the ventricles of the brain. The brain looks like a cauliflower. Imagine turning a cauliflower upside down. The ventricles would be the large area of the stem. In 'normal' people, these ventricles are quite large. The ventricles of some, but not all, schizophrenics are much smaller and look atrophied. Some psychiatrists argue that the literal lack of brain space 'causes' the illness. An extra strand of evidence comes from twin studies. These were much maligned in the wake of the scandal of Cyril Burt, the IQ psychologist who invented data but, with proper methodical safeguards and no cheating, they can give useful evidence. Now some Scandinavian studies seem to show that schizophrenia erupts at similar times in identical twins brought up in different families. Since their environments were very different, the only explanation is that the disease and its start must be genetically programmed. The impressive fact is that the disease hits twins in different settings at the same time. Nevertheless, all the findings are statistical rather than absolute and those with different ideologies have different interpretations. For Fuller Torrey and NAMI, these findings offer ultimate proof. For Professor John Talbott of the Univerity of Maryland Psychiatric Hospital, also no lover of Laing, the findings are less absolute. Talbott twinkled that he had seen too many fashions come and go to have complete faith in any one theory. The pendulum would swing back; biology would be out of fashion; families would be villains again; it was all good theoretical fun.

NAMI has no such sophisticated doubts. Its charter states that schizophrenia and other major mental illnesses are organic brain disorders. Its newsletter for August–September 1986 approves of Dr Samuel Keith of the National Institute for Mental Health who reported the latest twin research and pleaded for an end to the 'destructive blaming of the family'. Another report praised 'the search for genetic markers' which are (or would be if they were found) precise genetic combinations that make people vulnerable to specific diseases. There is a real irony here. Families want to show that it is the genes that are to blame for schizophrenia. You may transmit your genes to your children but you can hardly be held responsible for any defects in your

DNA. We can live with biological guilt more easily than personal guilt, it seems.

In its enthusiasm, NAMI is forgetting that some of the evidence is not so solid. Only 15 per cent of schizophrenics have gaps in the ventricles. Do these gaps cause the illness or were they the result of it? How much do such gaps matter anyway? One of the most striking neurological findings of the last ten years concerns a study of students whose brains were filled with fluid where there should have been cells and cortex. They had bloated heads because they had water on the brain. Many had less than half the brain mass of the average human. Some had as little as 10 per cent. Most of them, however, functioned normally and some had got to university. A few even obtained first-class degrees. This may mean we can succeed academically with only half a brain or it may mean we should be cautious in attributing major defects to holes, gaps or leaks in the grey matter. Still, the new interpretation of schizophrenia as a brain disease cheers families, making them feel more confident in fighting for the rights of their loved ones.

NAMI is now campaigning for a variety of legal and fiscal rights for better funding for existing services, for more money for research, for more community services. NAMI helped get the Protection and Advocacy for the Mentally Ill Act through Congress. This called for spending of 11 million dollars. In the face of Reaganomics, NAMI has had to learn to lobby. Its newsletter carries a model letter to send to politicians, asking: 'How did we get into this mess having to drastically reduce or eliminate necessary programs or services? It is appropriate to write to your members of Congress expressing your anger and disgust.'

NAMI is succeeding. Davis said, 'We are having affiliates join at the rate of one group every thirty-six hours.' He believes families need to feel less helpless which is perhaps why an approach pioneered by Robert McFarland of the New York Psychiatric Institute is proving popular.

McFarland is a psychiatrist who was interested in family therapy but he found, like many family therapists, that people did not keep appointments. There was great resistance.

McFarland was disheartened by the drop-out rate and wondered if it might be connected with the power of the therapists who were in complete control. Families and patients knew very little about mental illness, its causes, its likely development or, even, what triggers relapses. Julian Leff, a psychiatrist from the Maudsley, argued in the late 1970s that high emotions triggered relapses. A spot of repression might be healthier than endlessly expressing feelings because many sufferers found emotions too hard, and too hot, to handle.

'Basically, we give the family information. They are given detailed information about the disease, about its likely prognosis. It is an education kit for surviving schizophrenia. Families often feel relieved that their ignorance is going.' McFarland makes large claims for this approach. It has reduced the drop-out rate to 10 per cent, a vast improvement, and the rate of relapses has dropped too. McFarland argues that understanding the dynamics that trigger relapses makes them easier to avoid. Though McFarland claims the family atmosphere contributes to relapses, NAMI is not hostile to him – perhaps because he offers the families hope of redeeming themselves through self-knowledge.

The growth of NAMI is politically important. American administrations will have to take their lobbying into account. Unfortunately, there is little evidence that NAMI will have any impact on two of the root causes of America's problems – psychiatrists' obsession with private practice and the lack of housing. In *The Care of the Seriously Mentally Ill*, Torrey and Wolfe address only one of these problems – the role of psychiatrists – and draw attention to a programme in Maryland which succeeds in keeping psychiatrists in the state hospitals.

The Maryland Programme

The Maryland programme is the result of high ideals and historical accident. It is based in Baltimore, a city which houses the University of Maryland and the rather more famous Johns Hopkins University. Hopkins has been one of the powerhouses in American psychiatric and psychological research. It offered a PhD programme before most universities. In 1908, it even had a sex scandal when James Bladwin, the Professor of Psychology, was caught in a brothel and forced to resign. With competition from Johns Hopkins the University of Maryland concentrated on teaching and its medical school concentrated on training physicians for the state. 'In fact, for a while, it was illegal to raise private money,' John Talbott smiled. He is the Professor of Psychiatry and runs the programme for psychiatry graduates.

Talbott took his post after a scandal ten years ago. Maryland brought in a new Commissioner of Mental Health. 'He was young, naïve and did all the right things,' Talbott said. The new commissioner ignored the sage advice that warned his aims were impossible. One of his priorities was to keep trained psychiatrists working in the state. Otherwise, Maryland spent money educating highly skilled doctors and got nothing for its investment. Talbott smiled that they had been successful. '160 doctors have gone into the state system.' Unlike New York, where shrinks shrink from contact with the truly disturbed, in Maryland they are prepared for it. 'The students get a lot of psychiatry and patient contact from early on. We get double the national average of graduates who go into psychiatry: 20 per cent of all our graduates go into psychiatry,' Talbott added. The students spend some time in the state's large mental hospitals and, also, in the medical school's other facilities. 'I'm responsible for a department which has seventy-two beds here, 109 at the Community Mental Health Centre, twenty-two at the Research Centre, twenty at the veterans and seventy at the alcoholism facility.' Talbott believed that the fact that Maryland is a southern state helped because 'doctors are in charge more than accountants' and because doctors care more about clinical needs than management needs.

I had arrived in Baltimore by train. Unlike New York or Washington, Baltimore station seemed clean. No one seemed to be sleeping or living on the platforms or streets. Talbott said it was true. 'I'm a runner and you don't see them in Baltimore. I don't know why. You certainly see them in other cities.' He had jogged past them in Seattle, Los Angeles and Philadelphia where a homeless man lived on the corner of his street.

Talbott could not claim the absence of street people was due to his programme. 'Maybe crazy people tend to go to Washington,' he said. In their assessment of Maryland, Torrey and Wolfe ranked it seventeenth and pleaded for 'a more visible commitment to change at the level of the governor and the state legislature.' They approved of the Maryland plan because it had allowed both the university faculty and the new mental health state leaders to take risks. Eighty per cent of the psychiatrists trained by the state were still working for its public hospitals.

For all its success in retaining the loyalty of expensively trained psychiatrists, Maryland's scheme has not been imitated widely. Centralizing services is, of course, easier in a small city like Baltimore than it would be in a big one like New York. But it is the professionals who run New York's all-too-fragmented services who bitch most about how hard it is to do anything because of that fragmentation. Fuller Torrey told me: 'If the same team followed a person after they left hospital, that alone would improve services immeasurably.'

Voluntary Agencies

The voluntary agencies complain about the fragmentation and yet they are part of it. Without fragmentation they could not be as independent as they are. Voluntary agencies provide reach-out services, small shelters which are much better run than the city armouries, and stable-low-cost accommodation. As in other parts of this book, I am about to describe good services which are the exception rather than the rule. Between them, Project Reach Out, Community Access and Ellen Baxter's house on West 178th Street cater for less than 200 people. Community Access can take forty-six clients; Baxter has fifty-five tenants and Project Reach Out reckon they can deal at any time with perhaps eighty to ninety people. The work is impressive but it covers a tiny proportion of the need.

According to Diane Sonday who runs Project Reach Out, the psychiatric and social need 'out there' is far greater than anyone imagines. Sonday started out as social worker for the city and now runs her project from the basement of a block on West 88th

Street. It tries to 'reach out' to those who avoid the shelters. They run two vans which scour the streets. Whenever they see someone who looks mentally ill, they stop to offer a brown paper bag. This paper bag is called 'our engagement package', as nice a piece of jargon a social scientist could desire for fruit juice, a bar of soap and a sandwich. 'When times are good, it's a ham-and-cheese sandwich,' Sonday smiled, 'and when times are hard, it's a peanut-butter-and-jello sandwich.' Project Reach Out's workers just hand the bag over. No one is asked to talk to them in return, though 'engaging' is their main aim. But it's a slow business because New York is so riddled with fear and suspicion. Many people take the food and scorn the sympathy. Persuading clients to come to Reach Out's offices requires patience.

It took Margarita Lopez, a project worker, four months to persuade 'Mary' to come to the office. Mary is a middle-aged black woman who claimed to be Mary Magdalene, sometimes, and, at others, 'the greatest genius specialist doctor in the world'. She lived under a bridge in Central Park and, at first, would flee from Margarita. The cold, and the fact that Margarita gave her some gloves, finally persuaded her to come to the office but she refused to give workers her name. Her social security number, she said, was zero 'because I am the beginning'. Mary's secretiveness is typical. She came to Project Reach Out covered in lice, bugs, shit and urine. Some of the mentally ill have severe physical wounds from lice. Many suffer from malnutrition 'after living out of garbage cans'. For years, the Project had to take clients across town to public baths but Sonday finally raised funds to put in a shower. 'That way the client can be more comfortable and the worker can be more comfortable interviewing them.'

Mary smiled as she explained she liked washing her hair especially 'as I have brains in my hair. All geniuses have brains in their hair.' Though she was still suspicious, she came to the office every day and was talking in English. When she was found she talked a gibberish language. She had agreed to see a doctor but it would take months to work through her delusions. Until recently, Project Reach Out had no regular professional help in a city with more psycho-professionals than any other spot on earth. Eventually, Sonday cajoled two psychiatrists into giving half a day every week 'pro bono' and 'it's amazing the difference it makes'. The doctors can write prescriptions, offer quick diagnoses and, if necessary, get people into hospital fast.

Such quick, unofficial help is vital because many of the street people do not exist for the bureaucracy. They have lost all tags of identity. They have no medical cards, social-security numbers, records or proof of identity. Sonday finds it hard to prove they are entitled to services, welfare or any benefit at all.

No one admits it, but this confusion is to the advantage of the state, city and federal governments. For the past 100 years, there have been bureaucratic battles to avoid paying for the care of the mentally ill. Every arm of government tries to shuffle it off on to another one. If people are in hospital, the individual states pay. If they are in the shelters, the city pays in New York. The federal government chips in, however, with Federal Supplemental Income, Medicaid and food stamps. Residents have to pay these benefits back to the shelters. Fuller Torrey argues, 'It's to the advantage of the states to keep people out of the hospitals.' The complexities are such that Project Reach Out workers sometimes have to shuttle between five offices to obtain the food, medical help, housing and clothing their clients are entitled to. It's a hassle for the professionals; for the sick, it's an impossibility. The bureaucracy is so convoluted, Fuller Torrey lamented, only experts know who can claim what, from where, and when.

Sonday has her triumphs. Her favourite is an old Jewish tramp lady who persisted in refusing help because she knew she owned a grand mansion in the upper 80s. Sonday finally persuaded her to live in a hostel till the tenants left the mansion. Sometimes, the Project persuades hospitals to see poor 'patients' and persuades 'patients' to get monthly shots of drugs like prolixin to keep them stable. But, for all its energy, the Project has to work within a system that often defeats good intentions and intense effort.

Margarita likes Mary and has done much to transform her. Mary is clean, speaks English and will see the doctor as long as he doesn't insist he is the medical expert. 'In a few months,'

Margarita believes, 'I will have begun to work my way through her delusions.'

Margarita believes that Mary will eventually be able to live with other people 'in the city, like you, like me, like anyone'. Mary might be fit but there will be no housing to fit her. New York has less and less low-cost housing. Old tenement blocks either lie abandoned, as in the Bronx round the armoury, or have been gentrified into residences fit for yuppies. Mary may never find decent accommodation. She may improve but her progress is likely to be limited by that. She will be condemned to live in some form of shelter.

Community Access's office is at the corner of Avenue A and East 6th Street. Two blocks away, Bob Couteau sighed, the city becomes really unsafe. Many people sleep in Tomkins Park opposite the office – usually in the porch of the lavatories. In December 1986, however, someone built a shelter out of beer crates, shopping trolleys and plastic sheeting. A banner on one of the slum blocks overlooking the park proclaimed a rent strike. The area is poor but property developers are moving in to gentrify. Community Access has smart offices but, at night, they have to secure them with metal shutters. The agency may cater for only a few but it is not poor. Its computers work; its newsletter is handsomely printed. The most recent issue carries articulately bitter pieces on how to survive the mental health-system. Max Harding, for example, went into hospital after an acute episode of schizophrenia. He received medication but little else and, when he left, he was sent to a therapist who fell asleep on him!

Steve Coe, the executive director of Community Access, came from the New School of Social Research as a housing specialist. He found that planning and administration expertise wasn't very relevant since the project really needed someone who could hang doors and fix the plumbing in its apartments. After a crash course in being a handyman, he became able to concentrate on policy. Now he also sits on the board of the Coalition for the Homeless, a pressure group that fights for better housing not just for the mentally ill. 'Our goal is to get people out of the mental-health system,' Coe said. The best way was to offer them

alternative accommodation and a range of services including
counselling and help with getting all their benefits.

Community Access turn down nineteen out of every twenty
people referred to them. They choose to concentrate on the most
motivated who are the most likely to change. Bob Couteau, the
director of counselling, concedes that those they don't take 'will
get lost in the mental-health system, some will end in the shelters,
some will end on the streets, some will die. It's a grim picture.'

The project succeeds partly because it is demanding. It insists
that residents put in thirty hours' work a week. Work can be
going to classes, participating in groups, or, like Paul Lee, giving
lectures on Browning's poems. Max Harding, who had a problem
with work, was found a clerical job; Geraldine Evarts goes to a
regular group outside Community Access. Residents cannot just
sleep, idle or daydream in comfort. After three or four years they
are expected to leave. Max Harding has already done so, lives in
his own apartment and works as a clerk for a religious organization. Another ex-client bought a card shop close to Community
Access.

The residents live in self-contained, decent, cheap apartments.
Two to four people usually share. Staff are on call for emergencies. And, added Couteau, 'we do visit residents two or three
times a week.' He has his own key to their apartments which
sounds intrusive. 'Residents have to accept some authority. They
have to accept that we will take them down to get their
medication when it runs out because if we don't do that, they
decompensate.' ('Decompensate' is the latest jargon for breakdown.) The office stays open late every evening and on weekends
so that clients have somewhere friendly to drop in.

The clients of Community Access certainly appreciate what
the agency offers. Geraldine is thirty-seven and has been in and
out of hospital six times with depression. As if she was presenting
a CV, she also listed three suicide attempts and two courses of
ECT. Despite her depression, she had worked as a bank clerk.
Her ability to keep a job had worked against her because the first
five times she was discharged from hospital she was given no
after-care programme at all. 'I was told to get back to the job
market and, within three to four weeks, I was breaking down

again.' Geraldine is articulate and charming, if a bit nervous, and so I was slightly surprised by how obsessive and how childish she can be. Teddy bears surround her bed. Gaudy red knickers are draped over her chairs and tables. She can't bear anything to be moved from its place. Geraldine blames her mother. 'I hate her for not giving me all the things a mother should, for making me feel small.' Her mother, she claims, told her she would never get married. Relationships with men were traumatic. Her fiancé was a drunk who set fire to their flat three times, 'so I'm petrified of stoves'. As a result, she hates cooking. Geraldine smiled that her choice of men hadn't been brilliant. 'I want to meet a normal man, a man who hasn't been hospitalized.'

Community Access has very practical benefits for her. She likes the privacy of being in a flat of her own and says she feels she is beginning to change, 'to see myself in a different way because I used to think that no one was as bad as me, not even someone in jail.' It is clear that living in a decent flat won't by itself 'cure' her or give her the emotional self-confidence she needs, but it is a base from where she may begin to find healing. Without such a base, her chances would be nil.

Paul Lee is sixty-four and has been schizophrenic since his thirties. He belonged to the first generation of patients to take thorazine. The drug gave him side-effects – mainly drowsiness and slurring of speech – 'But I managed to fight the drowsiness and have a job as a clerk. I often had to fight it but I did.' He built up a life for himself and settled into an apartment in Manhattan. He had over 5000 books and records he was proud of. Then he was taken off his medication by his doctor. The hallucinations came back. He found it harder and harder to leave his apartment. He fell behind with his rent. Within a few months, he was evicted, lost his furniture and was back in hospital.

Paul is appreciative of Community Access. It provided him with a home after the traumas of his eviction and of his stay in Manhattan Psychiatric. He said that the apartment provided was very pleasant though not a patch on the 'luxury apartment' he had in Manhattan Plaza. The only possession he had managed to get back from his landlords was his rocking chair. They had sold everything else to pay off his rent. Paul appreciates the accommodation and the regular contact. If the doctor who had taken him off medication had kept in touch, he might have seen Paul was deteriorating and he might have done something about it before Paul reached the abyss of panic where he couldn't step out of his door: 'I was sure the President and Mayor Koch were after me.' Paul knew he was lucky to find Community Access. It was even helping him sue his old landlords. But he said he had to add that he resented the lot fate had given him – thirty years of struggle against the demons in his head. He said that slowly, with dignity but with bitterness.

Many of Community Access's clients are less articulate. Clearly, the agency succeeds partly because it chooses highly motivated clients and partly because it is intrusive. Couteau feels free to pop in, free to chivvy. It is a little paternalistic and it can look like bullying but Couteau may be right in arguing he is being realistic.

Ellen Baxter runs a hostel on West 178th Street where there is less intrusion and more confusion. Or so I was told. I was also told it was because she relied too much on the residents.

When I first arrived, I was not allowed in. A man in a check shirt said I'd have to wait for Ellen so I stood on the porch, trying to guess if any of the women walking towards the house were her.

'Didn't they let you in?' Ellen Baxter is a fragile-looking blonde. She explained that the residents were nervous because one of them had died during the night. Of natural causes, she reassured quickly. Once inside, I found none of the chaos I was primed to expect. Everything was impeccably tidy and clean. Pine tables gleamed in the dining-room; the corridors were spotless; the bathrooms respectable. Baxter had spent a year at Geel, a town in Belgium, where the mentally ill have lived in family houses for generations. It was important for her to set up a house where they could take responsibility, man the doors, take the phone calls, help organize their lives. Too often, they were assumed to be helpless.

Ellen asked John, the thin man in the check shirt, to join us.

She did not tell him but asked as one would ask an equal. He had, I felt, a perfect right to refuse. She emphasized they were not 'patients' or 'clients' but tenants who had leases and legal rights. She held no keys to their rooms.

'This woman saved my life,' John declared.

'Aw, come on,' she grinned.

'I mean it,' he insisted. Before going to live in the house, John had been an alcoholic in ever greater trouble. Now he had a place to live and the incentive to keep off the bottle. She asked him if we could see his room. It was small, filled with heavy pieces of furniture and photographs. It had exactly the personal touches people can't create in shelters or RACCAs.

Baxter had spent years researching the homeless. Her reports, she smiled wryly, were added to 'five cabinets of evidence on homelessness and the need for alternative housing. Despite all that, 80 per cent of the budget goes to support large institutions.' Tired of collecting more and more dismal statistics, she set out to find a building to convert into the low-rent housing that was needed. She hoped that co-operating with the city – the house was owned by the city – would help cut red tape. But it took three years to get grants and permissions. The delays made her angry, especially when she began to suspect that the city was worried by her ambition of training tenants to manage the building themselves. 'We do have cleaners in but people see it as their home so they keep it clean. We also think we are showing that you don't have to segregate the mentally ill.'

Keeping the helpless helpless seems an unspoken objective. Steve Mollins, at the Franklin Armoury, found the shelter staff and the Human Resources Agency furious when he tried to teach residents to know and stand up for their rights. Assertiveness training is not for derelicts.

Like Coe, Baxter had trouble with tenants who took drugs but while he could throw them out of the programme, she had to take them to court to evict them. Baxter argues angrily that her house is not only more humane but cheaper than the shelters. Hospitals cost even more but state and city continue to make it hard to set up projects such as hers. Baxter is now trying to set up a second house and she faces a familiar snarl of difficulties, though this time she has tried working with private money so as to free herself from the city administration.

Small-scale community projects like Project Reach Out, Community Access and Baxter's house are impressive but the problem is how to replicate them to cover not just all of New York but all of America. Diane Sonday of Project Reach Out noted: 'If only the Human Resources Agency, the welfare departments, the housing departments talked to each other, it would make a big difference.'

I have been very critical of mental-health programmes in America but I would not wish to argue that liberal community care is a bad mental-health policy. However, it needs 'affirmative action' to make it a realistic policy. Good intentions, even decent funding, are not enough.

In their survey, Wolfe and Torrey argue for

1. A concerted effort to persuade psychiatrists to work in state hospitals.

2. A far better co-ordinated follow-up service for patients when they do leave hospital so that they do not get 'lost' in the community. They praise Dane County, Wisconsin, where there is a well-organized community service which includes 'assertive' work. Social workers seek out people who need treatment.

3. Local control over how the mental-health budget is spent so that communities are genuinely involved.

4. A more realistic attitude to how well patients can function. Fuller Torrey wants to see the laws changed back to allow psychiatrists to treat patients against their will without bringing them into hospital.

In many ways I agree with their analysis, but I would argue that imposing new legal handicaps on patients would be reactionary and wrong. Curiously, Fuller Torrey himself, in praising Dane County, highlights how well assertive social work does. If those who need it are offered help firmly, they don't often refuse it. Rikki, Juan Gonzales, Walter Reed didn't reject help but were themselves rejected by agencies. In the final chapter, I shall try to draw together more evidence on the value of assertive social work.

Many kinds of sheltered housing are also needed. Some ex-patients need totally independent, cheap apartments; others need supervised hostels; others something in between. To effect this requires a housing policy in favour of low-income housing. It will mean the city cutting back on licences to develop smart condominiums. Will New York have the political will to cut the profit of a few developers? Further, though it is a society with psychology on the brain, America badly needs some psychological education. A campaign has to make it clear to Americans the truth of what their hero, Freud, said long ago. Between the well and the sick, there is no great divide. There is far less of a gap than they imagine between the neurotic traumas it is OK and cool to suffer and the real mental illness they ignore.

It isn't just a question of summoning political will and fighting stigma. Some bureaucratic imagination is needed to make services more coherent so that people no longer 'disappear' in the cracks between different agencies. Phil Brown (1985) argued that it was precisely this lack of a coherent national policy that turned a promising liberal policy into a fiasco. The American mental-health system is more fragmented, more complex and richer than any other. It needs a national initiative, rather like Kennedy's, to fight that fragmentation. If that doesn't happen, a patient's lot will continue to be a lottery. Some will thrive like Walter at Community Access; others who are not that different will die. It is a scandal because America has the money, the power and the knowledge to make the necessary changes.

Paradoxically, America funds research on community care in Israel, a country which can summon up unity and where according to David Davidson, who trained at Johns Hopkins, 'you can make things happen quickly.' Ellen Baxter would approve of that and of much else, I suspect, in Israeli psychiatry even if the country has had to learn how to organize community care properly in order to survive in times of war.

5

Israel: Psychiatry at war

This book has so far concentrated on large countries. Israel, the Scandinavian countries and others like Holland have small, highly educated populations; Western medicine and psychotherapy are well established. For all their cultural differences, they have developed fairly similar patterns of community care. Israel, however has to provide community care in the midst of constant stress. Holland and the Scandinavian countries are not surrounded by hostile nations; since 1945, they have been at peace. Their worst military crises have been the snooping of Soviet submarines in Sweden and the guerrilla actions carried out by the South Moluccans in Holland between 1975 and 1978.

I learned how difficult it is for psychiatrists to operate under such circumstances when I made a film that traced the subsequent lives of those people held hostage during the Dutch train hijackings. The first train hijack lasted thirteen days; the second one seventeen days. The hostages lived through terror, trauma and uncertainty. Three people were killed in the first hijack and two hostages and two hijackers in the second.

Instead of being grateful as expected, many hostages complained they had been treated appallingly by psychiatrists and psychologists after they were 'rescued'. They were made to lie down on stretchers and rushed to hospital against their will. They were not reunited with their families at once but were made to 'debrief' with psychiatrists who told them they were bound to be unhinged by what they had experienced. Before he met any of the hostages, Professor J. Bastiaans of Leyden University explained on radio that they would suffer from the KZ syndrome which he had identified in victims of the concentration camps. In a grand denunciation of the human condition, Bastiaans said there were few stable individuals in the world. You had to expect thirteen days of torture to lead to years of depression, delusions and dementia. People had to be kind to the ex-hostages; if they criticized the government's handling of the whole train crisis, that just showed how disturbed they were.

Not surprisingly, the ex-hostages were furious. They became even more furious when many of them were visited by social workers demanding to know what was wrong with them and offering unsolicited help. Hans Prinz, a biologist who was one of the angriest of the hostages, said they felt as if they had been hijacked all over again. The government line that they were too disturbed to criticize the handling of the hijack denied them their human rights. Experts did learn from the Dutch experience. After the Bradford football-stadium fire of 1986, social workers offered assistance more sensitively.

Israelis often feel as if they live in perpetual crisis. The feeling is not unreasonable. In the Middle East, Arabs outnumber Jews by thirty to one. In 1967, Nasser threatened to shove Israel and all its Jews back into the Mediterranean, a threat that revived memories of Hitler and the Holocaust. Kalman Benyamini of the Hebrew University in Jerusalem has found that Israelis are deeply conflicted about Arabs. His surveys show they want to be accepted by Arabs yet they also fear them and feel superior to them.

Israel has fought four wars for its survival – in 1948, 1956, 1967 and 1973. In 1982 it invaded Lebanon, an operation which divided the country and has been described as Israel's Vietnam. some 9,000 soldiers have been killed in the wars; 50,000 injured. The psychological damage such deaths cause in a small country is vast. In 1973, the Israeli Cabinet was frantic that the relatively heavy casualties in the first days of fighting would wreck morale.

Stress is aggravated by the presence of many Arabs who live inside Israel and by the occupation of the West Bank. There, Jews find themselves in the unaccustomed position of holding power over others. To put it glibly, the persecuted have become the persecuting, a reversal that makes many Israelis uneasy. To complicate these conflicts, many survivors of the Holocaust live in Israel and while not all of them conform to Bastiaans's theory, many are still haunted. They suffer unpredictable nightmares, fears and inescapable anxiety.

Israel, also, is committed to accepting all Jews wherever they might come from. During 2000 years of exile, Jews spread from the Yemen to York. Communities sprang up in remote areas like Cochin in South India. These communities fought to remain Jewish but often absorbed much of their local culture. A joke says that, outside Israel, a Jew is first a Jew; inside Israel, you are first a German or a Russian or a Briton. Israel has its own very Anglo cricket team while its first Cabinet held some of their meetings in Russian. Much research (Rack, 1982) points to the stresses of immigration. In Israel, arrogance aggravated these stresses. The first 'settlers' were mainly European Jews and they looked down on 'black' and North African Jews who, on arrival, were treated with contempt and shunted into ghetto towns, like Kiryat Shemona on the Lebanese border. Recent arrivals, like the Falashas from Ethiopia, repeat this pattern. Discrimination by Jew against Jew has led to much bitterness and conflict. It has only added to the country's psychiatric needs.

Israel has some advantages, however. Early this century, Freud warned that psychiatry was in danger of becoming the Jewish profession. No one knows for sure how many Jewish psychiatrists and psychologists work in America and Britain but, from Freud on, Jews have been drawn to the profession. Many great theorists – Freud, Adler, Reich, Adorno, Ferenczi, Anna Freud – were Jewish even if they were not religious.

Some historians argue that Jews homed in on psychiatry because they had to cope with so many conficts between 1850 and 1900. In 1850, most Jews lived in isolated rural communities of which Annatevka, the village in *Fiddler on the Roof* is a schmaltzy version. In Annatevka, the Jews were farmers, milkmen and butchers but none of them had a degree in social or medical science. In his book *Souls on Fire* (1985), Elie Wiesel describes the rabbis who ministered to these communities. They lived simple lives, steeped in the Talmud, the Kabbala and Messianic dreams. The modern was truly alien.

Freud was born in 1856 into a world none too different. Pogroms were a constant threat. Freud told a story of how his father let an anti-semite knock his hat off his head. Freud's father did not protest: Jews had to put up with such humiliations and were grateful not to be hit, maimed or killed. It didn't matter if your hat got wet! Throughout the nineteenth century, Jews were in a curious position. In Eastern Europe persecution continued as it had done for centuries. The Tsar, or local officials, might decide it was time to slaughter some Jews. In much of Western Europe, on the other hand, Jews were being assimilated. By 1848, a Jew sat in the House of Commons. In Britain, Italy, Germany, even France, it became possible for Jews to be educated and go into the professions. This emancipation pitchforked Jews out of a narrow, exotic God-centred world into late Victorian Europe which was proud of its progress. Jews were not wholly grateful. They wanted to be accepted but they also wanted to cling to their own traditions and identity. The shock of emancipiation and the subsequent conflict bred much neurosis and it seems to have led many talented Jews into the field of psychiatry.

Israel has reaped the benefits. It has more psychiatrists and psychologists per capita than any other country. Many trained in the West because they were born in America, Britain or Europe. They were not gifted 'colonials'. Among the doctors I met, David Davidson, the regional psychiatrist at Ashkelon, was an American Jew who went to medical school at Johns Hopkins; and Moshe Avner came from Liverpool and was trained in Britain. Few doctors go to Israel for money. Any competent psychiatrist could do much better in Manhattan providing talk therapies for angst-ridden yuppies who subscribe to *Psychology Today* or *American Health*.

Israel believes in investing in psychiatry. The country needs every healthy Jew. Wounded and damaged soldiers are not neglected as happened to American soldiers after Vietnam. The Isreali Ministry of Health devotes 4.2 per cent of its budget to hospital psychiatry. A further 2 per cent is spent on preventive and community care. The Ministry of Defence, aware of the need to maintain morale, will not say how much it spends but it provides rehabilitation services and counselling for wounded soldiers and bereaved families. Israel's state of crisis also stimulates charity. Jewish law says one must give one-tenth of one's income to charity, and many American Jews donate generously. Medical buildings often have a plaque recording, for example, that the 'Strudel Institute of Therapy' was set up thanks to the generosity of Mr and Mrs Strudel. It is not just private American funds that find their way to Israel; the American National Institute of Mental Health finances projects, especially in community care, that may offer models on how to improve American services.

The stress placed in Israel on being fit and capable is, itself, stressful and, while it motivates professionals to provide good services, it leaves some mentally ill people to cope with a stigma that is even harsher than usual. Israelis are vicious about anyone suspected of malingering to avoid military service. There are severe penalties, not just for those who do malinger but also for those who cannot cope with the stress of military service.

For years, the Israeli armed forces used what was known as a 21R or discharge on mental grounds. These were recorded on a national computer so that every time the discharged person went for an interview for a job or for entry to further education his status on the computer would come up, making things difficult for him. A discharge from the army on mental grounds can also ruin a young man's sex life. In Israel, it seems that one of the first questions asked on a new date is, 'when are you going on reserve duty'? If a man has no reserve duty (one month a year), girls are put off – what is wrong with him? To save face the young man becomes evasive or lies, citing a date far ahead. The girlfriend becomes suspicious and leaves him. Not to be a soldier in Israel is not to be a man.

It has taken seven years and much pressure from voluntary groups like ENOSH (which in Hebrew stands for Mental Health Association – see page 146) to get the conditions surrounding the 21R discharge partly lifted. Even now it is still a cause of stigma. It is understandable that there should be no easy escape from military duty by faking mad. What is less just is that, in order to make sure that no one is tempted to malinger, those who are genuinely mentally ill suffer considerable stigma if they are young men. There is plenty of compassion for the elderly demented but little for the young.

Hospitals

Though it was never a colony, Israel had to develop its services out of the rump the British left behind when they gave up the Palestine Mandate in 1948. There were two large mental hospitals – Bat Yam, a grim set of buildings in Jaffa which housed up to 1500 patients, and the hospital near Haifa caled Atlit. The other institutions that have patients in Israel tend to be either general hospitals with psychiatric wards, private hospitals or hospitals run by Kupat Holim. Serious cases ended up in Bat Yam, making it hard for families outside Tel Aviv to visit relatives or maintain contact. For all the Jewish expertise in psychiatry, patients stayed for many years, as abandoned as in other parts of the world.

There has been progress. Inpatients have declined from 8,700 in 1975 to 7,700 in 1985. The state hospitals are less crowded. Bat Yam is down to 600 patients, Kfar Shaul, set up in 1950, down to 420, Shermenache near Hadera in mid-Israel houses 500. The hospital buildings are less bleak.

The close connection between war and psychiatry is made clear at Kfar Shaul psychiatric hospital. The hospital is at the top of one of the dry, baked hills of Jerusalem. It offers a magnificent view of the hills that stretch, turrets of yellow earth, towards the Dead Sea on one side and, on the other, of well-designed apartment buildings. Jerusalem these days is packed with American real-estate dealers putting up condominiums for zealots from Brooklyn. Inside the hospital gate is an old Arab village, packed with little houses and small alleyways. Flowers bloom; creepers grow up the walls. The setting is charming. Patients wander around looking rather relaxed.

Dr Barel, the director, a dark, gloomy Argentinian, welcomed me to his dark office.

'Do you know what this hospital used to be?'

'No.'

'It was Dir Yassin. Do you know what Dir Yassin was?'

Dir Yassin was an Arab village which was the site of a controversial 'massacre' during the 1948 war of independence. According to one version, the Hagganah, the Israeli freedom-

fighters under Moshe Dayan, slaughtered 248 Arabs to terrify
the Arab population and persuade them to flee. The Israelis
counter that it was a battle, not a massacre; the Arabs wouldn't
surrender. Both sides suffered heavy casualties; both sides
wanted these strategic heights.

Now, it's a hospital.

Barel offered the history of the location as a fact, neither ironic
nor picturesque. The site was taken over in 1950 because
Jerusalem needed a psychiatric hospital, especially for those who
had survived the Nazi camps. In 1980, 62 per cent of the patients
were over forty-five – many of them Holocaust survivors. 'Now,'
Barel smiled, 'we also cope with the tourists' who become over-
excited by the holy places. Barel handed me the brochure that
the hospital produces to seek American funds. It made no
mention of Dir Yassin but waxed lyrical about the landscape.

The hospital consists of a number of scattered stone buildings situated
on a hilltop in one of Jerusalem's suburbs. This pastoral landscape
contributes to the uniqueness of the place and even facilitates the
consolidation of the therapeutic community.

The brochure was franker about the clinical problems faced,
saying: 'The upkeep of these old buildings is difficult and they do
not comply to the required standards.'

Dr Avner took me round the wards at Shermenache hospital –
apart from the one closed ward. They were bright and airy.
Pictures decorated the walls. Most patients shared a bedroom
with two other people. The atmosphere did not seem oppressive.
Avner suggested this was because they tried hard to convince
patients that they could improve and get out. They aimed to
have a therapeutic programme for each individual.

Many of Israel's patients don't go to state hospitals but to
facilities which, in theory, are better. The trade-union federation,
the Histadrut, runs a huge medical-insurance scheme, Kupat
Holim. Kupat Holim owns hospitals, clinics and even health
centres for community care. Some Israeli psychiatrists working
for the state resent the fact that it can buy better facilities but, in
general, the two systems run in tandem. They certainly share

one principal aim – to keep people out of hospital or, at least, to make their stay as short as possible. In most places, that is just the therapeutic trend; in Israel, it's an economic and military necessity.

Community Care

Ashkelon is a ninety-minute drive south from Tel Aviv; 50 kilometres on is the Gaza Strip. Ashkelon is a small port. On the road in, posters urge you to buy your retirement home here. The town, however, has more of a reputation as a problem area than as a happy resort. Dr David Davidson, the local psychiatrist, explained there was a high working-class Arab and North African population. Many Falashas from Ethiopia had settled here. Europeans preferred Haifa or Jerusalem or, if they were inclined to the ascetic, the real desert to the south.

Davidson came from America in the 1970s. He had worked at Johns Hopkins and decided that life would be more fulfilling in Israel. His senior social worker, Miriam, had made a similar decision, though she often goes back to America for a quiet year to indulge in consumer goodies. Davidson is a tall man with a bushy beard. His rather tatty office is at the end of a long, dark corridor in Ashkelon's main hospital. In the US, his office would have been plush. He makes do with a battered sofa. Old copies of the *American Journal of Psychiatry* line the walls. He is committed to community care and has only ten hospital beds. His aim is to have community services good enough so that he needs to admit only the most acute cases.

As it happened, they had an acute case to handle when I visited. Miriam had asked the team to meet urgently to decide whether or not to hospitalize a woman against her will. Under Israeli law, as the regional psychiatrist, Davidson has the power to do this on his own. The meeting convened – Miriam, dark-haired, Brooklyn-accented, plump; Jenny, who had been a social worker in Barnet; and a tall student doctor who was the only native Israeli. The woman, Miriam explained, was known to them. She claimed her husband was to blame. He had pawned the colour television set to buy drugs. For her this was the final indignity. What would her friends say when they saw she had no television! It wasn't strange she had tried to kill herself. If the team believed the attempt was serious, then Davidson would bring her into hospital even if she resisted. Otherwise, they would see her as an outpatient. Briskly, Davidson asked them to rate her 'lethality'.

'Do you know what lethality is?' Davidson asked. He gave a brisk run-down, explaining that it was a way of predicting how likely an attempted suicide was to try again and how successful such an attempt would be. One of the paradoxes of coping with attempted suicide is that patients become 'successful' when they die. Miriam rated her lethality as three. That is, not that high. Davidson fretted, though, because she was known to them and unstable. He had to balance the disadvantages of bringing her in against her will – she would be upset, there might be legal difficulties – against the risk of letting her stay out. She might be more successfully lethal than Miriam guessed.

In most Western countries it takes two doctors to hospitalize someone. In Israel, the regional psychiatrist can detain a person for seven days. Odder still, the psychiatrist does not have to see the patient. He can accept the word of a general practitioner that the patient is dangerous and unco-operative. That is enough to allow him to send in the police. 'If the family doctor is right, that's OK, but if he's wrong, that's bad. Usually we don't do it without an examination. But if the case sounds convincing . . .' Davidson nodded, he does sometimes do it, 'or if the person is known to us.' He sections between six to twelve people a month and cannot explain why the rate varies so drastically. These powers to detain date from the British Mandate. It also seems likely that giving psychiatrists such power reflects the obsession with catching malingerers from the army.

Davidson paused for a moment, looked at Miriam and said that probably they had better bring the woman in. Miriam would go to fetch her, with the police if necessary. He justified this decision quickly. With her past history of instability, the risk was too great. If she calmed down fast, they would take her home.

Davidson sat down, the crisis resolved, to explain that it really was unusual. Ashkelon is better known, he hopes, for its community care programme which aims to defuse crises long before they explode. Distances across the desert are huge, so Davidson has set up satellite clinics throughout the area, in towns like Sderot, thirty miles into the desert. Their purpose is to avoid just such emergencies.

Sderot is a town of 20,000. Its streets are wide and dusty. Most houses are bungalows – apart from one large estate at the edge of town where the desert resumes. The satellite clinic is next to the Polish club. It will move soon to a purpose-built health centre but for years they have managed in rather cramped quarters. People can drop in without appointments. The social workers see 'patients' at the centre and also go visiting. The clinic was part of the town's life. Davidson explained he had been careful to nurture good relationships with many local bodies including the police. That was not too difficult since 'everyone knows everyone else in a place like this'. Dinner with the local police chief would lead to Davidson giving seminars to officers on how to handle psychiatric emergencies. The police saw many such emergencies and it was important they should know how to handle them, especially with many new immigrants in the area whose ways might be odd. (In London many psychiatrists preach the same message, but few dine with the Commissioner of the Metropolitan Police.)

The morning of my visit, Sderot had an emergency. A girl had not kept an appointment. It could be a serious problem, Leila, the social worker, warned. She had a new baby and was living with her mother. The family had come from Russia recently and spoke poor Hebrew. Davidson sniped that Russians were often a problem and he thought it sentimental hypocrisy to see them as harrowing refugees. The mother, the social workers suspected, took to a bit of whoring when she was short of cash. She had fits of temper, dominated her daughter and would be jealous of her baby. It was ominous that the daughter hadn't turned up.

Our two cars stopped at the housing estate on the outskirts of Sderot. The back yard was the desert. Leila made us wait at the bottom of the communal stairs while she checked to see if the girl was in. When she called us up, the door was not open. Inside, voices were raised, fluttering. Leila muttered that they might be

hiding a man and grinned that, if it were so, he probably
belonged to the mother. The daughter wasn't living with the
father of her child but seemed to know who he was – something
of an achievement given her parenthood. The door opened on to
a dramatic scene. The daughter was standing in a flimsy
dressing-gown beside a pram. She held her baby in a Madonna
pose. Her mother, a skeletal woman with a gaunt but attractive
face, wore a red dress and had a scarf tied across her grey hair.
She looked angry. She was not pleased to see social workers and
sat down in an armchair. Like all her furniture, it was heavy and
ornate. There was an unexpectedly stylish sideboard with twirly
struts and gold-edged mirrors, decked with photographs and
tasteful ornaments. The smell of nappies and washing powder
filled the room. The team politely ignored banging which came
at intervals from another room. Was this the concealed lover or
a client who hadn't bargained for being locked in a cupboard?
No one investigated.

The mother seized the initiative. She launched into a diatribe.
The only problems her family had were financial not psychological or emotional or mental. Just money. Take the electricity bill.
Or the price of eggs. Or the price of fuel. Or the rent. All of them
were exorbitant, far worse than in Russia. The mother argued
with vigour as if she were making a case. Perhaps she feared they
might take the baby away. The state, she obviously believed,
owed it to her to provide a decent flat, enough fuel and a good
standard of living, making me wonder how she would have fared
in New York, or London.

Leila let her have her first, fiery outburst. Then she suggested
there might be better ways of managing money.

Perhaps, the mother smiled, not very convinced.

It was something they could look at in detail, Leila added, if
the family kept appointments.

There were more things to worry about with a baby around
than appointments.

During these exchanges, the daughter paced by the pram. She
picked the baby up. Then put it down. Then held it again. Was
she trying to show that she was a competent mother?

It was vital to keep appointments if you wanted the system to help, the social worker stressed.

The mother looked chastened. Perhaps she worried they would stop some benefits if she broke their rules. The atmosphere changed subtly. The other social worker stood up, went over to the daughter and purred at the baby. It didn't look as if she was examining it but that was what she was doing, subtly.

If she didn't keep appointments, there would be trouble. Leila looked at the daughter who nodded. Then she turned to the mother and offered help in seeing if they could get them extra benefits.

Then, abruptly, we left. The social workers wondered just how effective they had been, mixing offers of help with threats. But they had taken a good look at the child and were reassured it was clean, fed and not bruised. The mother did know about babies. An English social worker would, I suspect, have done more to reassure them that the baby wouldn't be taken away as there was no hint of violence. But, in Sderot, they were not unhappy to keep this difficult family slightly on edge. 'That way they might keep the next appointment', Leila grinned.

As a reaction to someone not keeping an appointment, it was impressive. The size of the town helped. The estate was a five-minute drive away and the team accepted that they were not too badly overworked. Usually it's all too easy for patients to slip through the net, though the social workers themselves were not sure just what they had accomplished. Still, the baby was safe and the mother would be helped to get more money. Though, Leila said, she was not sure what she would do with it when she got it.

It is in times of stress that Israel most needs effective community psychiatry. In 1981 I visited Lionel Davidson, a psychiatrist from Glasgow who was in charge of the regional psychiatric services in Safed, high in the hills of northern Galilee. You reach Safed by driving through hairpins and hills of pine forest. The desert could be a continent away, though Ashkelon is, in fact, less than 200 miles away.

Jews came to Safed in medieval times when, under famous

rabbis, it was a centre of mystical learning, especially of the
Kabbala. The town is full of old synagogues. The picturesque
landscape shouldn't fool me, Davidson warned, we were close to
a war zone. In 1973 the area was heavily shelled; in 1976 some
twenty-two children from Safed were killed by guerrillas in the
Ma'alot disaster; a few months before I visited, the border town
of Kiryat Shemona had been shelled from across the border. It
was such attacks that precipitated the Israeli invasion of Lebanon
in 1982.

Like all other men, male psychiatrists aged under fifty-five
spend a month every year in the army reserve. They often spend
their month preparing for just such crises.

In the Safed area, the local psychiatric team learned, Davidson
said, to resist the temptation to interfere too much. 'The local
people on the spot must know that psychiatric services are
available if you want them, but you must not swamp the place
with outside experts'. Davidson was particularly sharp about
foreign volunteers who liked to drop in on a crisis to assuage
their guilt by serving Israel in her hour of need. 'They get in the
way. Raise all kinds of expectations and then disappear'. In the
1973 war, the Safed team learned lessons in Kiryat Shemona
which the Dutch could well have heeded.

'We found that the local people didn't know who the hell we
were and were not too keen on discussing their feelings with
perfect strangers.' As a result, in 1976, when Palestinian guerrillas held children hostage and killed twenty-two of them, 'We
assembled a team of local people including teachers to talk to the
parents and relatives. The regional psychiatric team only inter-
vened if someone erupted into obvious illness. All this was
stressful for local people so the regional psychiatric team became
a back-up group: the local team could express their anxieties and
feelings to them. When Kiryat Shemona was shelled in 1981, the
same policy was followed. The experts were kept at a remove,
intervening as little as possible.'

Kalman Benyamini of the Hebrew University in Jerusalem
suggests a similar approach in schools. In times of tension and of
war, schoolchildren often show 'emergency reactions'. You see
shock, grief, fear, confusion, perplexity. The temptation, Beny-

amini pointed out, is for mental-health workers to invade the schools and elbow teachers out of the way. Both in the 1967 war and the Yom Kippur war, they had found that it was much better for the mental-health workers to provide back-up. Let the teachers handle as much as they could, and interfere only as a last resort. Benyamini found how well schools had coped during the Yom Kippur war depended on how much contact there was in 'normal' times between the mental-health team and the school. If there was little contact in 'normal' times, there was confusion. The moral was for mental-health teams to keep in regular touch, to be really part of the community, before emergencies required action. Given its peculiar circumstances, Israel tends to put this into effect more than other countries, but it holds a general lesson: community care has to be nurtured slowly; it can't be created quickly or out of Ministry of Health recommendations.

Davidson might be unimpressed by foreign visitors but not by foreign money. In 1981 he obtained a large American grant to help establish comprehensive community services in the Safed area. Israel was too poor to provide all the services needed. He had enough funding to hire six doctors and seven psychologists. He was grateful and did not think it at all bizarre to use American money to fund his centre in Galilee. He took me round the old hospital, set in a pretty park, which will be the headquarters for the new facility. As in Sderot, satellite clinics will be set up so that patients won't have to travel far to get specialized help. The woods, full of lovely scented pines, Davidson grimly pointed out, also house a nuclear shelter – a reminder of the stresses Israelis have to cope with every day.

The Enemy Frontier

All the facilities I have mentioned so far cater for Jews, though Shermenache also has a good proportion of Christian Arabs. When I asked the Israeli Ministry of Health about psychiatry on the West Bank I was urged to talk to Dr Mohammad Kamal. Kamal was 'a good man'. He ran the Bethlehem Hospital. He had been trained at the Maudsley in England. When I telephoned Kamal he said he was happy to be interviewed as long as I got clearance from the military governor of the West Bank. This I was denied a number of times. I was asked why I wanted to interview a Palestinian doctor, he would be bound to criticize the Israeli government. It was no use pointing out repeatedly that the Israeli Ministry of Health itself had suggested I see him. My interview was seen as a political threat. I made threats of my own to the governor's office: Israel rightly made a huge fuss about the Soviet abuse of psychiatry, how would it look if I had to write that they would not let Arab psychiatrists be interviewed? All these arguments were in vain till my cousin's husband, a vet who was in the right brigade during the right wars, phoned up some mysterious major. Immediately, permission was granted. With such a cousin, I could be trusted. Nevertheless, I could only visit Dr Kamal with a 'minder', a doctor who was, ironically, called Dr Kafka.

Dr Kafka, an East European Jew, fidgeted with embarrassment as we drove out to Bethlehem. He started to read a book once we got to the hospital because he did not want to look like a censor. Kamal smiled wearily at his presence. His chief nurse, an elegant woman, winced, though, and it was hard to escape the feeling that, as far as she was concerned, Kafka and I (also a Jew) were enemies. I had to be shown round but it would be with icy politeness. Kamal was welcoming and, after all the hassle of fixing the permissions, I was amazed at his grace and good nature.

The Bethlehem Hospital is a different world. Where Shermenache and Ashkelon are relatively modern hospitals, Bethlehem is a fine old building. Inside the lovely façade, conditions are poor. 'They give us far less money than they do Israeli hospitals', Kamal said as he walked me through corridors. The wards were large and dark though not crowded; one had an isolation cell which was nothing but a cage. Kamal explained unaggressively that the occupation of the West Bank caused many psychological problems. People felt angry, defeated, helpless. There was constant tension. Arabs did not like to admit to emotional or mental problems so they spoke of feeling 'heavy' or 'tired' or of mysterious psychosomatic pains.

In the garden of the hospital, Kamal showed me a touching

sight. A nurse was having tea under a Eucalyptus tree with twelve female patients. The sun shone; some of the patients looked dreamy and blank; others smiled. It was one of the few times when I was struck by how peaceful, even happy, patients looked. Kamal encouraged them to sit in the garden and laze. Some maintained the gardens and the icy nurse proudly showed me some beautifully tended areas. In many cases, though, families had completely abandoned relatives, Kamal said. The political situation provided an excuse. Kamal had got permission for relatives from Amman and other parts of Jordan to come to visit the hospital but few had taken up the offer. He shrugged. There was only so much one could do. He was kept too busy, and, unlike Israel, the West Bank did not have good facilities for community care. It was not in the interests of Israel to keep the Palestinians healthy. Depression helped them accept the occupation. Despair was a powerful weapon. He drove me back to Jerusalem and smiled that, of course, he saw Jewish patients too. Many North African Jews were appalled by the snootiness of European Jewish doctors and preferred to see a doctor who understood an important part of their background.

Kamal let me off in the middle of Jerusalem, on a street where the night before sirens had blared because of a bomb scare. We shook hands in his car and smiled. I watched him drive away and recalled that there was a time when psychologists and some psychiatrists believed that their new disciplines would cure the world of war. Optimists proclaimed that they could analyse the aggression out of politicians. Wilhelm Reich, a disciple of Freud's who then quarrelled with him, praised the healing qualities of the orgasm. The world needed more orgasms. It was frustration that led to fascism. But, as in Ulster, few psychiatrists and psychologists have tried to use their expertise to promote peace between warring 'tribes'. A few Israeli psychologists have tried to organize encounter groups in which Jews meet Arabs. They carry out role-playing exercises to learn what it is like to be one of the others. It is useful and it does shift attitudes a little. Yehuda Amir and John Hoffman who run such groups at Haifa and Tel Aviv universities have both met with hostility, however. Arabs are suspicious; so are orthodox Jews who argue that such enterprises might lead to cosmic calamities and, even worse, to mixed marriages.

Despite the fact that psychology and psychiatry ought to offer techniques for transcending hostility, experts on both sides rarely question the political orthodoxy. One psychiatrist explained to me that it was 'normal and necessary' to dehumanize the Arabs because they were the enemy. If you feel too soft about Arabs, seeing them as other human beings, you might have qualms about killing them. He was an exception in his bitterness but few Israeli psychiatrists were trying hard to build bridges – even with Egyptian colleagues. And those that did received little encouragement.

Legend has it that war brings communities together. We huddle together against the enemy. I have argued that Israel knows how much it needs good community care and provides it. Yet, for all its cohesion in war, for all the golden dollars, Israel is as ambivalent as other countries about having mental patients in the community. Instead Israel concentrates on the psychiatric 'technology', the methods by which patients can hope to survive out of hospital. Hospitals can teach the skills patients need for independence but they can only preach at the 'community' to be tolerant and caring. Not surprisingly, institutions devote resources to improving the patients' skills. That is their job. It also happens to be easier than changing the attitudes of 'normal' people.

Rehabilitation

Staff at Shermenache and at Kfar Shaul have developed a technology of rehabilitation. Patients graduate through a series of well-defined stages. They return to the outside world step by psychological step, in theory at least. But though the 'technology' is impressive, being in the community is defined in a curious, negative way: it just means not being in hospital.

Kfar Shaul is a good example of preparation for community living and its contradictions. It has an 'intramural rehabilitation unit' which encourages patients to become less dependent on nursing staff. Graduates proceed to the 'extramural rehabilitation unit' which was set up in 1980. Those who graduate can hope to live outside hospital in the 'follow-up unit' as housing becomes free. It is likely to take five years to get 'really' out into the 'real world', if all goes well.

The rehabilitation villa is at the top of the same hill as the hospital. Patients are expected to clean and tidy the house on their own, no mean achievement since most of them are chronic schizophrenics who have spent over twenty years in hospital. Preparing them to live more independently is hard work. Dr Barel explained that the staff try hard to teach patients to groom themselves better, with classes in hairdressing, beauty and make-up. All too often, psychiatric patients look like psychiatric patients and don't give themselves a chance in the world. As in New York, Kfar Shaul teaches patients how to cook, clean and do the laundry – all things they never had to bother with in hospital. More ambitiously, they try to teach them how to manage relatively superficial social relationships. But since they live together and share bedrooms, something adults only do with someone intimate, how superficial can, or should, such relation-ships be? As in New York, they know of Julian Leff's findings about high emotions triggering relapses. Many patients find emotions hard to handle. Superficial calm may be more helpful, but isn't it odd to ask patients to live so closely with others and not get that involved?

Israel does have one advantage over New York. Patients can realistically look forward to a place to go. The skills they learn will get practised in a proper home.

It can take over a year, Dr Barel explained, to make someone ready to try the first 'unit'. The time offers a reasonable chance of spotting those who will never cope with the demands; those who get too anxious even after they have been given prolonged lessons in how to cook a simple meal.

The villa is a new house, built, as ever, with a contribution from America. As I went in, two men were by the cooker, preparing lunch. They were slow but competent. They told the nurse who accompanied me that they were having spaghetti and they obviously wanted her to approve the menu. A dark man sat in a pine armchair – everything in the villa is pine – and showed

her a cut on his finger. He wanted her to deal with it at once.
She looked, said it was nothing serious and that a plaster would
do. He seemed disappointed. Two elderly women competed for
the privilege of showing us their bedrooms. We visited both, both
equally tidy. Identical plaid bedspreads covered identical pine
beds. They opened the cupboards to show how neat they were.
Awkwardly, we smiled our approval which they wanted or,
perhaps, felt they should want.

A social worker is available to cope with crises. Barel emphasized that most of the patients here would in the past have been
abandoned to hospital for ever. Planned rehabilitation improved
their chances of a normal life. Since 1981, the hospital has been
moving patients out to sheltered housing in Ramot, a new suburb
of Jerusalem. Three or four patients share a flat. Barel insisted
on a contract between the patients so that each of them was
guaranteed as much freedom and privacy as possible. 'We
continue therapy, of course,' Barel stressed and the hospital is
always a phone call away.

Eventually, some patients will be competent enough to move
out of the Ramot apartments into 'real life'. Will that be ultimate
success? If so, why? Dr Moshe Avner, who runs a similar
coherent scheme at Shermenache, believes that it is essential for
both ex-patients and the community to know that the hospital is
still accessible, and easily so, if things go wrong. Israel seems to
succeed in this better than America or Britain. There are few
stories of needy patients being turned away from hospital.

Such success, however, has not meant the end of stigma or the
start of true community involvement. For all the ideals of its
pioneers, Israel is usually as 'careless' about care as Britain,
France or America. It is left to a few enthusiasts to provide
compassion, companionship and vital voluntary services. The
enthusiasts have to fight both for recognition and for money.

Chanita Rodney is a freckled, energetic woman in her fifties.
In 1978 she began to organize ENOSH, a group of parents whose
children were mentally ill. She had had to struggle for a long
time with a mentally ill child. She felt alone and isolated. No one
seemed to understand what caring for the child involved or the

strains it imposed on her family. Today, a practised publicist, Rodney explains her anguish with professional polish. She has it down to a patter, unlike one of her organizers whom she sent me to meet. Mrs A., a heavy-set German woman, kept on interrupting our conversation to minister to the latest demand of her leather-clad daughter. She almost trembled before her daughter. It seemed this girl could, if not appeased, turn dangerous and make life unpleasant. The girl, conscious of her power, whined. Her mother placated. Rodney, in public at least, displays none of that rawness. She seems comfortable with herself and her lobbying. But, she smiles, it is much easier now – partly because of ENOSH.

The charter of ENOSH talks of the 'spiritual and emotional plight of families faced with this problem'. It now has members in branches all over Israel. After nine years it is being slowly accepted as part of the mental-health system. The Ministry of Health funds some of its activities and ENOSH joins in the favourite Israeli game of looking for money from American Jews and their charities.

Anyone can join ENOSH – patients, ex-patients living in the community, volunteer helpers, relatives of the mentally ill. It offers its members support, mainly through evening clubs and discussion groups.

Chanita Rodney took me to a meeting in Ramat Aviv, 20 kilometres south of Tel Aviv. 'We have our meetings in the fall-out shelter,' she explained. It's hard to forget the sense of crisis when nearly every psychiatrist in Israel ends up working in or next to a fall-out shelter. The shelter was in a white building in the middle of a shopping precinct. Downstairs, tables had been piled with cakes, sandwiches and soft drinks. Though it was just an ordinary meeting, a few festive streamers were draped across the white, bleak walls. People, the well and the ill, milled around, chatting.

There are similar meetings three or four times a week depending on how active local organizers are. Such routines, Rodney argues, are vital if patients are to be kept out of hospital. Without them they get isolated and depressed. The whole cycle of crisis starts again and ends with them back 'inside'.

Social clubs do little, however, to make ex-patients feel useful. For all the good fellowship in the nuclear shelter, it had a feeling of charity. Do-gooders were doing good to the deserving disturbed. The ex-patients looked pleased to be there but few were totally independent. Most who worked had unskilled manual jobs. Anything more taxing might create stress which might create a crisis. ENOSH has recently taken the radical step of seeing if patients can work at a relatively skilled level. The Tel Aviv branch set up Mashap, an office business that provides a variety of secretarial services. What is no more than a small business took eighteen months to organize because they met so much hostility. The office offers typing, duplicating, photocopying and a messenger service. The twelve patients who staff it work at their own pace but they are fast enough to be relatively competitive.

'All along the way,' notes ENOSH's annual report, 'we met with doubts and discouragements from those who were supposed to encourage and to help.' The report notes, wryly, that probably the greatest help came from the Chalamis Company which provided premises. 'True, we are far from being in the fashionable part of town but our place is spacious, well lit and, most of all, relaxed'. In that relaxed atmosphere, ex-patients can earn a respectable living. They have surprised themselves – and others – by how much they have achieved. Yet it is exactly the kind of scheme that is needed if community care is to be more than a pious dream.

The military get the best rehabilitation, but for most of them the question is not one of resuming a normal life but of tolerating a grossly abnormal one. The Ministry of Defence has its own rehabilitation hospital which experiments on the best way to deal with badly injured soldiers. Most have had severe injuries, especially brain damage. Families have to adjust drastically. Wives have to cope with husbands who have become child-like. Bad as the injuries are, soldiers could recover a surprising amount of brain function even a year or more after being wounded. Britain could have used such initiatives after the

Falklands war, but, unlike Israel, it does not need its manpower badly enough.

Severely damaged soldiers who end up in hospital for months, even years, are an extreme example and prompt one crucial question: how do you rehabilitate people who have spent years in institutions? And what do you rehabilitate them to or for? Talk of patients living 'in the community' is upbeat, but what does it mean in practice? How much 'in the community' can they hope to live? Psychiatrists rarely confront its implicit contradictions.

One of the few to examine them is Alexander Leighton (1982) who concluded sadly that 'the community' doesn't really exist. He found fifty-six different uses of the word 'community', and most expressed fantasies. Arguments about it tend to come down to simple practicalities. Are there facilities for ex-patients to live in and spend the day at? Larger issues get forgotten. I want to raise some here because Israel probably has one of the best systems of community care. Yet no one asks: what is 'normal' involvement with the community? Do 'ordinary' people always mix in with the community? Are we asking ex-patients to conform to a kind of existence that is abnormal and that we, the 'normals', would never lead? Ordinary people live very different daily lives. Some love to live in a crowd; others choose lonely lives. If I want to be a hermit, I'm entitled to my isolation. It may not even be a question of my personality but of the particular time in my life. When I was married and we had small children, we lived in a semi-detached house on a street of semi-detached houses. The couple next door were much older but had a teenage daughter who liked to babysit; the house on the other side was bought by a couple with three small children. Life on Boyne Road was quite communal. When we moved out to a larger house, our children were older. There weren't any compatible next-door neighbours. In four years, I had a drink once at a house next door and invited people to my house twice. In each house (they are half a mile from each other) I had a very different level of involvement with the community. Not being a psychiatric patient, I could do what I wanted. No one could tell me that I was healthily involved in the first house and neurotically detached in the second. Patients are not given the same freedom. They are expected to participate 'in the community'. Ex-patients are expected to share houses, even bedrooms, with people who have been chosen for them by the hospital. They are expected to get along in this group and, also, socialize every week. Not to attend the group or the social club is interpreted as a danger signal.

'Normal' people can be as messy, forgetful and wayward as they want. No one is going to commit me to hospital because my kitchen is filthy, I miss an appointment or I snap at my partner. But the ex-patient has to be neat and organized, living a tidy life with tidy moods. Otherwise he might have to go back to hospital. For all the studies of the efficacy of community care, few researchers raise these contradictory issues.

Like the Scandinavian countries, Israel has evolved a good system of community care – and one which seems able to handle national crises reasonably effectively. It is, of course, privileged, because it not only has well-trained psychiatrists but it also has access to American money. Other Middle Eastern countries have to make do with little of that. Some Israeli psychiatrists would be willing to share their expertise but they find it hard to be accepted. Politics intervene. The World Health Organization has its Middle Eastern offices in Alexandria. Narendra Wig, the WHO's regional officer, is a distinguished Indian expert on community psychiatry, but Israel is not part of the Eastern Mediterranean section of WHO. The Arab countries have excluded it. Saddest of all, perhaps, is the experience of Moham-mad Shalaan a Cairo psychiatrist. Shalaan believes that the Middle Eastern conflict is not just political but personal too. Jew and Arab fear and do not know each other. They are suitable cases for treatment. There are enough Jewish psychiatrists in the world so, surely, it would be possible to arrange some fertile meetings. Shalaan told me that he thought some of the political impasse between Israel and Egypt was aggravated by the psycho-logical problems of politicians and civil servants. This view was not very popular among politicians and civil servants, but he thought exploring such hostilities might help pave the way for peace.

It does not take much to be convinced by Shalaan's view. Ever since Sadat's historic visit to Jerusalem, Israel and Egypt have argued about who owns Taba – a strip of beach 600 yards long, six miles south of Eilat on the Red Sea. It at present houses one luxury hotel (or, rather, part of it) and a nightclub. For five years, politicians and civil servants in Cairo and Tel Aviv have scrapped as to whether 1907 maps drawn up by a British major gave this strip of sand to Israel or to Egypt. They have fought about whether the dispute ought to be settled by negotiation or arbitration. In Cairo, Egyptian doctors explained that the unwillingness of the Israelis to hand over these palm trees proved that they were warmongers at heart; in Tel Aviv, I'm sure, it would not have been hard to find opinions equally illogical and childish.

Shalaan met with less response than he hoped for from Israeli colleagues. On his own side, the reaction was even worse. He found himself cold-shouldered and denounced in the Arab press as a Zionist renegade. It was a little frightening and, he sighed, sad. The world prefers psychiatrists to mend the brain-damaged and shell-shocked. Shalaan's experience illustrates the conditions Israeli psychiatry has to work under and fight against. In Israel, war and peace is a daily issue. In Egypt, it is not. Across the Sinai Desert they have less money, less expertise, less immediate affinity with Freud, and rather different crises.

6

Egypt: Care and the Qur'ān

'When I was director of Abassia, I decided we should take the schizophrenics camping by Lake Suez. When I had prepared all the arrangements,' Dr Gamal Abu Al Azayem paused to create the proper suspense, 'I got a telephone call from the prefect of the governate. He was a very worried fellow. He said "You are responsible".' Dr Gamal smiled at such pettiness. He waved his hands expansively. 'I told him that he should come to see the schizophrenic camp. And when he came, he said it was very nice.' In Egypt, local government has real powers. Once he was convinced, the prefect did more than approve. He acted. Gamal hoped his camp would push his patients back towards the community and re-establish contact with their families some of whom had not seen them for years. The convinced prefect ordered the police to fetch the families and bring them to the camp. 'They would see their "crazed" relatives whether they wanted to or not.' Gamal beamed. For him, it was a triumph. He did not question whether he, or the prefect, had the right to compel the relatives to visit or if it would do any good. In Egypt, the doctor reigns supreme.

I first heard Gamal tell this story to a meeting in London of the World Federation of Mental Health. In the middle of a paper on community care in the Pacific, a dumpy man shambled in. He was elaborately courteous to delegates as he made his way between the chairs, like a Byzantine courtier who had strayed into modern times. He had an oval, very semitic face, with a long nose and heavy jowls but, when he smiled, he looked impish. At lunch, I manoeuvred myself next to him. When I said I wanted to come to Egypt, he was effusive: I must visit his hospital.

Gamal Abu Al Azayem's career as a psychiatrist began in

1943 and covers many of the contradictions of Egyptian psychiatry. 'As soon as I studied medicine I was interested in psychiatry'. His father who was learned in the esoteric philosophy of the Sufi masters encouraged him. 'Now three of my children are psychiatrists and I have to ask whether it's infectious,' he laughed, pleased at his own joke. Many Egyptian doctors see him as a father figure, though one psychiatrist tut-tutted when I said I was visiting Gamal's hospital. 'He doesn't see what his hospital is like,' his colleagues criticized.

Gamal's hospital is very much a 'family business'. Two sons and one daughter are psychiatrists; two sons run the business side; a fifth son manages a farm which produces food for the patients. Another daughter is a biochemist and runs the chemical lab which specializes in analyzing urine samples (many of their patients are drug addicts). 'My wife is the chief administrator,' said Gamal. Nadia saw her administrative job more poetically: 'I am a mother to all the patients. I love them and they love me.' She is a stern mother, for she holds the keys to every door on the premises. 'These keys are the power.' The keys open, among other doors, those that divide the hospital into deluxe, second class and basement class. The keys also open the doors to the lift which is the only way of reaching all the floors, and which Gamal speaks of only in French as *l'ascenseur*.

I am sure that Gamal and his family will feel betrayed and upset by some of the criticisms in this chapter. However, many important issues in the West, such as patients' consent to treatment, are treated in Egypt as irrelevancies. Doctors and health officials talk as if patients are lucky to have any treatment at all.

Such an attitude might be understandable if psychiatry were new to Egypt. It is not, however. Egypt has had over a century of Western-style psychiatry. Many of its 200 psychiatrists have been trained in Britain, America and France. In a report to the World Health Organisation, the Egyptian Ministry of Health declared with some satisfaction that Egypt was far more advanced in this field of medicine than any country from Morocco to Pakistan. 'One of our problems,' smiled Dr Okasha, who trained in Edinburgh and is now Professor of Psychiatry at

Cairo University, 'is that our doctors can earn twenty times what they earn here in Saudi and the Gulf. They are very much in demand.' This general complaint causes real problems, but Cairo psychiatrists complain with pride. They are not slow to remind the Western observer of the antiquity of their tradition. The Pharaohs coped with the mentally ill. The Qur'ān has rules on how to treat them. To criticize Egyptian treatment is not to pillory a poor, backward country but, rather, one whose leading doctors see themselves as a Middle Eastern élite. There are plenty of Egyptian psychiatrists in Harley Street and, 'Many of them feel guilty, of course, because they are not here', added Dr Okasha.

All the psychiatrists I talked to believed that patients had not yet developed the nasty, Western, neurotic trait of complaining about their doctors. Okasha smiled that, naturally, Egyptian doctors did sometimes make mistakes but he could not recall one case of a patient impertinent enough to sue a doctor. Okasha approved, because faith was an essential part of the doctor–patient relationship. I am not entirely sure that all Egyptian patients are quite so uncritical. Two complained very readily in private of the quality of care they had received in private hospitals. Furthermore, everyone agreed state hospitals were far worse because money was short.

Conventional Egyptian psychiatry dates from the founding of Abassia Mental Hospital in Cairo in 1880. Today, it lies on the outskirts of Nasser City, a new town on the way to the airport. Tower blocks peer down on the wards, walls and gardens. When the hospital was built, the architects imitated Western fashion and placed it in the countryside outside Cairo. Abassia was set on 70 acres. It housed 5000 patients in wards that could sleep up to 100 patients. Gamal was its director from 1965 to 1977. He reduced the population to 1500. Now, it has risen to 3500. For many years it was the only state hospital. Now there are also Chanka, and Mamoura in Alexandria which has 600 beds. Beds in general hospitals increase the total number of state beds to 6192. (Egyptian government figures for WHO, November 1985).

Egypt also has a complex system of private inpatient and outpatient care. Government psychiatrists often run their own private practices. While he was director of Abassia, Gamal also had a thriving outpatient clinic in Cairo. No one criticized him for doing private medicine part-time.

In 1907, an English doctor started a small psychiatric clinic in Hellwan, a resort in the hills thirty miles outside Cairo. Hellwan was known for its clean air which attracted tourists and invalids. It had German, French and British hotels. Seven patients, Dr Fatieh Loza explained to me in his opulent study, were given treatments like remedial baths. He added: 'We have preserved the baths in a little museum'. In 1920, the hospital was bought by Dr Behman, Dr Loza's father-in-law. It now takes over 200 patients and the truly rich can have a villa of their own, complete with swimming pool.

Another six private hospitals have been built since and they offer a variety of care from 'deluxe' to 'basement' class depending on what you can pay. Some hospitals insist all patients get the same food and treatment. Fees only affect whether or not you share a room. Other hospitals are less precise, half-admitting that patients who pay less may get worse food and poorer treatment. Private hospitals provide perhaps another 600 beds. For a country of 53 million, the total provision of beds is small and community care is haphazard.

Twenty-five of Egypt's twenty-six provinces do not have, at present, a comprehensive, local, mental-health-care service. General practitioners provide the services. Egypt has 70,000 doctors but they receive only about ten hours training in psychiatry, according to Dr Kotry, the director-general of mental health at the Ministry of Health. 'That is sufficient,' he added. GPs could go to refresher courses at two universities but, in fact, less than 500 a year attend. Even the government's showpiece district, Fayoum, where the World Health Organization has invested £25,000 for special training, has only sparse services.

Tension between different approaches complicates matters. At his hospital, for example, Gamal likes to boast that he has the latest Western technology – rich private patients expect it – but he also likes to recall that he uses the ancient principles of Islam – the mullahs like that. Gamal straddles these contradictions easily and patients are whisked from ECT to the mosque and back, but other psychiatrists are much less happy with it. They see the use of Qur'ānic principles in psychiatry as, at best, a fad.

'In Islam,' Gamal explained, 'the doctor is called *hakeem* which also means wise man.' He added that they were now rediscovering the wisdom of the Qur'ān and that wisdom 'is very good'. The Qur'ān teaches that every human being belongs to a group and the group has to care for him if he gets into trouble. This did not rob people of their individuality, Gamal defended. 'The individual is still responsible and the Qur'ān insists, for example, that everyone works and starts work early.' It also safeguards the rights 'of those who cannot control their emotions. They must be fed and respected. They should not be punished for their madness.' They had to expect, however, that the group would control their lives. For example, they should not be allowed to administer their property but, 'and this is very nice,' Gamal wagged his finger, 'the family must not use their money badly'. Swindling is a sin. The sick person ought not to be isolated; he still belonged to the community.

Not every Islamic country takes such a benevolent view. Bangladeshi psychiatrists, for instance, said that families there saw a mentally ill person as a punishment on them. In Egypt, the consensus is that the Islamic background makes the culture particularly tolerant. 'We are a country that is very tolerant of eccentricities,' Dr Okasha smiled an elegant smile, 'and we all have our eccentricities.' Dr Al Rahawy of Cairo University said there were few norms for acceptable behaviour. Families would cope with a sick relative by giving him 'work for his level'. That might be easy work at the bottom of the field. His assistant, Dr Hatem, mused that the mentally ill were accepted as long as they did not interfere with village life. Slow, rural life, not much changed since the Pharaohs, could make space for the disabled and the damaged. 'There is a natural kind of community care,' Okasha said, so Egypt did not need that many hospitals. Everyone was eager to have me visit a model of community care – Fayoum.

Community Care

Some six kilometres outside Fayoum, Mohamma Said lives in a small village. She is a tiny woman with sharp features and excited movements. Her daughter, Maha, is much fatter and restlessly stood up and sat down throughout our conversation. I guessed Maha did not like being discussed but she had no choice, for Dr Sikri had brought us there to survey her. Five years ago, Maha began to behave strangely. 'At first I neglected it because I thought it was just headaches.' When the headaches began to get worse, and Maha started to smash their furniture, Mrs Said took her to a traditional village healer. The healer offered a variety of remedies including draping quotations from the Qur'ān round her waist. 'But she wouldn't do it. She's my only daughter and she is my life.' After a year of failure, Mrs Said took Maha to the local hospital which has a psychiatric outpatient clinic. Dr Sikri, one of the two psychiatrists there, sees 150 patients a week and a further fifty in his private clinic. Dr Sikri explained that Maha was diagnosed as a schizophrenic with some mental retardation and was given chlorpromazine. In the West she probably would have been put in hospital for a spell. In Egypt, she went home. Every two weeks she walks half a mile to get the drugs from the local rural health centre. Every six months she takes the bus into town to be assessed, though Dr Sikri said that her condition is 'contained'. He did not expect her to get better or worse. She is at high risk of developing tardive dyskensia, since she started drugs young. The long gaps between assessments means that treatment aims to keep her calm or sedated enough for her mother to cope with her. Maha needs supervision. 'I don't allow her near the fire or to cook because of it.' With a devoted mother, Maha can stay in the village in her mother's house. 'My friends are very sad for me,' Maha smiled.

Egyptian psychiatrists like to claim that their more tolerant society will allow people like Maha to be more integrated. Maha, however, said that she spent most of the day in the house waiting for her mother to tell her what to do. Her mother said she was willing to help but couldn't do much. It was hard to know how much part of the village she was. Dr Sikri did not make any large claims for the treatment they could provide but confirmed that if she lived far from Fayoum she would get far less.

If the structure of life in the village provides 'natural' community care, are there no drawbacks? No one raised the issue of whether family closeness made parents too demanding and children too dependent. Gamal laughed that this question of the Arab family 'would need a panel'. Theoretically, close family life with everyone destined for a well-set role, should create its own tensions and repressions. Many psychiatric theories emphasize the role of family conflicts. Depression might be provoked by what, in the West, would be small challenges to the authority of parents. Parents might claim a rebellious child was mad. No psychiatrist saw these as questions of any urgency. Rather, they insisted on a honeyed vision of how ancient country life creates its own asylum. To the Western sceptic it seems too good to be true. Do villagers really tolerate the mad? Don't they sometimes lock inconvenient relatives away? Probing did reveal some cases of neglect.

Ironically, it was Dr Okasha who introduced the most drastic of these cases – a young Saudi who had spent twenty years shut up in his room. He also had just admitted a young woman who suddenly revealed that her family had neglected her. Gamal spoke of families who failed in their duty to take relatives back: one suggested putting the man up in a hotel. Tolerance is not total.

It is also threatened by Egypt's rapid changes. The country is fast becoming modernized. Cairo is a vast building-site. A new airport, a new metro, new roads and hundreds of new apartment blocks are being built. This is a source of pride. One psychiatrist told me that she hoped I would not make a film 'full of ridiculous images' of Egypt. There was more to the country than rural hovels and streets full of goats and chickens. There was industry, progress and, certainly, traffic. Cairo traffic jams rival anything the West can offer. Dr Kotry sighed that this was proof of psychological inadequacy. Egyptians, he moaned, 'always look to their self-satisfaction, and they get a car as soon as they have a little money even if they have no sanitation where they live.' As more people have drifted to the city – Cairo has some 13 million inhabitants – the strain on the psychiatric services has increased. The extended family functions less well. The traditional healers who flourished in the villages and dealt with many a rural neurotic are being outlawed. Egypt has a powerful medical lobby. A group of GPs explained to me that the traditional healer has no proper qualifications. He is, therefore, more liable to harm than to help a patient. But will there be enough doctors who know about psychiatry to replace them? Planners, like Dr Kotry, recognize the problem and create splendid plans on paper. But will there be the money and the will to carry them out, especially as, for all the talk of tolerance, mental illness still carries fear and stigma?

State Hospitals

Initially, I was told it was not possible to visit Abassia, Egypt's oldest mental hospital. I ought to have made the request from London. After a meeting with Dr Kotry and Dr Atif Shonka, his deputy, I was told that there would be no problem. A day later, there was a problem. I needed to be cleared by the security police. Shonka, a smooth man who is a pharmacist not a psychiatrist, loves political jokes and, skilfully, turned the problems with Abassia into a joke, sniping they were worried 'in case you see that we are building nuclear missiles at Abassia'. Eventually, after much negotiation, Joan Shenton and I visited the hospital. In October 1986, returning to film, it was not to be so easy.

Abassia is built like a prison. The grounds are guarded by a green fence. Inside the fence, 100 yards back from the main road, the hospital is ringed by a high wall. To enter, you first drive past a sentry post. The road then runs through scrubby woodland. To the right is the long, pink-tinged hospital wall. The road hugs this wall for 100 yards and stops at a second gate. Police and troops guard this gate.

The office of the director is near the entrance, down a dark corridor. After Gamal left, he was succeeded by a woman, Dr Naheed. She is in her fifties and seems peculiarly shy and retiring to be running such a secure institution. She offered the ritual tea. She explained it was not easy to allow visitors to see their work but that, of course, they had nothing to hide. A faded picture of President Mubarak hung above her large desk. She took out a map of the hospital. It had been built to house 5000 but now it had 2500 patients, she said. (Other psychiatrists said 3500.) But

not all of them stayed a long time. 10,000 patients 'flowed' each
year in and out of the hospital. There is no way of checking these
claims because there are no audited statistics. Dr Naheed sighed
that some patients had been in for twenty years. Often they were
not that sick but their families did not want them back. As a
result, they could not leave the hospital. They had nowhere to
go. The public worried about Abassia patients. She did not
reveal that a patient who had just been discharged committed
suicide the day after his release. At first it was impossible to
confirm this had happened, though when I mentioned it to Dr
Kotry he said that 'we' didn't want to talk about such things.

When he first worked at Abassia, Gamal said, 'It was the old
asylum. Everything was locked. I was given many keys and, if
you lost these keys, there was big trouble. Patients stayed in their
cells all day and there were no activities.' He shook his head.
'This exaggerated the symptoms of the patients.' As soon as he
was appointed, he went to Britain which, being 'advanced',
would teach him better, modern methods. He went to Aberdeen
University and the Maudsley. He was most struck by War-
lingham Park Hospital, but the highlight was staying with
Maxwell Jones, 'the father of the therapeutic community', at
Dingleton. Gamal shook his head still at the wonder of how Jones
would have meetings with 100 psychopaths. Inspired by these
liberal ideas, he came back to Abassia and 'opened the hospital'.
Patients were let out of their cells. They started doing occupational therapy. He began to 'listen to the life of the patients'. As
he originally told it, Gamal conveyed the impression that the
entire population of Abassia – between 2000 and 3000 patients –
were taken camping. In fact, it turned out to be forty-nine, but
the move was symbolic. They did not have to be confined to the
hospital. 'I brought up my children in Abassia,' Gamal added,
'and they were taught to be kind to the patients and to make sure
they had enough food.' It was suspected the staff had been
stealing patients' food.

By the time that he left Abassia, Gamal had reduced the
number of patients in the hospital and he was proud of the fact
that those who had to stay led a more open life.

Dr Naheed often referred to Gamal with admiration. She

recommended, and there was no quarrelling with her, that we visit three blocks. First, she took us to one of the residential blocks. We had to drive as it was so far away. Dr Naheed stopped her car in a small courtyard. Cats lay in the shade of a Eucalyptus tree. The ward itself was dark; five beds were placed in the dining area. Tables and benches were stacked against the walls. High up a television droned offering, a nurse said, 'entertainment therapy'. The hospital also encourages patients to play football. The main room was a long dormitory with 100 beds, each six inches to a foot apart. No patient has a private locker or a cupboard; it is wall-to-wall bedding, much like New York's shelters! Few patients were lying down in the middle of the day. The hospital discourages idleness. 'Every morning, of course, we give the patients drugs. Some refuse and put it under their tongue but when they see their colleagues take it then it's OK,' explained Dr Sokhal, the head of occupational therapy.

A male nurse with a missing tooth greeted us at the next block. He presided over occupational therapy and led us into a room which had an exhibition of patients' work, marquetry, pottery, Donald Duck puzzles and trains. Dr Naheed added, 'I thought it would be more interesting for you to see the patients working.' A line of patients sat docilely, putting blocks of wood together. In smaller rooms to the side, patients were pressing and tailoring rather like in an East End sweatshop. A bald man who would fit nicely into a film of *The Hobbit* was mending and making shoes. The shoemaker has been in Abassia for twenty years. He displayed no obvious sign of madness and applied himself to banging nails into leather much as he might in the bazaar where he had once worked. No one was entirely sure what was, or had been, wrong with him, though Dr Sokhal thought his family did not want him back. He was unlikely to leave for years.

Opposite the shoemaker twenty-five men were crammed into a dark cavern of a room. They were making carpets, some holding hoops of wool while others ran it on to the carpet-making frames. Most stared ahead without a word. Did they stay like that most of the day? Dr Naheed and Dr Sokhal introduced the scene as if it offered an impressive tableau of the possibilities of therapy. They accepted, however, that if these patients reached the outside world, they could not make carpets for a living. But in hospital, they smiled, such efforts were rewarded with cigarettes and a sense of dignity.

In the West, union laws make it hard for hospitals to use patients' labour for anything 'real'; in New York, there were complaints about the Shelter work-experience programme which only pays 12.50 dollars a week. In Egypt, the attitude is quite different. Where patients can work, they ought to. The hospital was more of a real community, Sokhal claimed. Working made patients feel useful and they did not mind not getting paid for it. It prepared them better for going back to the world. She smiled enigmatically, though, 'All this is hard to evaluate.'

Any therapy is hard to evaluate. Few suggest occupational therapy is a cure. At best, it may teach something about social contact, self-discipline, self-esteem and even specific skills, though the cobbler did not need more skill. All mental hospitals seem to struggle to find enough to fill the day and occupational therapy helps patients pass the time. Few professionals are honest enough to admit that that may be its main achievement. In her studies of unemployment, Marie Jahoda (1981), a very distinguished psychologist, argued that when people lose a job they not only lose money, status and friends, but also a way of passing time. Occupational therapy may be more of an occupation than a therapy.

'We don't mix men and women, even at work. Our culture wouldn't allow it,' smiled Dr Sokhal. She knew that in the wicked West there were discos – indeed, there was a Lunatics Ball in the 1840s – where male and female patients danced together. For Egypt, such mixing was shocking. The women's wards are in a separate part of the grounds guarded by a large blue gate. The buildings beyond this gate resemble the men's though the wards are more spacious. In one, beds were tucked into corners of a huge dark hall. The hall doubled as a common room and occupational therapy centre. Women's work was daintier. They could do embroidery, knitting and needlework. Sokhal held up to be admired a tablecloth with a Chinese design and beckoned to a lady who was wearing pink bows on her dress. The coquettish patient walked forward. 'See,' cooed Sokhal, 'she combs her hair all by herself,' displaying her much as she had done the tablecloth.

Many of the women patients have been in hospital for ten to twenty years. Families abandon them, Sokhal sighed. A woman in hospital was a total loss. No one would marry her; her fate, if it were known, might make other members of the family less eligible. Sokhal introduced two ladies who had been in Abassia for many years though she couldn't be sure just how long. One wore a green dress and had smatterings of French, enough to complain when asked if she enjoyed her work. '*Mais, docteur, nous ne recevons que 50 piastres.*' 'You see,' Dr Sokhal commented, this complaint proved how free the regime was. She promised she would look into it. Then, she walked out saddened almost by the ingratitude of the patients. How many piastres did they expect?

In the West, mixing male and female patients on wards has been taken to be a sign of progress. Many hospitals still have single-sex wards but patients usually function better on mixed wards. In Egypt, the Islamic revival has made any such progress impossible. The few mixed facilities that existed such as a mixed cafeteria at Mamoura State Hospital in Alexandria are being shut down. Justifying this, Dr Faiwal, the director of Mamoura, pointed out, 'The women don't like staying there. The nurses bring them and they stay just as long as they need to buy their goods.' In his new hospital, this one concession to unisex will end; there will be two cafeterias. Almost all Egyptian psychiatrists defended this separation as culturally necessary though, at Mokattam Hospital, the sexes mixed freely without attracting the wrath of the religious (see page 170).

The shop at Abassia stands just outside the blue gate. It sells the carpets, cloth and pottery the hospital produces. Eagerly, Sokhal showed what patients can achieve, holding up item after item for admiration. I looked past these across the courtyard to the grim, acute ward. Men were hunched up on the windowsills of the barred ward. Some stared out, immobile. Some swayed against the bars. It looked like a prison. Cats screeched perpetually. Sokhal drew my attention back to her collection of nice tableclothes, nice rugs, nice plates and nice carpets. As I wanted permission to film in the hospital, I did not dare alienate her so

I exclaimed with pleasure over these, bought some plates and
napkins and never mentioned the macabre acute ward behind
us.

At the end of my visit, Dr Naheed served tea in her office. Tea
was interrupted, however, because three policemen brought in a
young man. He was handcuffed to one of them. The policemen's
boots were unlaced and too large so they looked like players in a
comic opera, but there was nothing comic about the scene. The
'prisoner' looked pathetic. Dr Naheed hardly deigned look at
him. The paperwork was wrong, Dr Naheed snapped. He would
have to be admitted but the forms were not filled in correctly.
She did not examine the handcuffed man and, with no more than
a quick look barked two questions at him. I didn't see much
therapeutic sympathy. She dismissed him brusquely. He was
marched away, handcuffed, while she sat powerful at her desk,
consulting the all-too-imperfect file.

The other main state hospital is Mamoura in Alexandria.
Mamoura was built in 1967 because Abassia and Chanka had
far too many inmates. The pressure on beds was enormous.
Already, much of the hospital is decaying. Its director, Dr
Faiwal, complained it was expensive to maintain. The wards are
overcrowded. At Mamoura I witnessed rough handling of
patients. As Dr Faiwal showed off the long hospital corridors, a
patient approached him. Not speaking Arabic, I don't know
what Dr Faiwal said but he seemed in no mood to listen. A nurse
grabbed the patient and bundled him away. Faiwal did not refer
to the incident but continued to stride down the corridor to show
me the large, hygienic kitchens. There was no chance to talk to
patients alone. For all its modernity, Mamoura did not seem to
be an active therapeutic centre any more than Abassia.

Few governments are proud of, and open about, their psychiatric hospitals. In Egypt, there is certainly an air of secrecy
surrounding them. It was made clear that visiting Chanka was
out of the question. To get permission to see Abassia and
Mamoura had required endless pressure. Such secrecy inevitably
makes one wonder what is being concealed. By the time I left
Abassia, I felt sure that I had not seen everything. Some of what

I had seen, however, seemed reasonable given that Egypt is not a rich country.

By the time we left Egypt, Central Television had been given permission to film. In the three months between the research visit and arriving with a crew, a time and date for filming was fixed. Telephone calls from London confirmed the arrangements without anyone raising objections. When we got back to Cairo it emerged that there were difficulties, first with the board of the hospital, then with the Security Department of the Ministry of Health and then with the local prefecture. It was never clear who really made the decision to refuse us access to film. Was it Dr Naheed? She said it wasn't her. Was it Dr Kotry, director-general of mental health? He said it wasn't him. He was all for filming. Was it the head of the prefecture? I was not told of his existence till it was too late because he had made a decision and couldn't possibly reverse it without losing face. 'These Freudian problems,' sighed Dr Kotry, and went on to blame bureaucrats, known and unknown, 'people who cannot take responsibility. Of course if the Ministry of Health had ordered him then it would have been different.' But when I pointed out to Dr Kotry, that he was the director-general of mental health in the said ministry, he only smiled, 'Oh, but I have no influence.' I have no way of knowing just what the truth was. Later in the week, the story was that the real obstacle was a new head of the local prefecture who, the psychiatrists said, failed most tests of maturity and was a 'poor servant and a poor master' lacking ego resolution. For all the imperfections of his ego, this prefect came up with an ingenious excuse. It would be unpatriotic to let a foreign film crew into Abassia before an Egyptian film crew. And no Egyptian film crew had ever been allowed in.

It is hard to judge a hospital which gives such limited access. The buildings were old and often dirty. Only a few patients got to do occupational therapy. The patients squatting on the interior window ledges of the acute ward looked in poor shape. The doctors at Mokattam Hospital, Dr Al Rahawy and Dr Hatem, criticized Abassia for offering nothing but sedation and drugs; there were no activities, no real therapy. Dr Hatem said, 'You have seen our old public hospitals. The patients are kept drugged and isolated from society. It is not very human.' He added that this was not an exclusively Egyptian problem. Hatem's superior, Dr Al Rahawy, emphasized that 'doctors have been brainwashed by the pharmaceutical industry' which made him 'angry because I ask myself what it would be like to be a patient shut in with drugs'. It was brave of these doctors to be critical of their colleagues. Unfortunately, Egypt has no patients' organization to help trace and talk freely to ex-patients of the state institutions.

A 'Family Business' Hospital

By contrast with Abassia, Gamal was very generous. He let us see much of what went on in his hospital. It is some five kilometres on from Abassia, in the middle of Nasser City. The five-storey building looks out on to a square green. Gamal uses the green for his patients. He believes they need to go out, for all the balconies and windows of the hospital are covered with an iron lattice of circles. These round bars are small – you can put an arm through them, which patients often do – and Gamal claims they stop patients throwing themselves out. He laughed, 'We have made them into circles so they are really decorations.' There are similar decorations inside the hospital where bars and steel doors separate different classes of patients. I saw one assistant who guarded a steel door push a patient back down the stairs. He was restricted to the basement, the lowest class.

The Al Azayem Hospital can be viewed as a hotel of many classes. The top floor is the penthouse suite with private rooms, nicely panelled in plastic pine. 'The pine is waxed because the patients are always destroying and dirtying things,' explained Dr Ahmed, one of Gamal's sons who has been infected with the psychiatric 'bug'. On this floor, a room can cost anything from 40 Egyptian pounds a day (the hospital's version) to 90 pounds a day (the rate one patient claimed to be paying). Sharif Shoubagy said that he had been admitted because he drank too much and had made a suicide attempt, taking twenty valiums. He could afford the room because he was a 'very successful' banker but he was also, improbably, interested in make-up. This cosmetic banker lay in his bed surrounded by flowers and a telephone, though he complained he was 'so doped up I feel dizzy'. Despite the 90 pounds a day he had found neither a doctor nor a nurse on duty when he had woken up in the morning. He wandered down the corridor till another patient offered him a cup of tea. Shoubagy was annoyed by this lack of service and staff.

Exotic patients were to be found on the deluxe floor. One man, resplendent in goatee beard and magnificent yellow silk dressing-gown with dragons, appeared to belong in a Noël Coward play. Stairs lead up and down from this 'best' floor. A barred door leads to the private flat of the Al Azayem family: the stairs lead down to another barred door which is the entrance to the second class. Here, rooms have two beds; there is no television and no pine panelling; the bathroom is more basic. The ground floor is the outpatient clinic. An attendant stands by a large steel door to stop patients wandering into it. Below is the basement where they did not want us to film.

In the basement, eighteen male patients live in three cramped rooms – two dormitories and a small central chamber where they eat, wait and pass the time. During the research visit, pieces of wood which had been ripped off the walls were piled in one corner of the small space. 'I want my freedom,' shouted a large man who had worked in Britain and Germany. 'He's going through his hostile phase,' smiled Dr Ahmed, who added, 'I am your friend.'

'You are not my friend.'

'In two days he'll be okay,' Dr Ahmed reassured. Being OK also meant not complaining.

In the first days at the hospital, they use medication heavily. Unlike his father, Ahmed prefers to rely on drugs and ECT rather than the Qur'ān. Medication before meditation. Dr Ahmed is proud of a new way of giving ECT. 'Every morning that we do it, we don't like to worry patients so we tell them not to eat the night before because that is like an examination.' The patient has no reason to panic at the prospect of ECT. It comes as a surprise. 'Then in the morning we come to their bedside and give it to them.' Ahmed insisted that an anaesthetist is always present. Giving ECT in this way helped the patient. They

returned, asking for it. New technological developments made it
possible to give ECT without side-effects. Ahmed could measure,
for each patient, the precise level of voltage that would trigger a
seizure. The hospital had bought a new machine to perform such
computerized EEGs which would indicate the lowest voltage
needed. The EEG machine was waiting for its software in July.
At the end of October the software was still not working. In the
interim, ECT was given without these technological frills. The
hospital was happy to let us film ECT being given with an
anaesthetist but Ahmed was certain we wouldn't see anything.
ECT was so tranquil. In fact, the camera recorded dramatic
twitches and contortions. The anaesthetist held up the patient's
arm and dropped it like a lifeless thing. The patient's body shook
and juddered, which proves nothing about the merits or demerits
of ECT, but it is curious that doctors perceive ECT as being so
uneventful that there is 'nothing to see'.

Dr Ahmed is a firm believer in ECT for depression and in
acute episodes of schizophrenia. He pitied American psychiatrists
who had to get patients' consent for every minuscule item of
treatment. Asking for such consent destroyed the doctor–patient
relationship. The patient had to trust the doctor, the modern
equivalent of the wise *hakeem*. 'If the patient is mental he has the
right to expect that we think for him. To say schizophrenic is to
say you have no insight and how can you expect a patient who
has no insight to make decisions about his treatment.' The liberal
notions of the West were cruel really. Ahmed employed Western
technology and yet rejected Western notions about patients'
rights. He saw no dilemma in that.

The Al Azayem Hospital claims to offer patients a constant
round of 'activity therapy'. Every day there are prayers because
Gamal believes that is, in itself, healing. Every day, about twenty
patients go out by bus for a trip; others sit in the square in front
of the hospital. There seemed, however, to be rather less activity
than Gamal claimed. Like many private psychiatric hospitals,
his seems torn between the desire to give good therapy and the
need to make a good profit.

The hospital boasts it has a facility known as Fountain House,
Egypt, named after Fountain House in New York, one of the first

programmes for social rehabilitation. In July, the Egyptian equivalent was deserted. The large rooms which 'housed' it had no equipment, no therapists and no patients. When we returned to film, Fountain House had been tarted up for the cameras. There were tables, each prettily covered by a tablecloth. Prints of the Nile and of Tudor cottages had been glued on the walls. Patients had a choice of playing dominoes, making clothes-pegs or putting blue tops on white biro stems. In a side room two patients were working an old Gestetner on which Dr Gamal explained, as part of therapy, patients printed, guillotined and collated an Islamic mental-health journal he edits. 'All the patients and their relatives ask for this journal,' he smiled. No one supervised these activities. No one explained how these menial tasks would be healing. There were no qualified staff who used the work in any therapeutic manner. At best, it seemed a way of killing time. Two ex-patients said that they had never done any such therapy. Fountain House was reserved for men: women seemed to do even less on their wards.

It is appropriate that Gamal should be President of the World Federation for Mental Health. Many of the criticisms I level against his hospital can be levelled against psychiatric care in many countries. Patients are given drugs or ECT, tranquillized and given little else. There seemed to be virtually no individual attention paid to individual problems.

In Egypt, only the affluent can go to Gamal. The poor either have to rely on such services as exist where they live or seek something more unusual.

Alternative Communities

The lack of resources has stimulated experiments in Egypt which would seem very esoteric in the West. With far fewer professionals, the community becomes more involved.

With his belief in prayer, Gamal has become involved in what he likes to call 'community care in the mosque'. He helped set up a clinic in Fayoum which offers a number of services separate from those that Maha used. 'It is very nice, Fayoum,' Gamal

sparkled. It also happens to be the national showpiece. Despite
calling itself a psychiatric facility, the mosque mainly concerns
itself with drug addicts and, skilfully, uses religion to badger
addicts to give up hashish or heroin. The Qur'ān forbids the use
of any stimulant. Those who come to the mosque for help may
see a doctor or a social worker but they may also see an imam.

Psychiatric patients are seen in the outpatient clinic. I was
introduced to an ex-addict who had 'kicked the habit'. Moham-
mad was an electrical engineer who had become hooked on
drugs. He claimed friends had led him astray. His family life
began to suffer. 'I shouted at all my children,' he said and added,
slyly, 'and I have many.' Then he began to lose money at work.
Finally, after two years, he came to the mosque. He was treated
in what seems to have been an effective manner with a mixture
of religious bullying and vitamin pills. He had found an environment which condemned drugs totally and where there was
enormous social pressure to conform. In an analysis of therapy
at Fayoum, Gamal has claimed that 63 per cent of drug addicts
withdraw and stay clean. It's an impressive claim but it is not
certain that such Islamic moral pressure helps cure ordinary
psychiatric diseases which don't yield to moralizing. And the
study is flawed because it relied exclusively on what ex-addicts
said. A number of Gamal's colleagues are frankly critical of the
mosque providing community care.

The medical elite in Egypt is as capable of theoretical bickering
as psychiatrists in the West. Most doctors cling to the medical
model. Some defend it aggressively, like Dr Ahmed; others
concede that it may not be always perfect but that it is usually
the most appropriate; a few dissent and offer the Egyptian
equivalent of radical chic. Mokattam Hospital is perhaps the
most radical of such ventures. It is a small private hospital run
by Dr Al Rahawy, a balding, lean man. He believes that
psychiatry needs to treat the whole person and that therapists
need to get personally involved. The distance between the doctor
and the patient that Egyptian doctors see as perfectly natural
seems wrong to him. Al Rahawy describes his basic approach as
'milieu therapy'. He is out to create an environment, a milieu,

which is therapeutic. It is crucial 'to activate the patient'. Being passive, lazy, out of it, is not allowed. Each patient spends two days in the countryside. They leave in a bus at six o'clock. On the way they buy newspapers, an interesting act since it's rare for anyone to admit that 'lunatics' take an interest in current affairs. Then they sing songs. Singing warms everyone up and, according to Al Rahawy, you can see patients begin to come out of their shells and their lethargy as they travel to the hospital's farm. The first hour they play volleyball and do exercises. Such games are not only relaxing but break down set roles. 'Sometimes our visitors ask who is the patient and who is the doctor,' Al Rahawy smiled. One patient, Shadia, had been twelve years in different hospitals and usually heavily medicated. She was refusing to put her heart and muscle into her volleyball so, when she served, she gave the ball a limp pat. Al Rahawy's colleague, Hatem, went over to her, took her arm and swung it so that she could feel what it might be like to hit the ball properly. He insisted she try again. She did a little better the second time. 'I have to put pressure on patients sometimes. The schizophrenic likes to sit in his autistic little world but we invite him back into society. Invite them back so they can tolerate the stresses imposed on them by society.' Patients like Shadia often resented the effort that was required of them. 'One way of coping with that resentment is to make patients see that the doctors care. If you go through a crisis with someone, they know you care.' After volleyball and a one-hour therapy session, patients and doctors dig. Again, Shadia did not want to take part. Again, Hatem coaxed and cajoled her into digging. 'If you work with patients, you have a completely new attitude because you share something common, very deep, with them,' Hatem added.

Unlike patients in other hospitals, Shadia felt she could complain in the hearing of the doctors. She hated all the activity. But pot-bellied Said and a girl who had not had treatment for five years for depression said the activities made them feel energetic. Said added that it was very different from Al Azayem's where he had received tablets, been interviewed for a little while by a doctor and felt 'it was like a hotel. Just tablets, medicine.' He appreciated that the groups at Mokattam tried to make them all see where their behaviour was bad. He saw he lied too easily to get his way. He felt he might now cope. The girl added that energy was not everything. She fretted very realistically about how she would cope back in the real world where volleyball didn't matter.

For Al Rahawy the approach offers a chance to integrate body and mind. He claims to be able to manage relapses better. Often, the patient knows himself well enough as a result of going through Mokattam to predict relapse and to ask to be readmitted before it happens. Milieu therapy here does not mean the doctor abandoning his authority. Hatem explained that, in the group, they confronted two paranoid patients. The doctors told them their paranoia was inappropriate and got them to pledge they would drop the aggressive posturing it led to. They were not so much exploring motives as exhorting. But they do this after they have all worked 'as a team'. Like Gamal's hospital, Mokattam does have classes but Al Rahawy said it was just a question of whether one paid for a single or a double room. There was nothing like the dormitory basement. Mokattam is attractive. Patients looked happy at the end of the day.

Patients might look happy but were they better? The evidence that milieu therapy cures is as mixed as the evidence for the success of other therapies. Mokattam may not so much succeed in curing patients as in managing them more decently, giving them a better life. Al Rahawy is more positive, arguing that his approach can integrate the patient back into society, making him more productive and creative. 'And I do not like to keep patients in prison chemically. I imagine what it would be like for me and I do not like it.' This is, perhaps, what is most impressive about Mokattam, the willingness of its doctors to see things from the patients' point of view. Hatem emphasized the equality: 'If you work with a patient, digging, for example, something very deep happens. You cannot be the superior therapist and you learn from them.' He learned from them. This humility, however, was not too deep. He never questioned that, as a doctor, his role was to guide the sick, to devise solutions for them. It seems very hard for Third World psychiatrists to conceive of any democratic treatment.

* * *

Egypt has many problems in coping with its mentally ill but there is also one mystery – the lack of brutality. I have described the apathy and poor physical conditions of its large public and some of its private hospitals. As in Japan, psychiatry in Egypt is good business for some doctors. Usually, such hospitals seem to breed brutality. Try as I might – here is the muckraking journalist in a ridiculous posture, deprived of his fix of muck – I could not confirm any stories of brutality. It may well be that the right sources were not accessible. Egypt does not have patients' organizations like MIND which are usually a good source for such material. The press does not have much tradition of critical independence and journalists tend to see doctors as founts of wisdom. I did not get access to Chanka, the hospital which houses the majority of the criminally insane. Nevertheless, there does seem to be very little physical brutality in Egypt and it is interesting to speculate why. Egyptian psychiatrists did mention, repeatedly, the splendid tolerance of their compatriots. It is, however, hard to be too convinced by the argument that slow, rural life prevents brutality. India, we shall see, is full of slow, rural life and its mental hospitals' treatment of the mentally ill is often brutal. It is not easy either to accept the view that Islam protects the insane. In Bangladesh, India's Islamic neighbour, the mentally ill are shunned, chained and thrashed. I can't answer why Egypt should have less brutality. But the comparison with the rest of the world is intriguing. It suggests again that public attitudes, some of which remain mysterious, may do more to affect the treatment of the mentally ill than doctors like to imagine.

7

India: Chasing the demons

Looking to the mystic East for wisdom is a habit that dies hard in the West, whatever the evidence. One of the most influential of the early seekers after Eastern truth was the psychoanalyst Carl Jung. In 1937, after he had written eloquently about Indian mythology, he visited the subcontinent at the invitation of the British Council. He found himself laid low by dysentery for ten days in Calcutta and was delighted because it allowed him to take stock of the 'Dreamlike World of India'. For Jung, India represented psychic wholeness. In *Analytical Psychology* he enthused: '. . . of course, we have an extensive amount of unconsciousness in our civilization but, if you go to other races, to India or to China, for example, you discover that these people are conscious of things which the psychoanalyst in our country has to dig for for months' (Jung, 1968:46).

Jung was enraptured by the dress of Indian women, especially the clinging saris which allowed them to show off their femininity. They did not have to pretend, like their Western sisters, to dress like men. Indian myths were profound: their gods and goddesses expressed powerful archetypes. Jung saw, in India, a model for harmony. He managed to ignore the poverty, squalor, disease and factional fighting between the Hindus and the Muslims. It was a psychological paradise.

Many psychologists and psychiatrists dismissed Jung as a crank but some schools continue to look East. Some gurus may be genuinely wise, like Krishnamurti; others are masters of hype, like the Bhagwan.

When research in the 1960s showed that the left and the right hemispheres of the brain specialized in different tasks, this was hailed as proof of the creative superiority of the East. The left hemisphere was Western: it controlled language and logic (in right-handers at least); it could find answers to specific questions – but where was its soul, its music, its imagination? Brutal, masculine Western logic had smashed such subtle qualities. The right, 'Eastern', hemisphere was where they survived. it was full of rich, juicy, oriental essences, brimming with soul. Robert Ornstein, a very reputable academic psychologist, argued in *The Psychology of Consciousness* (1976) that the problem of Western man was that he had been enslaved by the logical left hemisphere. A dose of the East would make him whole again.

Yet for all our visions of Eastern harmony, the history of Indian psychiatry is a history of very different influences, many of them surprisingly harsh. Indian philosophy saw madness as a form of possession by demons. Supernatural beings took over the body of the 'patient' and these spirits could leave him or her at whim and latch on to a relative. People were terrified that the bad spirit would move from one member of the family to another.

The psychiatrist L. P. Varma (1980) argued that some of the supernatural beings which possessed people corresponded to modern mental illnesses. If you were taken over by the demon Vatonmad, you were schizophrenic; if you were taken over by the wicked Pittonmad, you were manic. Other demons provoked other illnesses. Such an exercise, comparing contemporary diagnoses with old deities, is difficult, even suspect, since mental illnesses have been seen very differently at different times. What is more certain is that the traditional remedies on offer were a mixture of healing and harshness. Ayurvedic medicine was gentle. Sick people were treated kindly and given a balanced diet. Their heads were massaged with milk. Sleeping in temples and wearing charms might persuade the evil spirit to quit. If all this failed, however, there were more drastic remedies. Varma mentions sending in men dressed as bandits to drag the patient out of his room, and his depression. More violent yet, the patient could be terrorized by being put in a room with a snake. Usually, but not always, the poisoned fangs were removed. In September 1986, the *Guardian* reported that, near Ahmedabad, mentally ill people were taken to a shrine to be thrashed. This 'ceremony' was held openly and, indeed, was meant to be for the patients' good since a good thrashing might drive out the demons. But such rituals are also a way in which the community expresses its fear, rejection and even hatred of the mentally ill.

The thrashings at Ahmedabad were not an isolated incident. Pamphlets prepared by the National Institute of Mental Health in Bangalore (NIMHANS) recommend telling villagers that there is no 'need to thrash the devils out of the mad'. Dr Srinivas Murthy of the institute told me that because treatment only reached 5 to 10 per cent of the population, villagers often had no choice but to restrain the mentally ill. Sometimes they were locked in rooms. At other times, they were kept in chains. It isn't just poverty that leads to such cruelty, it's also ancient fears, fears which seem to have survived the arrival of the British with their scientific psychiatry.

The British, in the late eighteenth century, brought with them the best of European psychology. The first mental hospital was built in Bombay in 1745, the next in Calcutta in 1787. Its wards were reserved for the European mad of whom there were many, for running the empire and the unaccustomed heat took their toll.

Despite some good intentions, there were never enough hospitals and never enough money. Thirteen new hospitals were built in the nineteenth century. All of them offered custody rather than care, warders rather than nurses. Varma (1980) notes there were recurrent tales of brutality and torture on the wards. Yet Indian medicine was not isolated. There were medical students in London from the end of the nineteenth century. The Indian Lunacy Act of 1912 owed a great deal to the British Lunacy Act of 1890 which was committed to treating patients decently as well as keeping them out of society's way. Freud penetrated to India: by 1911 Bhose set up a psychoanalytic practice. But all this had very little impact on most of the mental-health system, though the European Asylum did have a few open wards and, at Agra, the hospital refused to become overcrowded.

When the Bhore Committee reported in 1946, it found that the mental-health services were desperately inadequate. The Committee noted:

Even if the proportion of mental patients is to be taken as two per thousand population in India, hospital accommodation should be available for at least 800,000 patients as against the existing provision of a little over 10,000 beds for the country as a whole. In India, the existing number of mental-hospital beds is in the ratio of one bed to about 40,000 of the population while in England the corresponding ratio is about one bed to 300 population (Bhore Committee, 1946:)

In an assessment prepared in 1982 for a series of debates on the National Mental Health Programme, Dr Srinivas Murthy of the National Institute of Mental Health was very critical. He wrote (1985): 'Before independence there were no clear plans for the care of the mentally ill. The approach was to build "asylums" which were custodial rather than therapeutic'. Murthy noted the criticisms of the Bhore Committee and added: 'The situation in 1984, 40 years later, is not very different. Though the number of mental-hospital beds is now 20,000, the bed/population ratio remains the same due to concurrent increases in the population.'

There are now forty-two mental hospitals in India. India in 1985 had a population of 750 million – which suggests there are 750,000 schizophrenics in need of treatment. A study by Professor Abraham Verghese of the incidence of mental illness in Vellore in Southern India suggests this may be an under-estimate (Vergese et al, 1971). He studied a random sample of 539 families in what would seem to be a perfectly average town. He found that 66.5 out of every 1000 people were mentally ill. If his findings were accurate for the whole of India, it would mean 51.5 million people in need of psychiatric help! Verghese found a predictable link between mental illness and poverty, illiteracy and low-status jobs. The age group that showed most illness was between thirty-one and forty-five. It is true that Verghese included epileptics and those with neurological conditions in his survey. But there is also evidence that people in Southern India are less prone to some forms of mental illness. Even if Verghese's figures are a little high, they are terrifying, for the 51.5 million will be competing for 20,000 hospital beds.

The psychiatric establishment doesn't try to hide the scale of the problem. Dr N. Reddy, the director of the National Institute of Mental Health said: 'In the country perhaps 10 per cent of the need is being met and most of that is in urban centres. In the villages, there is very little. People have to rely on witchcraft and

healers. The need is tremendous.' Murthy believes 5 per cent to
be a better guess and pointed out acidly that that over 60 per
cent of severely mentally ill patients will have gone without any
treatment for over five years. Holland, which has a population of
5 million, has more psychiatrists and more hospital beds than
India. In such conditions, the priority is to provide any care,
however flawed.

The resources and attention available for psychiatry are small.
The 1912 Lunacy Act, for example, has still not been repealed
and means that patients can only be taken into a state hospital
on a warrant from a magistrate. Legally speaking, there is no
voluntary treatment. The Indian health budget for 1985 was 70
million crore rupees, but India has very pressing problems of
physical disease. Malnutrition, cholera and dysentery are rife.
Mental-health spending was not the priority. 'You simply can't
expect too much,' said Dr Helmut Sell, the World Health
Organisation regional officer. 'India is a poor country and, at
this level of development, with a budget of 14 rupees for all
health care for each person, you just can't expect too much.' The
World Health Organization funds three projects to serve as
models for the rest of India, but Sell echoed Reddy and Murthy:
the need far outstripped the resources.

Bihar State Mental Hospital

On 5 September 1984, the doors of Bihar State Mental Hospital
in Ranchi burst open. 500 patients stumbled out begging for food
and water. They were starving and dehydrated. Forty-eight
hours earlier the hospital staff had gone on strike. The medical
superintendent, Dr Durga Bhagat, had made no arrangements
for patients to be fed or cared for. The 500 were lucky. Many
patients did not manage to escape. Some were left to rot inside
the hospital. When local people walked in, they found thirteen
bodies lying on the ground. Photographs show skeletal patients
who must have been denied proper food for weeks. Those who
survived looked much like survivors of concentration camps.
Four days after the patients burst out, there were still 102 people
missing.

Dr Bhagat claimed that he had not been told the staff were going on strike and would leave patients to fend for themselves. His arguments did not convince the subsequent inquiry and he was sacked. Later inquiries showed that in the month before the break out forty-four patients had died.

Perhaps what is most remarkable about this story is that the Bihar State Mental Hospital was already under critical scrutiny – as Utsonomiya had been in Japan. In 1982, a journalist from *India Today*, one of the subcontinent's magazines modelled on *Time* and *Newsweek* had visited the hospital. Chaitanya Kalbag was accompanied by a photographer, Raghur Rai. They assembled a horrifying dossier. Many of the 1580 patients were eating out of the same plates as dogs. Patients were tied to their beds or to bars on the windows. There was a 'shock shop', as the patients called it, where ECT was given with a pincer-like instrument dating from the 1930s. No anaesthetic or no muscle-relaxant was available. The hospital was badly underfunded, as most Indian hospitals are. It had to feed patients on three rupees a day. The 1580 patients had to be cared for by thirteen general doctors and three psychiatrists.

Despite the publicity, the hospital continued to function poorly. In August 1986, a patient called Subodh Singh had both his eyes gouged out. He was found unconscious in a pool of blood. The hospital claimed that another patient, Harendra Singh, had attacked Subodh. After some months, four warders were dismissed for negligence. But an independent doctor concluded that the eyes had been sliced clean out of their sockets with surgical precision – some feat for a patient. This supported the rumour that a gang of professional 'cornea smugglers' was working inside the hospital, removing eyes from dead patients. The new director of the hospital, C. P. Sinha, denied this allegation. He claimed Harendra had been hallucinating and had succumbed to the delusion that Subodh Singh was seeing with his, Harendra's, eyes. Dr Sinha was away when Subodh was found but, as soon as he returned, he ordered all operations at the morgue to stop. He personally removed the shrouds from all the dead patients' heads and confirmed that all the bodies, all the eyes, were intact. Dr Sinha did concede that there had been a kind of local mini-mafia at work before he was appointed. Patients were forced to pay fees illegally. Money for food might have been embezzled. But he had stamped out such practices. He had fired thirty members of staff for taking bribes and, he added, the cornea-smuggling story was patent nonsense. Without sophisticated refrigeration equipment to keep the eyes on ice, there would be no point in stealing corneas. They would, literally, go off. Dr Sinha insisted there were no such facilities in Ranchi.

Commenting on the situation in Ranchi, Dr Helmut Sell was not too outraged by the hunger and deaths. He said, 'It would be wrong to be too critical. Conditions in the hospital were not especially bad,' given the poverty and, when pressed, he said he had 'perhaps seen worse' in India. In that, Dr Sell was grimly accurate. An unpublished survey by Dr S. Sharma of all Indian mental hospitals suggests many have fewer doctors and fewer nurses than Ranchi. Sell also accused the press of sensationalizing, and denied the cornea-smuggling story too.

In his cluttered office which is dominated by old copies of his paper and a vast map of India dating from the mid-1950s, the editor of the *Ranchi Gazette*, Balbir Dutt, explained that the local press had tried to follow up these rumours. But the cornea-thieves tale did not stand up and, ever since 1984, it had been impossible to get a journalist into the hospital. Probably conditions were still bad. Dutt did not know, however, that a group of insurance salesmen (of all unlikely people) had petitioned the Indian Supreme Court. They argued that patients were being kept in inhuman conditions which contravened the Indian constitution. Their action had led to the food budget for the hospital being raised – from three rupees per head per day to ten rupees. The Supreme Court had also instructed a local magistrate to examine in detail the state of the hospital. The fact that the biggest local paper knew nothing of these developments emphasized a point Butt made with a little embarrassment: events in the hospital, however dire, were not a big issue in Ranchi. His readers had no urge to know what went on behind the huge, white wall surrounding the hospital. This indifference is surprising, given the town's many historical links with psychiatry.

Ranchi's Other Hospitals

A mile away from the Bihar State Mental Hospital stands the Central Institute of Psychiatry funded by the Indian government. This was originally an asylum for Europeans based in Calcutta but, in 1918, the citizens of that city complained that the asylum for the European mad was making life unpleasant for the European sane. In the best traditions of Victorian England, the lunatics were moved out into the countryside. Ranchi was a hill station, so the European hospital was sited some ten miles away in the village of Kanke which houses three hospitals and a collection of market stalls. The European Asylum named its wards after the greats of European psychiatry. There is a Freud ward, a Maudsley ward and a Pinel ward. After Independence, it became the Central Institute of Psychiatry. It tends to ignore the lowly, provincial Bihar State hospital, especially now after the scandals.

In 1955, the matron at the Central Institute was told she could not marry the hospital director, Major Brocklesby Davis, and keep her job. The matron walked out and 'with just £20, I started my hospital'. Her hospital, the third in Ranchi, the Davis Institute for Neuropsychiatry, offers private care for those who can afford it.

Mrs Eleyemma Brocklesby Davis was born in Amritsar. She is still bitter at never having been mistress of the great house that is the residence of the director of the Central Institute. The major, who soon joined her in her new hospital, died in America in 1983 where he and his son had gone to purchase, among other things, model aeroplanes. Since then, Mrs Davis has run the hospital herself with the help of two nurses and two part-time doctors for 300 inpatients. The doctors defer to her even though she is only a nurse.

The major had always wanted to keep fees low so as to be able to serve the poorer mentally ill. In 1986, Mrs Davis was charging 18 rupees a day or 540 rupees a month – three times the average rural wage. This covered food, medicine, laundry, 'barber service and ECT'. Though these charges are much higher than those for ordinary accommodation in state hospitals, Mrs Davis seems constantly harried about money. Having been trained at the Maudsley, she insists on her patients being clean. A barber shaves each man every day and she bathes patients herself. 'I worry sometimes about what is going on in the hospital so I sleep in the office over there. Then, I can hear if there is any trouble.'

Mrs Davis's patients come from all over India, even Nepal. Her records list that she has seen over 35,000 cases. Many arrive 'in a very miserable condition'. She estimates that 40 per cent of patients reach her hospital in chains: 'It makes things very difficult for me and very expensive.' She has to give antibiotics to prevent skin damage. Masir Khan had arrived at her hospital with his wrists and his feet both manacled. An iron bar joined the two manacles so that he was always bent forward. These restraints made it very hard for him to walk. Mrs Davis arranged for the local cycle-shop mechanic to hack through the chains. He often has to do that because she prides herself that no one enters her wards in chains.

Sometimes new patients have refused to eat and drink for weeks and sometimes, she admits, the families have been cruel: 'There are people who think that a bit of hardship will do them good' and she saw patients who 'had had good beatings at home.' Indian schizophrenics were, she claimed, particularly liable to withdraw completely. Often, they turned up close to death. In fact, one man died just as he arrived. Mrs Davis sees herself as something of a saint and told me, none too obliquely, that there were many Mother Teresas in the world, 'Not that I am saying I am like Mother Teresa.'

In some ways, Mrs Davis is doing her best in difficult circumstances. Her fear that there won't be enough money leads her into risky short-cuts. Her wards are overcrowded. We were not allowed into the female ward and, in the main male ward, the beds were tightly packed together. Money worries also make her favour certain kinds of treatment.

Mrs Davis gives up to seventy patients unmodified ECT every morning. It is cheaper without muscle relaxant or anaesthetic. This means that other patients have to hold down the person who is about to receive the shock. Patients watch, help and wait their turn. The Royal College of Psychiatrists in its report on

ECT in Britain (Pippard and Ellam, 1981) warned that unmodified ECT could lead to joints being dislocated and bones
broken. Mrs Davis defends the practice saying ECT has fewer
side-effects than drugs. She is specially pleased with the effect on
those who have refused food and water: 'You know, if you didn't
give them ECT, they would die and, then, you give them ECT,
the change is dramatic. They eat, drink, go to the bathroom, the
facial expression changes. It doesn't seem like the same patient.'

Still, ECT is given in poor conditions in a dark room. The
oxygen bottle which is vital to get patients breathing again has a
faulty dial. The voltage at which the shock is given doesn't seem
to be controlled. Patients are shocked, lifted off the 'operating
table' and put down on the concrete floor. Most have convulsions
and are confused – partly because they don't have a muscle
relaxant. With Mrs Davis looking on, two patients told me that
ECT did not hurt and that they needed it. Her daughters, both
psychiatrists, were very worried about filming the ECT; it might
ruin the reputation of the hospital they intended to run when
their mother finally retired.

Though she claims ECT has fewer side-effects than drugs, Mrs
Davis appears to enjoy the ritual of dispensing drugs. She sits in
regal splendour at one end of a corridor. Patients line up to
receive their dose. When it comes to their turn, they kneel at her
feet so that she can drop tablets into their mouth. Mrs Davis
keeps the pills in a large wooden board with separate compartments. They bounce in and out of these compartments. I saw a
number of pills fall on the floor. Mrs Davis picked them up,
dusted off any dirt and popped them into waiting mouths. Often,
she pats the inmates on the head for she is also dispensing love.

Institutions like Mrs Davis's remain hard to judge because she
operates in a country where there is so little treatment.

Nationally funded Hospitals

The Taj Mahal dwarfs everything else in Agra. It was built by
Shah Jahan in memory of his wife. He also built another palace
where he incarcerated his father – a good case of realizing
Freudian fantasies.

The mental hospital in Agra is not typical of Indian hospitals. For some years it housed a World Health Organization research project so that it had access to money and expertise denied to most Indian hospitals.

The hospital was opened in 1880 and is set in 200 acres of ground. Much of this land is a farm which patients work. There are 497 male patients who are mainly emergency admissions. According to Dr Yadav, the professor of psychiatry, patients usually first appear in front of a magistrate before they are admitted. Yadav believes this creates unnecessary stress. He would like to see patients brought straight to the hospital. The magistrate could certify them on the wards. Like many Third World psychiatrists, Yadav sees no objections on civil-liberties grounds. The procedure would be more practical. Dr Yadav is certainly not out to fill his hospital with long-stay patients, which is perhaps why it is so telling that he did not see any objection to deciding, inside hospital, if a new patient ought to stay there. In fact, Yadav tries to get patients out within a month though many schizophrenics have to stay longer. The best they can do is to cope with the worst of the acute symptoms. Then patients are generally sent back to their villages.

Bangalore does not have the glamour of the Taj Mahal or the tourists it attracts. Its hospital, the National Institute, is in the middle of the town. Bangalore is a stylish city with a sumptuous town hall, a turf club and elegant avenues. The hospital gardens give on to one of these avenues. In many ways, the hospital capitalizes on the fact that it is so much in the town. People walk in and out of it all the time. There are two closed wards but the rest is open so that patients, relatives and the public can walk freely through the grounds. On the large central lawn people chat, squat and wait. Laundry hangs from posts. Dr Reddy is proud of the openness as he aims to admit as few people as possible. There are 400 day-care patients, most of whom spend their time doing occupational therapy. The 700 beds are for those who are most disturbed.

At one end of the lawn is a rather grim-looking building with a grille. The mesh of the grille is fine. Inside the women's locked ward the atmosphere is not grim but a little bizarre. The women spend most of the day sitting in the courtyard. A few squat. Most of the women wear regulation-blue, hospital-issue saris which are made in occupational therapy. Some women were engrossed in combing each other's hair, gently removing any hair lice. One very old woman stood shaking and scratching herself till another patient gently took her hand and led her towards a group standing in the middle where she looked bemused. None of the women looked fierce as very disturbed women in European wards often do. The nurses, in starched, white uniforms, wandered around not being particularly bossy but they were stationed strategically. No patient could move from the courtyard towards the exit of the ward without passing by a nurse. Reddy emphasized that patients in this ward were the exception – they were likely to stay for months or even years. He hoped to get most admissions out in under a month.

Even though patients do not stay long, both hospitals place much stress on occupational therapy. In Bangalore, the patients bake bread and biscuits for the whole hospital. The head of OT explained that they were able to produce an 800-gram loaf of bread for under three rupees, which meant that they were the cheapest bakers in Bangalore. They sold bread to many other institutions in the city. They also produce all the bed-sheets, linen and curtains for the hospital. Each skill has its own room. Patients specialize in one activity. It would be too confusing to shift them around. The hospital staff stress that the work is therapeutic. Dr Murthy was proud of a man who had learned to make candles so well that he had, when cured, started a candle-making business. The reality, though, is that the hospital relies on patients to work, for its budget is too small. They can earn a maximum of 60 rupees a month for their work (which is one-third of a peasant's wage) but very few got paid so much. At Agra, Dr Yadav also believes in the value of work. The farm is his favourite activity for them. One legacy of the British is hospital farms which were a feature of all Victorian asylums. As late as the 1960s, they were common in British hospitals, like Napsbury outside St Albans, but making hospital patients do real work came to be seen as putting too much pressure on them.

They needed occupational therapy which was relaxed and gentle. Yadav, like many psychiatrists in the Third World, sees work as good in itself. He hopes to create an employment exchange to get patients back into jobs as soon as they leave.

At the Central Institute of Psychiatry in Ranchi, patients make most of the ward furniture and hospital uniforms. There is a surreal-looking lawn stacked with bedframes which patients repair. All the hospitals have signs which encourage or, perhaps, bully. In Ranchi, 'Work is Worship' beams down. In Bangalore, one notice said 'To be Lazy is a Crime' and another urged, 'Keep Your Attention on the Job'.

Agra, Bangalore and CIP Ranchi are exceptional. They are all nationally funded. Most of India's forty-two psychiatric hospitals are funded by the local states. In an unpublished survey of their facilities, Professor S. Sharma found much to criticize. Many hospitals had very few qualified staff. At Dharwad, for example, a hospital with 375 beds had to manage with three psychiatrists, a medical officer and ten qualified nurses. They dealt with 3033 new outpatient cases and 14,274 old cases. In Goa, one psychiatrist, three social workers and two psychiatric nurses handled a hospital with 372 beds. In Bareilly, one psychiatrist and three doctors handled 390 beds. Many of these hospitals did have unqualified ward attendants too but there were far too few staff. The nationally funded hospitals are showpieces with higher levels of staffing and, in reality, higher standards. The state hospitals, moreover, allow their staff to take private practice. In Bangalore and the other national hospitals that is forbidden. Dr Reddy claimed that private practice harmed the standard of service to poor patients, as 'money-making attitudes take over and there is much abuse'.

As in Egypt, one is initially shocked by the perpetual question of money. In all state mental hospitals, there were different rates for different standards of accommodation and food. At Ranchi, for example, patients could pay anything from 500 rupees a month (£29) for 'a first-class independent bed' to 60 rupees for a third-class government bed. At Agra, there were also three classes of patients though 268 were there free of charge. Bangalore allows an almost aristocratic existence in a special ward if you can pay 1400 rupees a month (£78). That buys you a private room and two servants. A more modest bed, in a room with six others, will cost 280 rupees (£15.50). Drugs, investigations and treatment charges are extra. At Vellore (see below), the ward for the poor is a large room where ten families sleep together on mattresses arranged around the room. The hospital fees range from 700 rupees a week (£39) down to 150 rupees (£8.30) with a few families being treated free of charge. The charges make it clear how expensive psychiatric care is given Indian earnings. The average rural wage in Vellore is 40 rupees a week which would buy one quarter of a bed. Nationally, the average wage in India is 150 rupees. Poor patients have to be admitted if they are deemed sick or dangerous enough but they often end up living in considerable squalor or deprivation. All the hospital superintendents administered the system of different classes of care without questioning it. There was no alternative in a society as poor as India but, ironically, many were critical of private hospitals. Dr Yadav hoped there would soon be legislation to inspect and control such institutions.

Families

In his enthusiasm for all things Indian, Jung rhapsodized about the role of the family. He would not have been surprised by one interesting Indian innovation. In most American and European hospitals, there are set visiting hours so that relatives cannot come and go as they choose. In some secure hospitals, like Broadmoor and Rampton in Britain, visits take place in the dining-room in an atmosphere which many patients compare to a prison. Most people will know the less dramatic conditions in which you visit people in an ordinary hospital. It is easy to feel uncomfortable and intimidated in an alien atmosphere where medicine rules and families do not belong.

Four hours by road from Bangalore is Vellore. It has 350,000 inhabitants. In 1971, Professor Abraham Vergese, the director of the Christian Medical College's department of psychiatry, completed his survey of mental health in the town which found more mental illness around than he had suspected. The results prompted him to improvise. New ideas were needed. Why not, Verghese asked, involve families more directly in the work of his hospital?

The centre at Vellore admits only patients with members of their family or close relatives. Families live with sick relatives and are encouraged to help in the treatment. They are expected to bring them for ECT, to sit with them during insulin treatment, to accompany them to occupational therapy and take part in outdoor games. Verghese believes that such participation will make families familiar with the patient's stress points and reactions to drugs. They will become better able to see a relapse coming. Vergese views this as a process of social education. Both the patient and the family should gain confidence. The jargon may be different but the concept is similar to that of 'information therapy' in America which tries to teach patients and families as much as possible about schizophrenia. The more you know, the better you can cope. At Vellore, the approach also allows the family unit to get by with few staff. Relatives often manage by themselves. The day Joan Shenton was there she saw only two members of the nursing staff on duty in the whole centre – two young nurses in the front office. The occupational-therapy section had been temporarily closed down and the whole atmosphere was sleepy. Families were very much left to their own devices. Dr Jacob John, Verghese's deputy, assured Joan Shenton, though, that regular therapy groups were held.

Residents included the family of the managing director of a multinational company in Calcutta. Father and wife had come to be with their son who was schizophrenic. They lived in two small rooms. They also had cooking facilities and a patio. The father had taken seven weeks off work to be with his son and help in his treatment. It is hard to imagine a Western executive doing the same, if only because the industrial structure would make it virtually impossible for him to take so much time off. The parents were not sure just how much progress had been made. The mother was very worried about going home because she was not sure she would be able to handle their son.

Dr John believed her fears were realistic. He had recently spent two years working in England, an experience which made him acutely aware of the lack of community back-up in India. Families he had treated went back into the community and, then, got no help whatsoever. There were no community nurses, no psychiatric social workers, no district nurses to ease the way back into home life. The family would have to face Calcutta on their own. It would not be easy, even though they were better off than most.

Other hospitals have followed Vellore's example. There are facilities at Ranchi, Agra and Bangalore for families to live with patients. It is hard to be sure how helpful such an approach is, especially if there is not much supervision. In Ranchi, one lawyer explained smugly that he had such a high concept of family duty that he had abandoned his practice for nearly a year to live with his violent and abusive daughter. She listened passively while he described her so. He hectored her throughout a meal they had together, nagging her to have more spinach. Their psychiatrist sniped that the main problem was that the girl wanted to get away from him because she hated him but, despite that insight, they had been allowed to stay for months in a family cottage. The concept of the family in the hospital seems warm but, in fact, it can be double-edged. And might not 'sane' relatives find themselves institutionalized?

Reaching the Unreached

Every month a team of seventeen professionals drives out from Bangalore into the countryside. There are few cars on the road and, by the time you reach a village like Madhur, the city seems very distant. Dr Reddy explained that this clinic was for the poor people from the countryside. They came by bullock cart and bicycle from up to 150 miles away. As soon as I arrived, a woman was dragged in dramatically. She hung, totally limp, between the arms of two relatives. Everyone could see how she looked and they let her in ahead of the rest of the queue.

Some 300 people waited. First they were sorted by a health worker into those who needed a psychiatrist, those who needed a neurologist and those who needed some other form of medical care. Mrs Jayashalmi had brought her skinny husband from thirty miles away because he kept on running away from home, wetting himself and begging. She had had to save the money to get an auto-rickshaw to bring him. At the clinic entrance, one man acted as a marshal keeping the queue in control. At the dispensary, people pressed their prescriptions urgently through the window almost as if they were afraid the drugs would run out. The clinic, Dr Reddy said, had never run out of drugs but that was only because he had inveigled local businessmen and rotary clubs to pay for them. To save money, they used only four basic drugs. The local contributions were essential. Reddy is very committed to such satellite clinics. He was the first boy from his village to graduate. He studied at Edinburgh University and, when he went back to India, he battled with his colleagues to set up such programmes. Most resisted going out into the villages. It was beneath their dignity – and, anyway, patients would not come. 'I proved to them patients did come and it helped prevent relapses.' Reddy didn't just want to repay a personal debt to rural India; he thinks it is an effective way of delivering services to remote areas. Reddy is an able politician and has some backing from the government, but clinics like the one I visited exist in three districts, serving perhaps 1 per cent of the population. Reddy, who is a neurologist, finds it easier to get money for brain surgery. Sending coachloads of psychiatrists into the countryside may be imaginative but it lacks the glossy hi-tech feel the Indian government wants to project. Obsessed by fear of the 'Oxfam image', that India is backward and full of beggars, the government likes initiatives that glitter with the latest science. If lasers could cure depression or if optical fibres could wipe away schizophrenia, there would be more money. So Indian psychiatry has a better reputation abroad than at home.

At NIMHANS, they have developed not just Reddy's beloved satellite clinics but an altogether more aggressive approach. 'Our aim is to deinstitutionalize and deprofessionalize mental-health care in India,' said Dr Murthy. The satellite clinic depended far too much on potential patients being aware it was available. Many would never come. Adequate treatment would require psychiatrists and paramedics to scour the countryside identifying schizophrenics, epileptics and others in need. Round Bangalore they have started to do that. Murthy displayed a map with flags indicating where they had been, and where they planned to go in the future. He took me to Banawadi, a small village two hours' drive from Bangalore. Its main street winds, just wide enough for donkeys and ox-carts coming in from the fields. Dr Murthy and his colleagues made for the house of Mrs Shivamma because she showed what such an approach to community care could achieve. The 'team' stopped at a house at the end of the village. Her daughter came out on to the porch and said her mother was working in the fields. Murthy was pleased. If she was working, she must be improving. Mrs Shivamma's daughter walked with us and explained that her mother had been very difficult. She had been violent and abusive. She slept little, refused to wash and scratched children, though only those of relatives. Mr Shivamma added that she had made their lives a misery.

For ten years, Mrs Shivamma had had no treatment. She had then gone into hospital briefly but, as soon as she was out, she relapsed. Her family took to locking her in a room. In much of India, that would have been her fate but, as she lived close to Bangalore, Mrs Shivamma was identified by the team from NIMHANS.

Though there had been some previous attempts to 'reach the unreached', co-ordinated efforts to do so started in 1975 in Bangalore and Chandigarth in Punjab. Teams of one psychiatrist, one social worker and a psychiatric nurse started to make house-to-house calls to find those in psychiatric need. Such forays discovered severely mentally ill and epileptic patients in every village. Many had been ill for years. Most had gone to traditional healers who had prescribed a familiar mixture of prayers and thrashings. Few were getting any treatment when they were discovered. With so few beds available, the initial survey concluded that only 4 per cent of patients absolutely needed hospital care. Many families were initially less than grateful and rather suspicious, as being identified meant having to pay for medication and follow-ups. It was only as their relatives began to improve that they became convinced.

Murthy and his colleagues found Mrs Shivamma and put her on fortnightly injections of modecate. She gets them at the primary-health-care clinic. The improvement was magical, her daughter said. She led us to the field where Mrs Shivamma, in a dark-brown sari, was picking tomatoes. Now Mrs Shivamma could take the cow to the field and tether it herself. Mrs Shivamma looked rather tense at first but grinned she did feel better. That was due to the tablets and injections, she thought. Perfect family peace didn't reign. Her daughter sniped that she often tried not to take her pills. Mrs Shivamma added that she quite liked working again. Her only problem was having to walk the three kilometres to the health centre. Mr Shivamma was more enthusiastic about the effect of the treatment. The illness had made his family suffer terribly. Life had not been worth living. He marvelled at how much his wife had changed. For Murthy, this little scene was proof of how much could be achieved without hospital. Using drugs to stabilize someone like Mrs Shivamma made it possible for her to be healed in her community. Picking tomatoes, looking after the cow, being with her grandchildren were better forms of 'occupational therapy', Murthy argued, than anything a hospital could offer. Here was therapy in the midst of life. Murthy also thinks that the attitude of Indian families is helpful. They nag rather than reject. 'They keep on saying, why don't you get up, why don't you go to work or to the temple, why don't you try this food.' They make it much harder than in the West for people to slip into the sick role. Once Mrs Shivamma did not behave destructively, the village accepted her because 'we tend to see mental illness as something bad which comes to us and then leaves.' The demons depart. The person resumes as before with less stigma than in most societies.

I have argued throughout that the West may be a little romantic in its view of India but, in Banawadi, modern medicines and an ancient way of life were in balance. The problem is that that balance is elusive – not just outside India but within it. Mrs Shivamma was lucky because she lived close to Bangalore where, after twenty-five years, she got effective help.

* * *

The 1982 Mental Health programme is ambitious, aiming 'to ensure the availability and accessibility of minimum mental-health care for all in the foreseeable future, particularly to the most vulnerable and underprivileged sections of the population.' The sentiments are fine; the likelihood of their being implemented is small. Dr Reddy, who is very dedicated to extending mental-health provisions, is training co-professionals in Bangalore. Even he, however, does not hope to see more than one 'outreach' psychiatrist for every 2.5 to 3 million people by 1997. It will take a long time, even though they can already point to excellent results.

Since 1981, Reddy has run 225 satellite clinics at which 15,512 patients have been seen. Only 22 per cent of them had psychiatric conditions. The rest had epilepsy or a neurological problem. Twenty-five per cent of the patients did need hospital care – far more than Murthy's 4 per cent. Nevertheless, the research indicates that serious illness can be handled outside hospital and without expensive equipment. The clinics have social value too, Reddy believes. They teach the community that mental illness is not so diabolical, which is important given Indian myths, and they teach professionals the value of taking psychiatry out into people's homes: 'In my institute, everyone has to spend a month a day taking services out to the community.' And, since Reddy insists on only providing 'professional help', the villages do have to take part because they see to the keeping of records, the organization of the clinic and everything that is non-medical. A little grandiloquently, Helmut Sell thinks that India does have a great deal to teach the West about using volunteers and instilling that community spirit.

To be over-optimistic, however, would be naïve. Murthy, for example, is far from satisfied. India cannot afford hospitals. 'No matter how many reforms are made at institutions for the mentally ill, they can never be the answer. The answer lies in a non-institutional approach. But I am well aware of the fact that at present we are only achieving a 50 per cent follow-up rate after initial contact in the community and we must address ourselves to this problem.' Half the people they see never come again. Many more who suffer psychiatric illness and live outside

Bangalore never get to see a doctor or a nurse. That is not going to change fast.

For a poor country with many demands, India's community-care programmes represent an impressive achievement, but the gap between what is needed and what is available is awesome. In many parts of the book, I have argued that it is simplistic to blame the lack of money for all psychiatry's failures. Usually, money is only part of the problem and can provide only part of the solution. In India, even in national centres like Bangalore, and far more in more ordinary places, the lack of money is crippling.

It is not just that there is not enough to pay for adequate programmes. Indian doctors know very well that, with internationally acceptable qualifications, they could earn far more in Washington, New York or London. In many Western hospitals you come across Indian doctors but, in India, I did not come across a Western doctor, apart from Dr Sell who was working for the World Health Organization. It is ironic that a country which has developed a good model of community care – and where there is a reasonable chance of its being accepted in the villages – should be unable to put it into practice except in a few privileged places. In the UK, we have been talking about community care off and on for thirty years and the obstacles are very different.

My thanks to Joan Shenton for her invaluable help with this chapter.

8

The United Kingdom: A caring community

Thirty Years of Community Care

Unlike America, Britain has had time to prepare for community
care. Legal decisions did not force hospitals into sudden releases.
Community care has been government policy for nearly thirty
years. It should not, as the House of Commons social services
committee sniped in 1985, have caught any government by
surprise.

In 1959, Enoch Powell, then the Minister of Health, introduced the Mental Health Act. It was seen as a reforming
measure. Its aim was to close large old asylums, relics of the
Victorian era, compared by Powell to the large London railway
stations. The 1959 Act pledged the government to transfer
resources to care for patients outside hospitals.

Despite this commitment, the number of hospital beds did not
begin to decline significantly till the early 1970s. A few areas like
Nottingham and Napsbury pursued a policy of reducing hospital
admissions and creating alternative facilities but these were
exceptions and were not always welcomed. Napsbury, for example, had a crisis-intervention service which ran into controversy.
Many psychiatrists accused it of obstinately refusing to provide
hospital care. Ten years later, as the first asylums start to close,
there is still confusion about what services are available in their
place.

By 1991, the Department of Health hopes to have closed sixty
of the largest mental hospitals and to reduce the present beds
from 70,000 to around 45,000. Without planning, this makes
many professionals very fearful.

The British situation is different from the American one

because there is a National Health Service on which to build. So far, not enough building has been done. The passing of the 1959 Act did alter psychiatric practice and general attitudes. The hospital population began to fall, though it fell slowly.

In 1955 it was 143,000.

By 1965 it was 120,000.

By 1970 it was 111,000.

By 1975 it was 87,000.

People also spent far less time in hospital. It is probable that the least-disturbed long-stay patients were the ones who were put into the community. The more difficult ones could wait till later. Few British hospitals, however, have introduced the stages of rehabilitation that Israel has.

After the Act was passed, campaigners began to focus on patients who were wrongly detained. Larry Gostin's influential *A Human Condition* (1977) showed that many patients were not really dangerous and were kept in hospital for far too long. It was, and is, an important civil-liberties issue, but it affected only 15 per cent of patients. It may seem that organizations like MIND paid too much attention to detained patients and too little to less dramatic cases. It is easy to understand why. There were many injustices, and some men and women had spent much of their lives in special hospitals for the 'criminally insane' like Rampton and Broadmoor having done little, if any, wrong. Further, the community would never accept patients if they believed they were all 'mad axemen'. Dispelling such myths was vital or tolerance would be just a dream.

The debate MIND promoted showed that many patients could be safely released and it did shift attitudes a little. The 1983 Act, for example, took away the Home Secretary's power to detain allegedly dangerous patients. Once, that would have provoked an outcry. Mental-health issues, however, only get so much media attention and it may be that this focus on detained patients made it easy to ignore what community care would involve. There was not enough of a fight for services.

Trends are never simple. There may not have been much campaigning for community services but, by 1970, there was a lot of interest in mental health in general. The American fashion for therapy began to affect the British media. Magazine articles, radio and television programmes about depression, stress and aspects of mental health became regular features. Both women's and science magazines began to pay attention to the work of Masters and Johnson on sex therapy. Some subjects became less taboo, and this helped to create a more tolerant climate. Such advances, however, were no substitute for proper research into what new services might be needed. This absence of research into alternatives is particularly surprising both because community care was government policy and because there were many small ad hoc experiments (many of which sprang up during the 1960s) which could have been fruitfully studied. But, in practice, no one translated the commitment to community care into action.

The absence of research meant that no one attended to a quirk the statistics revealed. Fewer psychiatric beds did not mean fewer patients. In fact, the reverse was true. More people than ever before were coming into hospital but for shorter periods. While the number of beds fell as I have shown, the number of admissions actually rose.

In 1965 admissions were 156,213.

In 1970 admissions were 272,931.

In 1975 admissions were 175,111.

In 1980 admissions were 185,514.

In 1985 admissions were 199,995.

Many were elderly patients. Others were short-term, going through the 'revolving door'. Each bed had a lot of use! In Aberdeen, while resident patients fell by 25 per cent from 1966 to 1975, admissions to hospital rose by 24 per cent. There were 37 per cent more emergency hospital consultations and 41 per cent more home visits, mainly to ageing demented patients. In Nottingham the pattern was similar. More, not fewer, services were needed but, with so little ongoing research, no one knew.

Imagine, however, planning another kind of medical intervention, a new drug. Animal trials would be the first step after a scientist had a hunch that compound X might be of some good. Successful trials would lead to modifications, small tests to larger tests leading eventually to experimental human trials. Slowly, knowledge would be accumulated on which to base the decision about whether or not the drug was safe, economic and effective. Drug trials don't always work out in this textbook way but, at least, there is a model of how they should go. Community care had to develop without any equivalent model for how to test it. Advance testing of how services will work if they are reorganized appears to involve so many variables that it is assumed to be impossible. A non-medical example is classic. The 1974 UK reorganization of local government was welcomed as a great initiative which swept away such quaint entities as counties dating back to 1066; within ten years it was classed as a disaster.

The English psychologist, Donald Broadbent, argued in *Behaviour* (1961) that intuition was dangerous. Zealots created all kinds of innovations in schools, therapy and business without doing preliminary research on their validity. Intuition had one specially damaging effect; it stopped people looking for alternative explanations or solutions. By 1960, everyone 'knew' that hospitals damaged patients and the obvious, intuitive answer was to open the hospitals. Only no one looked at possible alternatives in a methodical way. It led to some ironies. For example, the Department of Health had to appoint Sir Roy Griffiths at the end of 1986 to investigate whether community care was the right solution, after all, especially for the old. Such confusion reflects the muddled recent past all too well. If Griffiths decides that community care is wrong for the elderly (which is a distinct possibility), expect more confusion.

The right time to examine alternative solutions was in the 1950s and early 1960s. But the evidence against hospitals looked very persuasive. Many psychiatrists knew that inmates got stuck for life, as seems to have happened to the royal cousins, Katherine and Nerissa Bowes Lyon. Dr Stephen MacKeith, a psychiatrist who trained in 1933, reminded me recently that we have forgotten the social stigma that existed for unmarried girls who became pregnant. Many ended up in institutions to prevent that. So, according to an influential paper on mental handicap by A. B. D. and A. Clarke (1953), did many 'defectives' who could easily have been retrained to live outside. Clarke argued that many mental handicaps were minor and that those who suffered them could be re-educated. That would not happen inside hospital. Surveys showed that little happened to people once they were admitted. Inactivity ruled. At Severalls Hospital, in Essex, for example, patients spent five hours and forty-eight minutes of their waking hours doing absolutely nothing. At Netherne, in Surrey, it was better, a mere two hours and thirty-nine minutes of total inertia. The greater the 'degree of environmental poverty', the worse symptoms became. How long someone stayed in hospital was crucial. The longer they stayed, the less they cared about being discharged. Long-stay patients preferred a safe life in the limited institution they knew, to the uncertain outside world. The hospital sapped their will to make it on their own.

Psychiatrists knew that and, by the 1970s, there were many stories of people who had been kept in hospital for too long. In 1976, I met a number of patients who had been in Napsbury Hospital for many years. One was Vi who had been sent there when she had become pregnant in 1930. She was a maid and, in all probability, the father was one of the young men of the house. Vi tried to kill herself and was admitted to Napsbury where she stayed for forty-six years. The hospital had become her town. One of the other patients, John, had become her friend. He was a tall, imposing man with slicked-back hair and a moustache. He had been schizophrenic for many years but had found religion. He had qualified as a Methodist local preacher and I saw him preach a sermon full of sin, fire and brimstone. He became used to the oddity of going from hospital to church every Sunday. In the hospital, he was a patient, a subordinate; at church, he was a leader.

In the 1970s Napbury was a hospital with a distinct philosophy. It tried to admit as few patients as possible. Those who were admitted were usually expected to stay less than two weeks. After that, they would be returned to their homes unless their condition was dire. Allied to this admission policy was a discharge policy for all long-stay patients. They were assessed with a view to placing them in residences outside. The hospital bought houses in St Albans and turned them into group homes. Nurses were on call in case of trouble. There was a practical plan. The patients were grateful for the chance to have a home of their own and expressed remarkably little bitterness about their fate. I admired the way John had tried to make the most of what had been a stunted life and how much he relished his new freedom. He and Vi had gone on holiday together, a new experience.

Such powerful evidence, anecdotal and academic, confirmed the case against hospitals. It was taken as proof of the benefits of community care. It was not logical but it is easy to see how, without considered research, it seemed to be.

Funding community care continues to be a problem. Hospitals are funded through regional and area health authorities with money from the Department of Health. These 'local' bodies decide how to spend their allocation. Health authorities have to defend the budgets of their hospitals. Many facilities for good community care are not hospital-based and need fewer doctors and nurses. Day-centres, sheltered workshops, supervised housing for ex-patients to live in come out of the budget of the local authority. Health authorities have no administrative reason to give money to local authorities. If they reduce the number of beds in a hospital, they can use the spare cash for other health services. A local authority has to prove to the Department of Health that one of its facilities is cutting the load of patients the health authority has to care for in order to be given any health-service funds. The system is cumbersome. It creates unnecessary competition between different official bodies. Occasionally there has been downright misuse. After 1974, when the Butler Committee recommended setting up special interim secure units for patients coming out of top-security hospitals, funds were allocated to some health authorities to build these units. They did not do so for eight years and used the money for more popular health needs.

Closing Hospitals

The policy of closing hospitals is easy to devise, hard to execute properly. Banstead Hospital offers a good example of the muddle that can ensue. It opened in 1877 and at one time housed nearly

2500 patients. Like Abassia, it was once a world of its own with its own farm, bakery and workshops. Patients stayed on average between twenty-three years (male) and thirty years (female). The hospital had a cemetery where many were buried. For the last three years, the hospital has been scheduled to close and began to discharge its least-ill patients. Most were sent to live either with their families or in hostels. Some hostels, like the Richmond Fellowship, specialize in mentally ill ex-patients, but many others are simply bed-and-breakfast 'hotels' run by people with no professional qualifications. Without transfer of monies to a community-care budget, nothing better could be planned.

The 'best' patients were not so hard to place. Banstead began to experience real difficulties only with others. Some were sent to live at 83 Endell Street in the middle of Covent Garden which is a converted church run by the St Mungo's Association. The hostel was meant for single homeless men, not ex-patients. Two helpers deal with 110 residents. The hostel manager conceded that they could offer little to the mentally ill. But St Mungo's does not throw residents out during the day. They can stay in and watch television. The hostel has had to evict a number of patients like one schizophrenic who refused to take his drugs and set fire to his mattress; Endell Street had no way of coping with that. Other Banstead residents are due to go to Chiswick Lodge, a hospital which has been converted to mansion-style flats. MIND have attacked the Riverside health district for not making proper arrangements for these transfers. It claims that the landlords of bed-and-breakfast houses are sometimes collecting patients from Victoria station. The landlords know that putting ex-patients up is likely to be very profitable. Was 'warehousing' ex-patients in such accommodation, a bed-and-breakfast house or in a hostel where there are no facilities, what community care aimed to achieve? Surely not.

Banstead is not a unique failure. Setting up any community-care programme requires dedication and imagination. It had taken sixteen years to set up the programme at Napsbury. In 1985, the Richmond Fellowship warned that community care was so under-financed that patients would leave hospital and have nowhere to go. The Schizophrenia Fellowship have also complained that the lack of services means that impossible strains are being put on families.

Proper community care depends also on being able to get patients admitted in an emergency. In New York that has become a serious problem. In London, there is only one twenty-four-hour emergency psychiatric clinic – the Maudsley – and that is under threat because of inadequate funding.

Telephone calls come from all over the country. Social workers, GPs and other hospitals far away refer. Jo Brand, one of the Maudsley's charge nurses, has even had to deal with a man who was put on a train from Scotland. The most constant source of 'supply', though, is the police. Both times I visited, the clinic was quiet. The only noisy emergency was a young black man who walked restlessly in front of the nurses' counter, demanding a doctor. He was getting excited and irritated. The staff, Brand told me, knew him and had to watch him with female nurses. He would try to flirt, and, then, to grab them. A strange dance followed. The man hovered round a nurse. At once other staff members would surround her. After a moment he would walk back towards her, getting excited again. Finally, he lunged to kiss her. The staff moved in and told him that they would turf him out of the clinic if there was any more nonsense.

One strain in the emergency clinic was having to be ever-vigilant. They knew this patient and he was pretty harmless. A few minutes later he had calmed down and was sitting, meekly, reading an old magazine in a battered armchair. Other 'patients' were new, unknown and could be very dangerous. Jo Brand gave an example of how bad such violence could get. The police had brought in a man so disturbed they had to use riot shields to control him. Staff had to face knives. Anyone could come in off the street, often agitated after a struggle. The staff did not have a clue as to their medical history. The porters in the rest of the hospital were meant to be on hand to deal with such violence but they were often unavailable.

Joan Shenton witnessed far more drama one night. The police brought in a young woman who was fighting, kicking and screaming. She wanted to know why she had been kidnapped. It took seven nurses to move her into a small room. She was black and accused the doctors of trying to rob her of her baby. The duty psychiatrist told her she had to have treatment but, when she refused an injection, she was 'restrained' by three nurses. I put the word in quotes because nurses are taught how to restrain violent patients. Sometimes, there is no other way. It is an old skill that nineteenth-century nurses employed to stuff patients into the straitjackets that Clifford Beers hated so much. Restraining looks like a well-co-ordinated rugby tackle. They managed to hold her down and give her a tranquilliser. It was the only way to cope with such situations. Within a minute, she began to pass out. She should have been admitted to the emergency clinic's own beds but, in the confusion, she was sent to the Villa Ward which houses the Maudsley's most difficult patients.

The emergency clinic is in the middle of an area which has many problems that are apt, at least, to aggravate psychiatric conditions. Camberwell used to be a mixed inner-city area with a large working-class population. There were pockets of better housing. Peckham, which is now seedy, was fashionable in the early 1900s. The population of Camberwell has halved since then, however, and the majority of what John Wing, a psychiatrist at the Maudsley, calls 'the most healthy' have left. The presence of the Maudsley has contributed to this trend for it has spawned many day-centres and sheltered workshops, ideal for the less healthy. Camberwell has more working-class, more elderly people and more immigrants from the West Indies and India than average.

Since 1964, the characteristics of Camberwell residents – and those who seek psychiatric help – have been logged on the Camberwell Register which records all contacts between patients and the psychiatric and social services. There are six other registers in Britain and they allow doctors like John Wing to monitor existing services, though with a big time lag. Wing published in 1987 an incisive study based on data gathered in Camberwell in 1979.

On 30 June 1979, every patient in regular contact with psychiatric services was monitored. 208 patients were in the Maudsley's wards and had been there for more than a year; 107

patients had been in hospital for less than a year. Twenty-seven patients were in a day hospital. After excluding twenty-three people who refused to be interviewed, Wing concluded that of those outside hospital, ninety-four had their needs 'met' while fifty-five had their needs 'unmet'. He based that judgement on what professionals who interviewed the patients thought would be the most appropriate care. Wing warned that even those whose needs were being met tended not to be 'stretched'. Their therapy was usually too passive. They could manage more contact with the outside world. Wing noted acidly that in an area famed for its psychiatric services, one-third of patients were not being treated adequately. He looked, moreover, only at those patients who were in the system. If Project Reach Out were to appear on the streets of Camberwell, it would find plenty of dropouts and drunks hiding from the welfare. Workers from the Maudsley itself have started to study the extent to which they are ignorant of their area's needs.

Jo Brand is doing research for a doctorate and, as part of that, she and Eileen McGinley talked to a number of black social and community workers. They visited a project in the Walworth Road called the Fanon Project, after the great Algerian psychiatrist who wrote *The Wretched of the Earth*. In the Third World, no one quotes Fanon much; in south London, he is a radical hero. Brand and McGinley found that 'racism as a potent force of social injustice adversely affects the practice of psychiatry'. Many of the black professionals they met, were unhappy about the way in which the emergency clinic and the Maudsley worked. They felt that the 1983 Mental Health Act had failed in its reforms for 'it discriminates against black people'. Forty per cent of the patients sent to the Maudsley's most secure, most difficult ward, the Villa, are black. The senior charge nurse, Andy Gibbs, was worried because local blacks perceived the ward as a place where they were likely to be treated badly. They avoided it, if possible.

The Maudsley, like most other London hospitals, did not offer adequate services for immigrant groups. The Fanon concentrated on young black men who 'escaped' 'official' services. At Fanon, no one has to attend classes or therapy; the only commitment 'visitors' have to make is to eat lunch! Fanon workers justify this apparently 'lazy' approach because the hospitals are racist and 'white middle-class stereotypes are stamped on them'. Drugs are used to control the behaviour of blacks. Brand was upset by how angry black men were about their treatment. The Maudsley, she and McGinley wrote, had to change its attitudes for it serviced a multi-racial area. But the Fanon had little time for consultants and the consultants had little time for the Fanon.

The Maudsley doesn't just have problems with the local community. Its buildings are too old. Eric Byers, the administrator, said there were back wards whose physical condition he did not approve. The Mental Health Review Commission recently visited the hospital and its private report is said to be critical of the conditions on some wards. The library can no longer acquire many books it needs. Such lack of funds is ironic because the Maudsley is such a famous institution which has influenced psychiatry all over the world. In dealing with America, I tried to suggest that money is no guarantee of providing a decent service. But if there are deep cuts in funding (which has been the case in Britain since 1979) the services do suffer. The cuts meant that in 1986 it looked as if the emergency service would have to close. It would save a great deal since it cost much in overtime. The hospital itself mounted a campaign to save the clinic – partly to obtain publicity – and eventually managed to absorb its costs into its new budget. Creative accountancy came to the rescue.

In 1987, the Maudsley became responsible for all the psychiatric services in the Southwark and Camberwell Health Area. It should lead to more rational services, Eric Byers believes. His optimism is encouraging but the evidence so far is that a centre of excellence (which the Maudsley is) has signally failed to meet the needs of the local community.

The problems of the Maudsley are particular, perhaps. In 1980, the World Health Organization (1987) commissioned a number of pilot studies throughout Europe. In Britain, Aberdeen and Nottingham were chosen. Despite the oil boom, Aberdeen remained a rather traditional Scottish town. The population is fairly stable, 'God-fearing' and not very wild. Few people are homeless because new immigrants are oil rich. However, the town does have to cater for a huge area. Severely mentally ill people come from the Shetlands, the Orkneys and the far Highlands. There is one psychiatric hospital, the Royal Cornhill, as well as some psychiatric beds in general hospitals. The average GP in Aberdeen cannot be expected to give much time since s/he will have 1900 on the list – the WHO recommends 500 population per GP. The assessment carried out for the World Health Organization concluded:

Current problems concern, briefly, the demand for psychogeriatric beds; the shortage of nurses, due partly to competition from the oil industry . . . geographical difficulties which make it hard for outpatients to attend regular clinics or day hospitals and for relatives to visit those who are in hospital; the lack of a specific unit for adolescents: continuity of patient care, e.g. when patients are transferred because their illness has become chronic or when they are admitted as emergencies to different hospitals; the general lack of hostel accommodation for patients; and the lack of special facilities for the treatment of alcoholics.

It is a fairly severe indictment, and one which is echoed by rather different studies in London.

In Nottingham the situation is better, partly because there has been a clear policy at Mapperly to reduce inpatients. The hospital claims it initiated this in the 1950s well before it was flamboyantly fashionable. As in the rest of the country, admissions have risen but patients stay in hospital less than in any other part of England. Mapperly prides itself on its facilities which include six day-centres offering 550 places, an ECT clinic, two psychiatric day hospitals and centres for children, addicts and alcoholics. The WHO assessment praises the range available. Nottingham has, in thirty years, achieved a co-ordinated plan, though they still feel there are problems related to the age of the buildings:

. . . the inadequacy at times of social and other services which should meet the needs of former patients now maintained in the community; the shortage of suitable and supervised residential facilities for the increasing number of elderly patients with dementia; local municipal difficulties in financing community facilities; and the high rate of attrition among the outpatients and day patients for whom the majority of the psychiatric services cater.

In Camberwell, Aberdeen and Nottingham, there is considerable dissatisfaction with how community care is working and the Maudsley and Nottingham are both, perhaps, exceptionally renowned for psychiatry.

A study for the York Health Authority found things were a little, but not much, better. It followed fifty patients. Only thirty-four could be surveyed since the others had either died or refused to be interviewed, a pretty remarkable fall-out rate. Five of the thirty-four were living at home a year after release from hospital. The others were in a variety of hostels. One was on the streets and two were back in hospital. One man had shuttled twenty-one times between different addresses and hospital; he had hardly 'settled'. Ex-patients complained they were not consulted about their new homes and that, often, they did not get a chance to see it before being taken there. The idea that they had a choice did not occur to officials. The survey confirmed that, in private hotels, there was 'a dearth of activities' and the city had too few community psychiatric nurses.

The Mental Health Act Commission's report published late in 1987 adds to these concerns. It points out that while its remit is limited to detained patients, it is 'very much concerned at the lack of hard information on the destination of patients'. Patients may end up either homeless or 'in premises which are unfit for human habitation'. Detained patients face a particular Catch 22. The law obliges the relevant District Health Authority to effect aftercare once the patient is released from hospital. But the patient can't be released from hospital till proper aftercare arrangements have been made. The Commission cites one case in which a patient asked in September 1985 – two years before the report was published – for housing to be made available to him after he was recommended for discharge. As the report went to press nothing had been organized and 'there is still no firm date for discharge'. The Commission's report is a thorough and radical document. It pinpoints the deficiencies of care for detained patients but also suggests many ways in which ordinary patients fare badly.

*   *   *

In all these areas, community care is not working easily and not fulfilling its expectations. Interestingly, most of these assessments, which were commissioned by doctors from doctors, make no mention of a different obstacle to establishing good community services. It is not just lack of money, public hostility and political indifference that make it so hard, it is also the conservatism of doctors themselves.

Changing the Professional Role

Britain has the big advantage over America of having a well-established National Health Service. In theory, GPs are in an excellent position to provide the basis for community care. Everyone can go to see the GP. Surgeries are in the middle of communities. The GP ought to have the influence to get a seriously ill person into hospital quickly. Over the last few years, many surgeries have started to employ specialists. At Haywards Heath, for example, the local surgery is a health centre which has the regular services of psychologists (to cope with phobias) and community psychiatric nurses (to attend to patients in their homes). But the system has not managed to deliver adequate community care. Why?

The traditional explanation is that doctors are trained to look on the body as a machine. This makes them unsympathetic to psychiatric ills even though these account for 40 per cent of all consultations. In addition, doctors are under terrible pressure since they have endless queues of patients and spend, on average, less than six minutes with each person. That's no time in which to explore any emotional issue.

A recent book, however, *The Wound and the Doctor* (Bennett, 1987), draws on much research to hint at a different explanation. The book summarizes the evidence of many studies which show that doctors themselves suffer acutely from emotional and psychiatric symptoms. They have a high rate of alcoholism, suicide, attempted suicide, drug addiction and stress diseases. The physicians have utterly failed to heal themselves. Doctors, moreover, are trained to see themselves as heroes. With scalpel and stethoscope, they fight back the terrible tide of disease. That heroic self-image does not fit with the psychological symptoms they often show. So doctors often repress and become defensive when it comes to psychiatric problems because these are all too close to home. It is patients who suffer.

The classic instance, perhaps, of how GPs fail to understand the nature of the problems they are being presented with is depression. Throughout the 1970s, patients were complaining that they came to see their GP because of real problems. They had been bereaved, a spouse had walked out on them, they were terrified of losing their job. The GP put his head down in the prescription pad and wrote a 'script' for Valium or some other anti-depressant. Talk was then of surprise when a depressed patient went home and, instead of behaving sensibly, swallowed a bottle of pills. There was an epidemic of attempted suicides. The GPs' failure to listen to harrowing problems was remarkable. Eventually, GPs came under political pressure as self-help groups and organizations like MIND warned against the twin dangers of abetting attempted suicide and tranquillizer, or tranx, addiction. Many articles and films argued the same points. It has had some impact on GPs but it is a slow process, especially as doctors resent challenges to their authority.

It is telling to compare the status of GPs in Britain with that in India and Egypt. There, the departments of health (in Cairo) and major teaching institutes have the power to insist that GPs will attend refresher courses, that they will prescribe only four 'psychiatric' drugs and that they will go out to patients in the villages. There may not be the money to provide many courses but there is the power to compel GPs to attend. No one can wield such power over the British GP.

A surprising confession of difficulties with GPs comes from two Oxford psychiatrists, Stephen and Katharine Wilson. They have been involved in setting up a special service to establish a psychiatrist in GPs' practices. In theory, the hard-pressed GP will be able to refer the more recalcitrant cases to the expert. In theory, the Wilsons found that all the GPs welcomed this initiative. They gave parties to celebrate their new colleague. As the wine and cheese-and-biscuits flowed, GPs extolled the virtues of a valuable new font of advice and 'a bonus for the multi-interdisciplinary team'. In practice, they were nervous. Was the psychiatrist going to analyse them? Was he/she going to take over? Conversations between the psychiatrist and GPs were full of veiled hostilities and tense jokes about sex and power. The Wilsons found that the GPs referred virtually no one at first. There would always be referrals 'tomorrow' but, somehow, these never came. Relinquishing control and authority was very hard for GPs. The Wilsons believe that, with time, attitudes will change. They have to, or professional rivalries and fears will undermine good initiatives.

An equally honest analysis of the ways in which professionals in the caring industries often don't realize what they are doing comes in a brave book published in 1985, *The Politics of Mental Health* (Banton et al., 1985), which I criticized earlier for its lack of interest in the Third World. In it, five psychologists and social workers describe their work. All of them see themselves as feminists and socialists, committed to giving power to the people. Individuals, they knew, often needed money rather than therapy. Their worthy, radical self-images began to be dented as they read each other's descriptions of their daily work. They all noticed the painful fact that they had decisive power over 'clients'. They could give or deny them access to services and benefits. They had practised for years without facing that fact. It made them too uneasy. Their uncomfortable discovery forced them to confront their roles as agents of the state, which conflicted with their ideology. It shamed them to admit that they preferred their unthinking radical view of themselves. They wondered just how this confusion – seeing themselves as power-less while they wielded power – affected the way they treated clients. The authors were not examining what effect this had on their attitudes to community care but their experiences, and those of the Wilsons, suggest some subtler reasons for profes-sional hostility to it. There are also more obvious ones. Well-run community care takes power away from doctors. It undermines 'imperial' psychology. Psychiatrists are only human and prefer not to lose privileges.

It may seem odd that Britain, with its reputation for stiff reserve, should see such examples of self-analysis on the part of professionals who, the world over, tend to leave revelations to the patients or clients. But the results offer rather an unusual insight into why there is so much resistance to real change.

New Needs

Community care has coincided with profound changes in British society in the last thirty years. I want to examine two new areas of need – new immigrants and the elderly. In both cases, but for very different reasons, there are large failures. If community care is to succeed, it needs to be more responsive to the needs of new groups.

In May 1986, MIND held a conference on racism in psychiatry at which a number of black doctors and social workers voiced bitter complaints. Much research suggests that the needs of West Indian and Indian patients are not met. At the seminar, Maurice Lipsedge, a consultant at Guys Hospital, gave an update on a study he had carried out with Ronald Littlewood (Lipsedge, 1986). They found that men and women born in the West Indies were far more likely to be diagnosed schizophrenic than whites. Some forms of exuberant Caribbean behaviour looked crazed to the more subdued doctors of London. Not only West Indians were wrongly diagnosed; Indians fell halfway between the native and West Indian population. Lipsedge believed that doctors had to acknowledge their own prejudices which led them to see black patients, particularly young men, as more of a risk, who deserved more readily to be hospitalized. Aggrey Burke, the only Afro-Caribbean psychiatric consultant in London, told Jo Brand that British doctors thought West Indians were 'stupid'. Such an absence of senior Afro-Caribbean doctors points to racism within the profession.

Lipsedge and Littlewood have been only partially successful in modifying practice. Lipsedge, very honestly, told the MIND conference that he had sometimes gone too far the other way and not admitted a black person who needed hospital care. It had been a terrible mistake on a number of occasions.

Lipsedge's paper was greeted with enthusiasm by the seminar. He was telling them what they felt, from their own experience, to be the truth. That is not an objective test but it is surely worrying that projects like the Fanon are in danger of becoming black ghettos. An effective community care policy would seek to integrate immigrant patients. Instead, the lack of acceptable services is driving them into more social isolation and resentment. Given what Brand and Lipsedge have found, it is understandable, but it is also a mark of failure.

There is a London-wide project called Nasisyat which aims to provide counselling both for West Indian and Indian clients. They claim that the British simply do not manage to treat people from different cultures even when they employ psychiatrists from those cultures. Often, of course, a hospital may have an Indian psychiatrist but he may be a Hindu who speaks Gujerati which is not that useful in treating Sikhs. But it is not just a question of language. Psychiatrists tend to adopt the attitudes of the elite and, in Britain, that is of middle-class whites. The fears of the Fanon are borne out in a new study (Littlewood, 1987) which shows more British-born blacks are also being diagnosed schizophrenic and being detained. It may be ignorance; it may be racism; it may be stress. The study highlights a need in community care that Enoch Powell certainly did not suspect in 1959.

With the elderly, the failure is not so much a question of prejudices against people but against institutions.

By the year 2001, over 2 million people will be aged eighty or over in the UK. Over a fifth will suffer from some form of dementia, probably Alzheimer's disease which creates plaque on brain cells and disrupts connections between them. Ironically, better physical medicine is creating a new crisis for psychiatry, for the brain often gives out before the body.

In 1976, I visited the back wards of a psychiatric hospital in Dingleton. At the far end of the hospital, were the 'psychogeriatric wards' where the old came to die. As in Israel, there were different wards for different stages of illness. But whereas in Israel the aim was progress to the community, on the back wards it was progress to the coffin. Each ward managed progressively feebler patients. On the last ward, patients were doubly incontinent. Many had tremors. They spent all day in bed. They could not speak. The nurses explained that it helped to pat their shoulders. The atmosphere was terrifying. Here were bags of skin, bone and brain where nothing human worked any longer. Though the nursing care was adequate, it was clear that once an elderly demented person entered they could only emerge dead. The wards smelled of urine and despair. It was such facilities that community care was meant to improve. Two recent studies suggest it hasn't succeeded.

A recent study carried out at the University of York (Norman, 1987) found that elderly demented people who were discharged from hospital ended up all too often in distressing circumstances outside. Some had died. Of the rest, 40 per cent were back in hospital within a year due to a lack of support and strain on the families.

In a study for the Centre of Policy on Ageing, Alison Norman (1987) found that the majority of old demented people were cared for by their families 'often at great personal cost'. Children sacrificed their freedom to look after old parents. It was nerve-wracking to have an old person who might wander away or set fire to the house. Demented people require twenty-four-hour care and easy access to a psychogeriatric team. Few get it. Norman argues that one should not be rigid in the commitment to community care. Even if 90 per cent of demented elderly could be looked after in their homes, there would still have to be 6600 more long-stay beds in the country. She doubts however, that 90 per cent is a realistic figure for those who could be so independent.

We are prejudiced against institutional care, Norman maintains, because we have been so heavily influenced by the grotesqueries of old asylums. Institutions do not have to be depressing. She examined fourteen homes for the elderly and some of them were more than adequate. Inmates had privacy and stimulation. Relatives were encouraged to visit. She suggests it is wrong to separate the demented from other infirm old people as that creates stigma. Without such new institutions old people are likely to be cared for at home till they become so difficult that there is no alternative but to put them in the back wards of a psychiatric hospital. There, they will decline 'far more quickly than they might under a care scheme specially adapted to their needs'. Such homes could include programmes designed to maintain the new capacities of elderly people, such as memory clinics which encourage discussion of their past. That does more than might be expected to counter dementia. We have become too prejudiced against institutions, Norman concludes, and deny them the useful role they might perform.

The Backlash

Some psychiatrists have used evidence of the failure of community care to argue for a return to old policies and to old hospitals.

In Britain, perhaps the most forceful exponent of this backlash is Maurice Weller of Southampton University who has noted that bed and breakfast places are full and that the prison and homeless populations are rising. Weller claims that this rise is due to patients committing minor offences. They are desperate to get back into an institution. The humane answer is to reopen the hospital doors. Weller does not seem to know of Cournos's work which shows there is no neat transfer between institutions in New York. The extra prison population there, at least, is not made up of ex-patients or even of those who ought to be in hospital.

A backlash would be tragic, almost perverse. There is now enough experience from different societies to see what framework will provide good services. It will differ from place to place and it will not be easy to evaluate, but that reflects the 'messiness' of psychiatry itself. Take the question of the criteria for success. If fewer people enter hospital, does it prove that community care is succeeding or that needs are being neglected? Then, in individual cases, whose judgement as to cure matters? The doctor's? The family's? The interdisciplinary team's? The patient's? In most branches of medicine, the doctor asks the patient if s/he feels better. The patient is the best judge except in a few conditions. Only a very peculiar doctor would say, 'Ah, Miss Jones, you may say you're fine but I know better.' In psychiatry, the patient is not the judge. At best, the patient is one of many voices. In judging the success of community care, it is important to acknowledge this diversity. Ideally, the patient will feel better living in the community. His family will not feel imposed upon and the community will feel it has gained too. The research done on community care, however, rarely acknowledges that the criteria have to be so complex. That is not surprising because there is no methodology that can easily handle how to decide if a policy works, given that it has to be judged from such a variety of viewpoints. So the main criteria tend to be simpler: whether community care programmes keep patients out of hospital and cost less. And even then 'successes' come under attack.

The reaction to a recent (1986) paper about Australia shows how some psychiatrists remain hostile. Hoult is a psychiatrist in Melbourne committed to community care. He allocated new patients randomly either to a community care programme or to hospital treatment. Each patient was given an envelope to open which determined his or her treatment. Hoult is at pains to reassure that the hospital programme was good. It included daily visits from doctors and a full set of activities on each ward. The experimental group was never let in the hospital. Hoult, or one of his team, took them home where all treatment took place. If drugs had to be given, they were given at home. Usually, the team first talked to the patient and his family for two to four hours. Patients were seen again the next day and the team stayed in regular touch offering medication, counselling, whatever seemed needed. As Hoult records it, the procedure sounds very similar to that at Napsbury.

Comparisons favoured those handled in the community. Three months after the first contact, they had done better. They had fewer symptoms and reported they were happier with the care they had received, as did their relatives. The group admitted to hospital had more stubborn symptoms. Twelve months later, the community group had improved more while those in hospital did worse on a number of psychological tests like the General Health Questionnaire (which assesses how well you feel and how your health has changed over time – Goldberg, 1972.) The programme did succeed in keeping patients out. Only 24 per cent were admitted to hospital, and most for less than a week. Only 6 per cent were admitted for longer. Those first treated in hospital stayed for longer.

Hoult concludes that a community care programme needs

intensive involvement at the start. The first two to four hours spent with the patient and relatives are crucial. It created the climate for the treatment and led patients to expect to stay out of hospital. One team, as with Napsbury, had to continue the treatment. Changing doctors, social workers or nurses was destructive. Hoult recommended a particular style of intervention, assertive but not intrusive. Unfortunately, Hoult doesn't give any specific examples of this rather refined divide. A personal case manager had to be available whom the patients could reach quickly. Often, they needed practical help with housing, social service benefits or other issues. Finally, Hoult stressed the importance of twenty-four hour cover. A proper service cannot be confined to office hours. The 'necessities' are considerable but Hoult calculated it was still cheaper than hospitalization.

The reaction to Hoult in the *British Journal of Psychiatry* has been critical. Two letters attacked his conclusions. One grumbled that it was unfair to compare ordinary hospital treatment with the enthusiastic care Hoult gave those in the community. A researcher in the unscientific business of confirming his hunches will pull out all the therapeutic stops. Where, complained T. H. Turner, was the null hypothesis. Further, Turner pointed out that 40 per cent of the sample did need to go to hospital. Hoult had set up a 'false dichotomy between hospital and community care'. Yet Hoult's conclusions fit in with other international studies which suggest that if professionals change their style of work slightly, then community care might have more of a chance.

Assertive Care

In their survey of America, Fuller Torrey and Sidney Wolfe (1986) were impressed with the services in Dane County, Wisconsin. About 1110 seriously mentally ill adults live in the County. Since 1977, the number of inpatient hospital days has fallen from 10,000 days to 2600 in 1985. The ill, however, are not to be found wandering the streets. 'Assertive case management' makes sure they get medication and that if they fail to turn up for appointments, professionals go out to find them just as the social workers did in Sderot. Vulnerable individuals are not allowed to disappear in the cracks between the bureaucracies. This pursuit of patients may well turn out to be a crucial feature of successful community care. I saw it at work in New York when social workers from Project Reach Out persuaded 'clients' on the street, like Wallis, to go in for his shot of prolixin. The last time he had failed to do that, he had been beating on their car trying to save them from a non-existent fare. Bob Couteau was assertive in obliging Walter to get his injections because otherwise the 'black cloud' would drag him down. In Britain, very few patients get assertive treatment. At best, hospitals and GP surgeries send out appointment cards asking why a visit was missed. The only exceptions are for patients who are under some form of probation like Tony. Tony had been in Broadmoor for two years and, though he lives in a flat, if he fails to turn up for his monthly injection, social workers or, at times, the police come to find him. But Tony is considered a potential danger. 'Safe' patients get no such 'privileges'. And the anxieties about power that social workers revaled in *The Politics of Mental Health* (Banton et al., 1985) suggests that British workers will need to drop certain 'radical' assumptions to impose treatment.

In Dane County, assertive case management means that the mental health workers can find reasonable housing, mainly through the YMCA, for their clients. Some jobs are also available through Goodwill Industries. Dane County succeeds, Fuller Torrey and Wolfe 'speculate' (and it is only that), because the county has full control of how money allocated to mental health is spent. The County could choose whether to invest in hospitals or in community facilities and how to balance that mix.

Torrey also believes that certain local factors in Madison make it a good territory for such an assertive style. It houses the University of Wisconsin which is innovative. Still, even Dane County is not perfect. Fuller Torrey and Sidney Wolfe give it 5 out of 5, but point out that there are waiting lists for many services. Some families complain it is hard to get people into hospitals in emergencies and some mentally ill persons still fall 'between the cracks'.

An evaluation by Stern and Test (1986) also found that the

system in Dane County worked well. Violent crime had not increased despite the drop in hospital admissions. There was no evidence that disturbed individuals spent longer in police custody or that the jail population had increased. But these plaudits are not unanimous. In a generally critical review, Tantum argues that there is evidence of an increase in suicides, and attempted suicides, in Dane County. The evidence in favour, Tantum snipes, is inconclusive. If the only facility to which patients can be sent is a hostel, do they do worse 'out' than they did 'in' hospitals? Tantum questions how ill patients were anyway. Do not the really ill end up in hospital? Additionally, he suggests that community care is probably not cheaper. Thirdly, he wonders if the results which claim that community patients show fewer symptoms might not be biased. Hospital patients would have mastered their 'sick' role and, to please doctors, would report more symptoms having become practised players of the medical game.

There is another side to the medical game, though. Research continually throws up the fact that many people who need psychiatric help do not seek it. A study of West London showed, for example, that perhaps 15 per cent of those with minor psychiatric symptoms had not gone to a GP. I am not conjuring a new panacea but assertive social work seems to have something to offer that more traditional approaches do not. It forces doctors, community nurses and social workers to pay attention to gaps in services, to the much quoted 'cracks' through which patients can slip to oblivion. It requires better co-ordination of services, more professionals talking to each other. The all-too-late research that has been done makes it hard to trumpet the magic of any one approach and easy to be wary of simple solutions. An assertive style is only part of the answer, at best, but it is a part worth fostering, researching and experimenting with – even if it means jolting professionals into 'odd' behaviour such as 'selling' their services to the needy.

One of the more curious aspects of the community care debate is the way it has remained a professional debate. Doctors have succeeded in dictating its terms and excluding many potential contributors.

Paradoxically, good community care may need both more assertive health workers and more assertive patients. Throughout this book, the question of self-help has not yet been raised. If that is a little odd, it reflects professional controversies about community care. Yet, not to involve self-help is almost perverse. Community care implies, surely, that the community should not just tolerate the mentally ill but get involved in helping them. Among the groups best placed to provide that are fellow sufferers or those who have managed to overcome their illness. After a 'career' as a mental health patient, someone may well have much to offer others. A well-organized community care system would draw in such self-help groups.

In America, NAMI is a good example of such self-help. In Britain, too, there is a solid framework on which to build. *Someone to Talk to*, a self-help directory, lists over 20,000 associations for depressives, agoraphobics, claustrophobics, even thunder phobics who meet at Waterloo Station during storms, according to Maurice Lipsedge. Other groups cater for those dependent on drugs, tranquillisers, gambling or alcohol. Some organizations are fleeting but many others, like Narcotics Anonymous and some local depressives groups, are solid. Meetings are held regularly, outings arranged, discussions thrive. Such groups have strengths professionals rarely have. Its members will know what it is like to be depressed, to have hallucinations, not to be able to step outside the house. They will speak a common language and will know the reproach of families and the fear of getting sucked under again. Self-help has its limitations, of course. It cannot offer twenty-four-hour care but it can offer advice, a voice on the telephone, some befriending, a personal concern that can make a difference. But little of the community care literature acknowledges the importance of such groups.

Self-help groups challenge the authority of psychiatrists. Ex-patients have the irritating habit of questioning the assumption that doctors know best. They have strong views about drugs and their side-effects. Sometimes, they find ways of coping not mentioned much in the research literature. Little of the knowledge self-help groups deploy is scientific or medical, but it has its place and ought to be heard. But for professionals really to listen is often harder than they imagine.

Recall the issues raised in *The Politics of Mental Health*. Idealistic, socialist social workers were shocked when they realized how much power they had and used. Doctors accept the power of their role which makes for conflicts with other professionals. Psychologists and social workers in some teams, for example, want a say in what medications are used. It is bad enough to be asked to share power with co-professionals, but imagine being asked to share power with patients or clients. *The Politics of Mental Health* showed how easy it was for professionals to deceive themselves that they were being democratic to their clients. Self-help groups challenge the authority of experts. If they work well, they are a threat; if they work badly, they are a nuisance. Either way, it is easier to exclude them from the planning of community care – even though they should be a key part of it.

Though it had time to plan, Britain will follow America unless there is rapid and imaginative action. The signs are not promising. The Treasury has cut the community care budget by £12 million for 1988 and, in the recent general election, no party made community care one of its major issues. The Labour Party seems tied to unions who want to fight for more hospital facilities within the NHS; more beds, shorter waiting lists are its focus. The Conservatives fantasize that good community care can be had on the cheap. The Alliance did not make it a priority issue either.

We are paying the price for a lack of research, of preparation, of commitment. Enoch Powell is a politician who prides himself on his sense of history. He has been very willing to remind the public of the dire warnings he issued about immigration and the changes that would flow in the composition of the British population. He has been rather more silent about the fate of the community care policy he initiated with such optimism in the 1959 Act. His silence is unfortunate. Powell knows better than most that the present confusion can be blamed, largely though not wholly, on government inaction. No Labour or Tory administration fought for – and financed – the ideals of the 1959 Act. Powell could have offered powerful reminders of an honourable commitment to a sensible, sensitive transfer of people from hospitals. In introducing the 1959 Act, he said, rightly, it would need money and changes in public and professional attitudes. The failure to provide these has not made Powell return to the topic.

Meanwhile, the House of Commons Select Committee on Social Services (1985) warned that 'any fool can close a long-stay hospital. It takes more time and trouble to do it properly and compassionately'; that inappropriately discharged patients 'may end up taking their own lives if not other people's', and that, 'community care on the cheap would prove worse in many respects than the pattern of services to date.'

I have tried to identify some ways of dealing with this situation and draw further conclusions in the next chapter but it is a sad comment on twenty-eight years in which so little preparation was done.

9

In Search of Solutions

Are there any answers? It would be easy to be completely pessimistic and give in to despair. I also think it would be wrong. It is possible to see some ways in which one could dramatically improve the situation of the mentally ill both in rich and in poor countries. It is not simply a question of money, though money is vital. It is also a question of better planning, better motivation among professional groups and more compassionate public attitudes. None of these is an impossible ideal.

In particular, I suppose, I would not like this book to be used as evidence for the need to retreat to the hospitals. Everything I have seen suggests that while community care is not a panacea and is not easy to implement, it offers patients a better life than anything else. Going back on it now would be retrograde. The critical knowledge we have acquired of the failures of community care so far ought to allow us to plan a better future – not abandon it. The following 'recommendations' are a start, they are not exhaustive.

1. The Law

We need a fair framework of mental health laws. It is not enough to rely on general declarations like the United Nations Charter. These were never drafted with the mentally ill specifically in mind and governments do not really see them as affecting medical minorities. Yet laws do make a difference. In countries with few safeguards, like Japan, patients fare worse. Good laws may not make good care but they help create a climate in which it is possible. The Kyoto group was surely right to emphasize the freedom of patients to communicate with the outside world. That will, at least, prevent the isolation which has led to many patients being incarcerated for years. A specific right to use telephones, to write un_____ _____ access to lawyers needs to be incor_____ all countries should have some _____ patients. It must be quick and _____ This is not sniping against ps_____ someone is not just a medical _____ l factor but so is the tolerance _____ the family to accept him. It is _____ dangers against what society w... _____ experts in the mental state but they have no specific experience in tolerance, public opinion or, even, family dynamics. The composition of tribunals and review bodies must reflect that. Some psychiatric decisions are too complex to be left simply to psychiatrists.

Finally, any charter has to guarantee a right to be treated. It is fine for the Kyoto group to call for voluntary treatment but it is also needs to emphasize the need for treatment, per se. In too many parts of the world, it is lacking.

2. *Funding*

Mental health needs a reasonable degree of funding to be spent on the mentally ill and not diverted to more popular needs. What is most galling is that money should be allocated and then spent on other facilities. *The Care of the Seriously Mentally Ill* (Torrey and Wolfe, 1986) suggested that, in America, the most cost-effective policies came when local communities controlled the spending of the budget. The federal and state governments determined the total sum which cities were then free to spend as they saw fit. Most concentrated on improving community services by making them more assertive, seeking out those in need. One of the most striking conclusions of the Torrey Wolfe report was that there was no link between the amount of money states spent per capita on mental health and how good community services were. Torrey and Wolfe did not go on to recommend slashing budgets but they did warn that everything depends on how the money is used. Wisconsin, they suggested, spent money wisely because its local bodies made decisions about whether to have a community clinic or a new ward; New York did not because its decisions were essentially bureaucratic and it was a long time since the 'chiefs' of the Office of Mental Health had been out in the streets. Local control of these budgets may be the best guarantee of good community service, not just out of compassion but precisely because what does or does not happen in mental health facilities affects life out in the street (unless, as in Japan, you lock everyone away).

3. *Hospitals.*

There is no doubt that hospitals will continue to be needed both for a small minority of very sick and very dangerous patients and for short periods for others when they are in an acute phase. Hospitals should not be seen as isolated facilities outside community care but as part of the community provision. In Bangalore they were astute at this, moving patients in and out of occupational therapy during the day and letting the public wander through the hospital grounds.

4. *Training.*

If community care is to work it will require changes in medical training. Most crucial, psychiatry has to become more fashionable as a speciality. Then, psychiatrists have to be more willing to share power and authority with nurses, social workers, psychologists and others because, as I have tried to argue, community care requires far more than just medical expertise.

This will not be easy for doctors to do. Doctors are used to being sought out by patients. They turn up at clinics and surgeries. Few doctors operate in an aggressive way, seeking people out. Yet they will have to develop such skills, much like outreach workers trawling for drugs addicts. Clearly, such a style is not impossible. NIMHANS do it a little; in Britain, the experience of drug workers show that it can be effective in finding those who need help. With addicts, the problems are just starting when you identify them; with the mentally ill, treatment is generally easier. All this requires changes in the training and attitudes of doctors. It is remarkable that psychiatrists, for example, still get very little grounding in psychology, sociology and even how to handle public attitudes.

5. *Changing public attitudes.*

There is also a clear need for public information campaigns. Even in the sophisticated West, fear and ignorance persist. New

York may be full of joggers brimming with insight but they still seem worried if there is talk of a hostel for the mentally ill next door. With less unnecessary fear, it might be easier to site that hostel in the street. Those who tremble because they fancy ex-patients will attack them should be better informed and know the risk is not that high. The community needs accurate information about mental illness if it is to accept the mentally ill. Governments are best placed to provide that through concerted information campaigns.

6. *Local needs.*

I argued at the start of the book that the international 'medical market' made Western psychiatry too influential. The training of psychiatrists must begin to reflect regional and ethnic differences far more. It may be a nuisance but psychiatrists need to recognize they are dealing with diseases which are affected by the local culture.

7. *Non-medical support.*

The evidence shows that, among the variety of services a community should provide, self-help groups could play a big role. It is not easy for professionals to accept the advice of non-professionals, even less ex-patients, but they should learn to listen. Groups have a great deal to offer both by way of support, like ENOSH in Israel, and also as a safeguard to take up patients' complaints.

Such groups can help remedy one oft-cited failure. Once they leave hospital, patients lose touch with helping agencies. Only after a crisis do they get noticed. Groups can keep in contact with patients and befriend them so they don't get isolated or lost when they come out of hospital. Many of the tragedies like Rikki's murder or the Staten Island ferry deaths were not the result of patients rejecting care but of their failing to get it. Luckily, few of those who are not treated react by killing someone but it would be perverse not to acknowledge the evidence. Patients go berserk, usually, when they slip through the 'cracks' in the system. There are exceptions, of course, but the answer would seem to be to dam the cracks rather than damn the patients. It would be a pity if this were forgotten as some experts search for arguments against community care and try to fuel an utterly inappropriate backlash.

None of these 'recommendations' will magically transform the lot of the world's 250 million mentally ill. But the despair and apathy the present situation breeds is neither realistic nor helpful. It is time to recognize that much can be done to improve it. After thirty years, the temptation for many seems to be to pillory community care as yet another solution that failed. To do that would, I think, be to draw the wrong lesson. Community care is not perfect but it is probably as close to a good solution as we are ever going to get. Making it work requires legal reforms, changes in attitudes, refinements, pressure, commitment and a sharp eye for different local needs. Many professionals see that; others need to summon up some new enthusiasm. Such an agenda is less glamorous than trumpeting 'We had it all wrong before, and, here, at last, hot off the press, is the new solution', but, in the end, working away at community care is likely to be more successful. That success will mean changing the lives of many mentally ill people for the better – which is surely worth fighting for.

Bibliography

Argyle, M. (1952) *Religious Behaviour*. London: Methuen.

Bain, T. (1873) *Mind and Body*. London: H. S. King Ltd.

Banton, R., Clifford, P., Frosh, S., Lousada and Rosenthall, J. (1985) *The Politics of Mental Health*. London: Macmillan.

Beers, C. (1907) *A Mind That Found Itself*. Republished 1981 by Pittsburgh University Press.

Bennett, G. (1987) *The Wound and the Doctor*. London: Secker and Warburg.

Ben Tovim, D. (1987) *Development Psychiatry*. London: Tavistock.

Benyamini, K. (1976) *School Psychological Emergency Intervention*. Mental Health Society, 3, 22–32.

Bhore Committee (1946) *Report on Mental Health Services in India*. New Delhi.

Brand, J. and McGinley, E. (1984). 'The Fanon Project'. *Bethlem Gazette*.

Broadbent, D. (1961) *Behaviour*. London: Eyre and Spottiswode.

Brown, P. (1985) *The Transfer of Care*. London: Routledge and Kegan Paul.

Butler Committee on Mentally Abnormal Offenders (1975) Command paper 6244.

Clare, A. (1976) *Psychiatry in Dissent*. London: Tavistock.

Clarke, A. B. and Clarke, A. (195?) *Mental Deficency* London: Methuen.

Cohen, D. (1981) *Broadmoor* London: Psychology News Press.

Cohen, D. (1987) *The Development of Play*. Beckenham: Croom Helm.

Cooper, D. (1971) *Death of the Family*. Harmondsworth: Penguin Books.

Deutsch, A. (1948) *The Shame of the States*. New York: Harcourt Brace Jovanovitch.

Digby, A. (1986) *Medicine and Morals*. Cambridge: Cambridge University Press.

Dyer, W. (1984) *Your Erroneous Zones*. New York: Bantam.

Eysenck, H. J. (1952) 'The effects of psychotherapy and evaluation.' *Journal of Consulting Psychology*, 16, no. 5, pp 319–24.

Eysenck, H. J. (1986) *The Decline and Fall of the Freudian Empire*. Harmondsworth: Penguin Books.

Fanon, F. (1966) *The Wretched of the Earth*. Harmondsworth: Penguin Books.

Freud, S. (1932) *The Future of an Illusion*. London: Hogarth Press.

Goffman, E. (1961) *Asylums*. Harmondsworth: Penguin Books.

Goldberg, D. P. (1972) *Detection of Psychiatric Illness by Questionnaire*. Oxford: Oxford University Press.

Gorman, M. (1956) *Every Other Bed*. Cleveland: World Publishing.

Gostin, L. (1977) *A Human Condition*. London: MIND.

Gostin, L. (1986) Paper presented to World Federation of Mental Health Conference. House of Commons Social Services Report 1985.

Higginbottom, H. (1986) *Third World Challenge to Psychiatry*. Hawaii: University of Hawaii Press.

Hoult, (1986) 'Community Care of the Acutely Mentally Ill'. *Brit Journal of Psychiatry*, vol. 149, pp. 137-44.

Hudson, L. (1975) *Human Beings*. London: Jonathan Cape.

Ishiguro, K. (1986) *An Artist of the Floating World*. London: Faber and Faber.

Ingleby, D. (editor) (1981) *Critical Psychiatry*. Harmondsworth: Penguin.

International Commission of Jurists (1985) *Report on Japanese Psychiatry*. Geneva.

Jahoda, M. (1981) *Employment and Unemployment*. Cambridge: Cambridge University Press.

Jung, C. (1968) *Analytical Psychology*. London: Routledge and Kegan Paul.

Kesey, K. (1962) *One Flew Over the Cuckoo's Nest*. London: Picador.

Klabag, C. and Raghur Rai (1982) Bihar State Hospital, February issue. *India Today*.

Kyoto declaration *The Lancet*, 26 March 1987.

Laing, R. D. (1966) *The Divided Self*. Harmondsworth: Penguin Books.

Laing, R. D. and Esterson, A. (1968) *Families of Schizophrenics*. London: Tavistock.

Leighton, A. (1982) *Caring for the Mentally Ill*. New Haven: Yale University Press.

Leighton, A. (1986) 'The Initial Frame of Reference of the Stirling County Study: Main Questions Asked and the Reasons for them', in J. Barrett and R. Rose (eds) *Mental Disorders in the Community*. Guilford.

Lipsedge, M. (1986) Paper presented to South East MIND Regional Conference on racism.

Littlewood, R. and Lipsedge, M. (1981) *Culture Bound Syndromes in Cross Cultural Psychiatry*. Beckenham: Croom Helm.

Mclaughlin C. and Parkhouse J. (1972) Career Preference of 1971, Lancet, II, 1018–20.

The Mental Health Act Commission (1987) second biennial report. London: HMSO.

Murthy, S. (1985) 'Mental Health Services', *India Community Mental Health News*, 1. Bangalore: NIMHANS.

Neki, J. S. (1973) 'Psychiatry in South East Asia', *British Journal of Psychiatry*, vol. 121 pp 25–69.

Norman, A. (1987) *Provision for the Elderly*. Centre for Policy on Ageing.

Ornstein, R. (1976) *The Psychology of Consciousness*. Harmondsworth: Penguin Books.

Pereschkian, N. (1985) *Oriental Tales as Tools in Psychotherapy*. Springer.

Pippard, J. and Ellam (1981) *Electroconvulsive Treatment in Great Britain*. London: Royal College of Psychiatrists.

Rack, P. (1982) *Race, Culture and Mental Disorders*. London: Tavistock.

Rahman, R. (1967) 'Psychiatry in East Pakistan', *Pakistan Medical Review*, pp 11–29.

Reddy, N. (1986) 'Implementation of National Mental Health Programme in India, *NIMHANS Journal*, 4, 77–84.

Scull, A. (1983) *Museums of Madness*. Harmondsworth: Penguin Books.

Sharma, S. (1985) *A Textbook of Psychiatry*. Vikis: Delhi.

Sharma, S. (unpublished) *A Survey of Indian Mental Hospitals*. Made available by the author.

Someone To Talk To directory (1985). London: Mental Health Foundation, (distributed by Routledge and Kegan Paul).

Stern A. and Test B. (1986) *Dane County*: Am. J. Psychiatry.

Szasz, T. (1972) *The Manufacture of Madness*. London: Routledge and Kegan Paul.

Tantum R. (1986) A reply to Hoult, letter in the *British Journal of Psychiatry*, vol. 149, p. 200.

Toffler, A. (1970) *Future Shock*. London: Pan.

Torrey, E. F. and Taylor, R. L. (1973) 'Cheap labour from poor nations', *American Journal of Psychiatry*, 130, 428–34.

Torrey, E. F. and Wolfe, S. (1986) *The Care of the Seriously Mentally Ill*. Washington DC: Public Citizen Health Research Group .

Turner, T. H. (1986) A Response to Hoult, letter in the *British Journal of Psychiatry*, vol. 149, p. 202.

Varma, L. P. (1980) 'The History of Psychiatry in India', *Indian Journal of Psychiatry*, vol. 23, p. 316f.

Verghese, A., Benjamin, V. and Sunderrao, P. S. (1971) *A social and psychological study of a representative group of families in and around Vellore*. Mimeo. New Delhi: Indian Council of Medical Research.

Walsh, M. (1985) *Parents are psychovermin: why are you being blamed?*

Watson, J. B. and Watson, R. R. (1928) *The Psychological Care of the Infant and Child*. New York: W. W. Norton.

Wiesel, E. (1985) *Souls on Fire*. Harmondsworth: Penguin Books.

Wing, J. K. (1986) 'Long Term Care in Schizophrenia', contributions from epidemiological studies in the UK in Barrett, J. and Rose, R. *Mental Disorders in the Community*. Guilford.

World Health Organization (1973) *The International Pilot Study of Schizophrenia*. Geneva: WHO.

World Health Organization report (1987) on pilot projects: Geneva: WHO.

Index

Paladin Reference Books

A Dictionary of Drugs (New Edition)   £2.50 ☐
Richard B. Fisher and George A. Christie
From everyday aspirins and vitamins, to the powerful agents prescribed for heart disease and cancer, this is a revised reference guide
to the gamut of drugs in today's pharmaceutical armoury.

A Dictionary of Symptoms   £3.95 ☐
Dr Joan Gomez
A thorough-going and authoritative guide to the interpretation of
symptoms of human disease.

Dictionary for Dreamers   £2.95 ☐
Tom Chetwynd
A comprehensive key to the baffling language of dream symbolism.
Over 500 archetypal symbols give essential clues to understanding
the ingeniously disguised, life-enriching, ofen urgent messages to be
found in dreams.

A Dictionary of Mental Health   £1.95 ☐
Richard B. Fisher
A useful, sensible guide around the confusing world of mental
health, mental illness and its treatment.

A Dictionary of Diets, Slimming and Nutrition   £3.95 ☐
Richard B. Fisher
How do diets really work? Are the claims made for them justified?
What does the body need to function properly? This is a comprehen-
sive, up-to-date compendium packed with information vital for those
concerned about the food they eat and what it does for them.

The Jazz Book   £4.95 ☐
Joachim E. Berendt
From New Orleans to Jazz Rock and beyond – simply the best modern
companion to jazz available. Completely revised and updated.

To order direct from the publisher just tick the titles you want
and fill in the order form.
                                              PAL14082

Paladin Reference Books

A Dictionary of Operations   £3.50   ☐
Dr Andrew Stanway
A lucid commonsense guide to hospitals and how they affect the
patient plus an A–Z of operations and an alphabetical list of
procedures and investigations.

A Dictionary of Symbols   £3.95   ☐
Tom Chetwynd
Tom Chetwynd has drawn from the collective wisdom of the great
psychologists, particularly Jung, to create a comprehensive and
thought-provoking guide to the language of symbols.

Halliwell's Film Guide (Fifth Edition)   £9.95   ☐
Leslie Halliwell
A new edition of the indispensable film reference work.

Halliwell's Filmgoer's Companion (Eighth Edition)   £6.95   ☐
A gargantuan compilation of film facts. 'Totally indispensable' – *Film
Review Annual*.

A Dictionary of Mythologies   £2.50   ☐
Max Shapiro and Rhoda Hendricks
The first concise yet comprehensive dictionary of world mythologies.
It is fully cross-referenced, so that the universal themes common to
all myths are easily recognized, and the cultural differences easily
compared.

The Paladin Dictionary of Battles   £4.95   ☐
George Bruce
For the historian, the student, the amateur and the professional, this
dictionary offers the key to all the major battles fought in the world.

A Dictionary of Historical Quotations   £3.95   ☐
Alan and Veronica Palmer
Ranging over 1200 years, this highly acclaimed reference work
presents the great moments of history as reflected in the pithy phrases
of its great figures.

To order direct from the publisher just tick the titles you want
and fill in the order form.   PAL14182

All these books are available at your local bookshop or newsagent, or can be ordered direct from the publisher.

To order direct from the publishers just tick the titles you want and fill in the form below.

Name _____

Address _____

_____

Send to:
Paladin Cash Sales
PO Box 11, Falmouth, Cornwall TR10 9EN.

Please enclose remittance to the value of the cover price plus:

UK 60p for the first book, 25p for the second book plus 15p per copy for each additional book ordered to a maximum charge of £1.90.

BFPO 60p for the first book, 25p for the second book plus 15p per copy for the next 7 books, thereafter 9p per book.

Overseas including Eire £1.25 for the first book, 75p for second book and 28p for each additional book.

Paladin Books reserve the right to show new retail prices on covers, which may differ from those previously advertised in the text or elsewhere.